WAR IN AFGHANISTAN

EIGHT BATTLES IN THE SOUTH

WAR IN AFGHANISTAN
EIGHT BATTLES IN THE SOUTH

SEAN M. MALONEY

CANADIAN DEFENCE ACADEMY PRESS

Sean M. Maloney, PhD

Published by Magic Light Publishing and the Canadian Defence Academy Press in co-operation with
Canadian Defence Academy and Public Works and Government Services Canada. All rights reserved.
No part of this publication may be reproduced, stored in a retrieval system or transmitted in any form
or by any means, electronic, mechanical, photocopying, recording or otherwise without the prior written
permission of the Minister of Public Works and Government Services Canada.

©Her Majesty the Queen in Right of Canada, (2012) Catalogue Number: ISBN :978-1-894673-49-5

Published by: Magic Light Publishing
                       John McQuarrie Photography
                       192 Bruyere Street
                       Ottawa, Ontario
                       K1N 5E1

                       (613) 241-1833
                       FAX: 241-2085
                       email: mcq@magma.ca

Design: John McQuarrie

Library and Archives Canada Cataloguing in Publication

Maloney, Sean M. (Sean Michael), 1967-
    War in Afghanistan : eight battles in the south / Sean M. Maloney.

Includes index.
Issued also in French under title: La guerre en Afghanistan. (ISBN 978-1-894673-50-1)
Co-published by: Canadian Defence Academy Press.
ISBN 978-1-894673-49-5

    1. Afghan War, 2001- --Participation, Canadian. 2. Canada--
Armed Forces--Afghanistan. I. Title.

DS371.412.M355 2012   958.104'7   C2012-900335-2

Printed and bound in Canada by Transcontinental.

                    Canadian Defence Academy Press
                      PO Box 17000 Station Forces
                       Kingston, Ontario, Canada
                              K7K 7B4

WAR IN AFGHANISTAN

EIGHT BATTLES IN THE SOUTH

Contents

ACKNOWLEDGEMENTS

I would first like to thank Lieutenant-General Andrew Leslie for the encouragement and support he placed behind *War in Afghanistan: Eight Battles in the South*. His unstinting belief, in the face of substantial bureaucratic inertia, that the Canadian Army had to have an honest and transparent record of its actions in Afghanistan ensured that I was able to repeatedly deploy to Afghanistan to observe these operations and interview the participants of many others.

Eight Battles would not have been possible without the assistance, frankness and protection of the officers and non-commissioned members of the Canadian Army whom I accompanied on these operations. There are too many to thank individually. If they are named in the text, they deserve my thanks.

I would like to thank all of the Joint Task Force A (JTF-A) commanders and staff who facilitated each trip, but I would particularly like to thank Brigadier-General Guy Laroche, Colonel Christian Juneau, Brigadier-General Denis Thompson, Colonel Jamie Cade, Brigadier-General Jon Vance and Colonel Rocky Lacroix. I encountered no opposition at the Battlegroup and operational mentoring and liaison team levels while deployed in Afghanistan recording these events. All Battlegroup commanding officers I encountered, whether Afghan, American, British or Canadian, recognized the value of what I was doing (though sometimes later…) and made every effort to accommodate me in their respective Tactical Headquarters (TAC) during the operations depicted herein. For the operations I did not observe, I would like to recognize those officers and members who spoke to me frankly of their experiences while I was visiting their unit or organization in-theatre. At Regional Command (South), I would highlight Lieutenant-General Marc Lessard and Colonel "Spike" Hazelton and their staffs who were of exceptional assistance.

I would especially like to thank Michael Bechtold from *Canadian Military History* (CMH) journal at Wilfrid Laurier University. A number of these chapters appeared as articles in CMH and benefitted from Michael's editorial pen. I would like to thank him also for drawing the maps to chapters 5, 7 and 9.

Similarly, I would like to thank Ian Macdonald at the Institute for Research and Public Policy's (IRPP) *Policy Options*. He originally published chapters 2 and 4 in his fine journal. Chapters 1 and 3 appeared in their original form in *Small Wars and Insurgencies*, for which I must thank my good friend Thomas Durrell Young at the Naval Post-Graduate School at Monterey.

And finally, I would like to thank my colleague Colonel Bernd Horn for accepting and then shepherding *Eight Battles* through the editorial and production process, no mean feat in this new era of publishing.

Foreword

It is a distinct pleasure to introduce the latest addition to the Canadian Defence Academy (CDA) Press body of Canadian military literature. *War in Afghanistan: Eight Battles in the South* is an important record of distinct Canadian actions in Afghanistan. Specifically, it details a number of operations west of Kandahar City following the initial battles against the Taliban in the summer and fall of 2006. These operations, or more specifically battles, were crucial in stabilizing the situation in order to buy time for development and governance processes and, ultimately, reinforcement. The Canadian Army played a significant, and at times even dramatic, role in leading the fight for southern Afghanistan. Working alongside American, British, and Afghan forces, Canada's soldiers ranged throughout Kandahar and even into Helmand province on several occasions when the British position was threatened. The fight involved airmobile, mechanized, light infantry, and mentoring operations, operations that would have been virtually inconceivable during the Decade of Darkness in the 1990s.

This selection of battles, some closely observed by the author, Dr. Sean Maloney in his capacity as historian to the Chief of the Land Staff, demonstrates once again Canada's soldiers at their professional best, in combat with an elusive and tenacious foe in complex terrain and under forbidding conditions. There were those who worried over whether Canadians could command allies and fight enemies after years of UN "peacekeeping" and this concern was not limited to Canadian commentary. However, although locations such as Howz-e Madad, Spin Masjed and Mushan will likely never be as well known to Canadians as Vimy or Normandy, it must be realized that the same fighting spirit of today's Canadian soldier was alive and well in all of them. They demonstrated to their allies, their enemies, and to themselves that they were among the best in the world.

It is for this reason that CDA Press is publishing this latest volume. It is part of our mandate to (a.) create a distinct and unique body of Canadian leadership literature and knowledge that will assist leaders at all levels of the Canadian Forces (CF) to prepare themselves for operations in a complex security environment, and (b.) inform the public with respect to the contribution of Canadian Forces service personnel to Canadian society and international affairs. Undisputedly, this book outlines the professionalism and capability of the Canadian Forces and its dedicated personnel.

In closing, I wish to reiterate the importance of this volume. It provides another perspective on the conflict in Afghanistan that has to date, cost Canadians so much in blood and treasure. Importantly, it provides another outside assessment and outlook on the conflict and how it was waged. As such, at the CDA Press, we hope that *War in Afghanistan: Eight Battles in the South* provides valuable insight for those who serve in, and for those who interact with, the profession of arms in Canada.

Colonel Bernd Horn
Editor-in-Chief, CDA Press

INTRODUCTION

From 2006 to 2009, Canada and its allies fought a series of battalion- and brigade-sized battles and numerous smaller company and platoon-sized actions to prevent insurgents from isolating and seizing Kandahar City in southern Afghanistan. The plethora of coalition forces involved (including those under Canadian command), the political constraints imposed by several governments, the complex governance and developmental environments, the extreme media scrutiny and the rapid and vicious adaptability of the insurgent forces had never been seen before by Canadian military leaders, particularly at the brigade level. The Oka uprising in 1990 gave certain commanders brief insights into media operations and influence activities; the Balkans gave everybody an idea of what it is like to operate in the ruins of a failed state; but those experiences were in no way comparable to the situation in Afghanistan. Indeed, Canada's war in Afghanistan has no parallel or equivalent in Canadian military history. It is not Korea, nor is it the First or Second World War. Using those conflicts as comparative tools to assess what Canada accomplished in southern Afghanistan lacks validity, as much as any attempt to compare Afghan operations to UN peacekeeping activities lacks validity. The conduct of this new war has to be assessed on its own terms. Before we can even attempt that, however, we need to understand what it was like to fight there.

Picture the Provincial Operations Centre at Task Force Kandahar, (TFK) Kandahar Air Field. This nondescript building with its collection of windowless rooms is surrounded by barbed wire and protected by several security systems. It is manned by men and women 24 hours a day, seven days a week, who deal with one of the most complex environments in Canadian military history. In the centre is a large room with several large flat-screen displays; some of them have computer-generated maps, others are direct feeds from Unmanned Aerial Vehicles, while still others have logistical data on them.

There are desks cluttered with myriad computers for each headquarters function – intelligence, logistics, air support, artillery, engineering, allied units and so on. If an incident or a TIC ('Troops in Contact') occurs, the staff locates the incident, uses several information systems to determine what is happening and alerts the duty officer who passes it on to higher levels for information purposes or for action, if required. In any given day there will be upwards of ten such incidents, many occurring simultaneously. All will have political implications back in Ottawa, so each must be addressed in some detail by the headquarters as much as to allow the Government of Canada to avoid political embarrassment as to provide an appropriate Canadian military response to alleviate the situation.

Next to the main room is the J-3 Plans area. Several majors and lieutenant colonels, communicating with their counterparts in either the Canadian Battlegroup, an American battalion or a British battalion, look at plans submitted by those subordinate units, or work on TFK plans where those units might be used. The J-5 Plans planners look to the future. What might the Task Force do over a period and what resources might it need? What contingencies are there? What if Regional Command (South), the divisional headquarters equivalent, wants something done, such as to move a hydroelectric turbine through two provinces? And what resources will have to be stripped away to do it? And how will that affect other operations elsewhere, either planned or ongoing?

The Operational Mentor and Liaison Team, or OMLT, liaison officer must be present for both processes because Kandahar province does not belong to Canada and there is an Afghan National Army brigade with three kandaks (battalions) operating here as well. 1/205 Brigade has its own operations in progress and they must be coordinated with TFK's battle groups and battalions, too.

Allied units like the Gurkhas have liaison officers at TFK as well and, as regional reserve forces, they have operations they want to conduct or circumstances they will be forced to respond to – perhaps in the TFK 'battlespace'. And then there are the mysterious Special Operations Forces conducting their nocturnal activities in pursuit of the enemy's leadership and improvised explosive device (IED) manufacturers.

Task Force Kandahar's job was to balance these and other resources and coordinate and facilitate the execution of the plans to accomplish the objectives set by TFK's commanders and their superior headquarters.

Kandahar province is one of the largest provinces in Afghanistan, with an approximate population of 1.5 million, and features diverse terrain from mountains to fertile 'green zones', to deserts. At its centre is Kandahar City, Afghanistan's 'second capital' and the transportation hub of the entire south. Kandahar City is also the key to attaining religious legitimacy in the region as it is the home of Kandahar Ulema Shura, a highly influential religious advisory body. The enemy wants Kandahar City very badly and has thrown considerable resources behind bids to get the city's population to change sides, as it had done in 1996 and 2001.

Task Force Kandahar existed to combat this threat. Although a brigade-sized headquarters commanding battalion-sized units, TFK performed operations-level functions. When reading about each battle, keep in mind the proximity of the battle-areas to Kandahar City. These actions were not isolated in time and space and were not focused solely on generating local and tactical effects. The generation of positive effects on the course of the war in the province was, on one level or another, central to the execution of each one.

The effects generated by TFK's operations were operations-level in nature and had far-reaching implications. During the 2007 to 2009 period, they were intended: to shield the emergent Afghan governance structures in the city; to buy time for the build-up of the Afghan security forces (army and police) and to assist with that process; to challenge the enemy for control of districts adjacent to the city; and advance governance and development in those districts as much as possible given the near-post-apocalyptic conditions and circumstances. The massive reinforcement by American forces in 2009-2010 essentially brought this era to a close.

The eight battles described in this book are representative of some of the key actions taken in the pursuit of these objectives.[1] The Howz-e Madad operation in June 2007 was representative of 2 Royal Canadian Regiment (RCR) Battlegroup incursions into Zharey district. November 2007's Operation INITZAAR ZMAREY, also known as Arghandab 1, mounted, in less than

24 hours, the coalition's response to insurgent forces who were able to seize a sizeable portion of an important district adjacent to Kandahar City.

We then move out west of the city to Maywand district which was, and remains, a vital link between coalition forces operating in Helmand and their Kandahar support-base. Operation SOHIL LARAM II was conducted in March 2008 by a Gurkha battalion air-assaulting in, supported by Canadian enablers; it disproved conventional wisdom about how much control the enemy exerted over the district and had the unintended effect of interfering, in a more sustained fashion than anticipated, with enemy forces in adjacent Zharey and Panjwayi districts. In time, Operation JALAY, in spring 2009, would seriously capitalize on this state of affairs when an American infantry battalion and a Canadian mechanized battlegroup took on the Taliban in that area in a combination air-assault and mechanized ground-assault.

Operation TIMUS PREEM, a tank-led mechanized operation mounted in August 2008, was in part designed to keep Highway 1 open and generate breathing room for the newly created 'stability boxes', protected areas where interagency governance and reconstruction activities could take place.

The roles of the Operational Mentor and Liaison Teams (OMLT) and their Afghan National Army kandak counterparts in the conflict were incredibly important. The defence of Strongpoint MUSHAN, conducted by the Afghans with a Canadian OMLT throughout 2008, was critical in applying pressure on enemy movements in and out of Panjwayi district. Two 'out of area' operations conducted by the OMLT and Afghans in Helmand province, Lashkar Gah and Spin Masjed, highlighted not only the practical problems of OMLT operations but also the political problems of command and control. They also provide us with some insight into the progression of Afghan National Security Force mentoring in the 2008-09 period.

The aims of this work are to highlight the style of operations, the types of forces employed, relationships with allies and the complicating factors inherent to the multinational environment, and to provide the reader with some knowledge of what it was like to operate and fight in southern Afghanistan during the 2007-2009 period. It is not intended to be a definitive text. That said, there are chapters that provide information on situational background and on the evolution of enemy activity in the province, plus an interlude at the Canadian-led Role 3 Multinational Medical Unit, written to remind readers of the human cost of operations and that some battles were fought 'inside the wire' as well.

Note

A number of chapters have appeared previously as articles and I would like to thank the editors. Versions of the lead-in chapters appeared in the following journals:

"Conceptualizing the War in Afghanistan: Perceptions from the Front, 2001-2006." (*Small Wars and Insurgencies* Vol. 18 Issue 1, 2007)

"Blood on the Ground: Canada and the Southern Campaign in Afghanistan."
(*Defence and Security Analysis* Vol. 23 Issue 4, 2007)

"A Violent Impediment: The Evolution of Insurgent Operations in Kandahar Province 2003-2007."
(*Small Wars and Insurgencies* Vol. 19 Issue 2, 2008)

"Taliban Governance: Can Canada Compete?"
(*Policy Options* June 2009)

Operation INITZAAR ZMARAY originally appeared in Bernd Horn (ed) *Fortune Favours the Brave: Tales of Courage and Tenacity in Canadian Military History* (Dundurn, 2009); while Operation SEASONS, Operation SOHIL LARAM II, Operation TIMUS PREEM and the Strongpoint Mushan fight appeared in *Canadian Military History* from 2008 to 2010. A version of "MASCAL at Kandahar" was used by the Medical Corps International website. The two chapters on OMLT deployments to Helmand province and Operation JALAY are unique to this volume.

Author's Note

I observed the planning processes and then went out into the field with the forces for the following operations: SEASONS (2007), SOHIL LARAM II (2008), TIMUS PREEM (2008) and JALAY (2009). As for the other operations in Arghandab, the defence of Mushan and the deployment of Strike kandak to Helmand, I interviewed key personnel and collected material within weeks, and sometimes days, after these operations were completed. I have voluntarily blurred or altered certain control measures and intelligence methods for operational security reasons.

1. A more detailed history of the Canadian Army in Afghanistan will follow as a separate work and will provide a coherent preliminary narrative structure for the 2001-2011 period. For a personal and impressionistic view of operations in Afghanistan, see the author's Rogue Historian series of books: *Enduring the Freedom* (2005) *Confronting the Chaos* (2009) and *Fighting for Afghanistan* (2010). These cover the 2003 to 2006 period.

PART 1:
SETTING THE STAGE

Operation APOLLO: The 3 PPCLI Battlegroup deployed in early 2002 as part of Operation ENDURING FREEDOM to protect Kandahar Air Field and project force into potential enemy sanctuary areas. (DND-Combat Camera)

CHAPTER ONE
CONCEPTUALIZING
THE WAR IN AFGHANISTAN:
PERCEPTIONS FROM THE FRONT
2001-2006

"WAR IN AFGHANISTAN IS VERY STRANGE."
-GENERAL KULIKOV

With all of the analytical attention directed towards Iraq and now the new American construct of "The Long War" it is easy to forget that there is another major counterinsurgency war in progress involving Western forces and that it is not the sole preserve of the United States. Coalition operations in Afghanistan evolve dramatically from year to year and there are several overlapping problems involving insurgent, political and criminal violence in Afghanistan.[1] Simplistic analysis conducted by those seeking to jam the insurgency in Afghanistan into a Maoist Procrustean Bed have only confused the issue for the non-cognoscenti. The situation is compounded by the fact that there were (and remain) two major international military coalitions, both working with Afghan security forces, in action against insurgent forces at the same time.

The first, Operation ENDURING FREEDOM or OEF, is American-led and is part of a larger regional effort, while the International Security Assistance Force (ISAF) started off as a UN-mandated European organization but then evolved into a NATO-led mission which operates solely in Afghanistan. To make matters worse, unskilled commentators referred to ISAF as a "peace-keeping" mission which conversely implied that OEF was a "warfighting" organization. The reality of the situation is that both organizations conducted stabilization, counterinsurgency, and counterterrorism functions, in many cases working together. They have to: the insurgency in Afghanistan adapts year to year, which in turn prompts constant adaptation on the part of the international community and their Afghan government partners.

This study will lay out a chronological and conceptual framework for understanding the war in Afghanistan from 2001 to 2006. The war in Afghanistan can be broken down into distinct periods. First, there was the removal of the Taliban regime and the hunt for Al Qaeda by OEF. This period lasted from September 2001 to well into 2002. From 2002 to 2004, international efforts were designed to stabilize Afghanistan to prevent a repeat of the 1993-1996 civil war while, at the same time, staving off insurgent attempts to interfere with that process. The insurgent forces re-organized and re-conceptualized their campaign so that by 2005 their efforts were refocused on southern Afghanistan. In 2006, the insurgents severely challenged Afghan government control of the southern provinces with a much more sophisticated and organized campaign. This conceptualization is not meant to suggest that insurgent violence was absent from 2002 to 2005; indeed, throughout that period there was a steady border campaign, low-level unrest in the south and east, and a growing urban terrorist campaign.

2001-02: Proxy War and the Al Qaeda Hunt

The situation in Afghanistan prior to the intervention in 2001 consisted of a civil war between various combinations of Afghan religious, ethnic and tribal groups combined with significant external support to the factions. The Taliban movement, created and supported by Pakistan, controlled most of the country. Dominated by Pashtuns, the Taliban enjoyed significant support from Pakistani military and intelligence, a wide variety of jihadists and ex-Soviet bloc mercenaries. When the Al Qaeda organization was expelled from the Sudan in 1996, it relocated to Afghanistan and there developed a network of sophisticated terrorist and guerilla training camps, biological and chemical weapons labs and facilities for religious/ideological indoctrination. Al Qaeda also had conventional military units, engineering companies and its own non-governmental relief organizations, in addition to the terrorist training and support infrastructure.

A cluster of organized armed groups resisted Taliban dominance. Known as the Northern Alliance by the media, there were a number of Afghan military leaders of Tajik, Uzbek or Harzara ethnicity who had no truck with the Pashtun

Taliban's radical Islamist orthodoxy. The Northern Alliance received material support from Iran, France and, ironically, Russia. It held a number of mountain citadels in northern Afghanistan as well as the vital Panjshir Valley north of Kabul. The action was primarily conventional in nature and even static on many fronts where the terrain precluded manoeuvres.

There were prototypical American proxy efforts against the Al Qaeda organization in the years prior to the intervention in Afghanistan after the 9/11 attacks. An incoherent anti-Al Qaeda policy under the Clinton administration resulted in the deployment (and later removal) of a small Central Intelligence Agency (CIA) liaison group, codenamed JAWBREAKER, into Afghanistan during 1996 to meet with the Northern Alliance that was at that time coordinated by famed anti-Soviet guerilla Ahmed Shah Massoud. Contingency planning was conducted to insert American special operations forces (SOF) to kill Osama bin Laden, but these plans were superceded by a plan to use Predator unmanned aerial vehicles (UAV) to act as spotters for submarine-launched cruise missiles. A variety of other covert operations designed to hunt and kill Osama bin Laden using the Northern Alliance as a proxy force, or cover, for U.S. covert activities were conducted without success.[2]

After 9/11 the gloves came off. The CIA's Northern Alliance Liaison Team (NALT) re-initiated contact to facilitate the introduction of American special operations forces to work with the Northern Alliance's conventional forces to effect the collapse the Taliban regime. At the same time, the intelligence relationship between the NALT and their Afghan counterparts was used to gather information on the Al Qaeda organization in Afghanistan and to track its leadership with the objective of killing them with armed Predator UAVs and traditional airpower.[3]

American special forces teams, working with CIA facilitation and intelligence teams, deployed across northern Afghanistan in direct support of Northern Alliance forces. These teams had access to significant air resources and employed them to support Northern Alliance tactical and operational moves on the northern front. Northern Alliance forces used a combination of bribery, PSYOPS and fighting to convince the Taliban and Al Qaeda forces to surrender, fight among themselves or otherwise quit the field. At the same time, an American air campaign was conducted against more traditional airpower targets, which included Taliban military bases and air-defence systems, until the U.S. Air Force virtually ran out of targets after the first two weeks of the war.[4]

In southern Afghanistan, American special operations forces established contact with anti-Taliban tribal elements, coalesced with them, provided material support and initiated a campaign designed to put pressure on the regime from the south. In many cases, this was a classic U.S. special forces task. At the same time, American and, later, allied Tier I special operations forces, conducted a hunt for Al Qaeda high-value leadership targets in the south using the newly liberated areas as a base and the new tribal allies as intelligence assets.

This squeeze play produced dramatic results; the Taliban regime collapsed much earlier than anticipated.[5] At this point, American CIA and special operations forces on the ground were trying to establish an 'Eastern Alliance' in an attempt to block retreating Taliban and Al Qaeda forces. Generally, enemy forces fled south from the northern front to Kabul, then east to Pakistan or south to a number of mountainous areas (Ghanzni province, etc.). Enemy forces in the west and north-west headed to Kandahar in the south with the intention of reaching Pakistan. Al Qaeda's leadership established itself in the Tora Bora region; they escaped and moved east to Pakistan while Al Qaeda fighters tried to establish defended areas in mountainous regions near the Shai-i-kot valley and in other rugged locations along the border. American special operations forces and their proxies in the south consolidated control over Kandahar City and commenced a massive, sensitive site-exploitation operation against abandoned Al Qaeda facilities. These operations prevented further large-scale Al Qaeda operations.[6]

The increased unreliability of Afghan proxy forces operating outside of their traditional tribal and ethnic areas of domination prompted the belated deployment of American, Canadian and then British light infantry to assist in the reduction of enemy-defended areas in 2002. More and more coalition special operations forces arrived, mostly from NATO countries, to contribute to these operations. After a series of light infantry/SOF operations in the southern and eastern provinces conducted throughout 2002, Taliban and Al Qaeda formations and units ceased to operate at a level above platoon-sized groups. Al Qaeda lost all of its infrastructure in Afghanistan. Al Qaeda affiliates like the Islamic Movement for Uzbekistan (UMI) also lost their safe haven and their ability to seriously interfere with Uzbekistan and its neighbours. Military operations in Afghanistan during this period essentially forced Al Qaeda to evolve its modus operandi: one result was the emergence of what analyst Marc Sageman calls the 'bunch of guys' model of Al Qaeda terrorist groups, like those who conducted the Madrid and London bombings in 2004 and 2005 and who planned attacks in Toronto in 2006.[7]

2002-2003: Initial Stabilization Efforts

The problem of what to do about Afghanistan once the Taliban regime was removed concerned planners long before the collapse, but there were no easy answers. There were two overlapping schools of thought in American circles. The first was to have a hands-off approach whereby pro-American proxies would dominate the country and ensure that Al Qaeda did not come back in. In this scheme, Afghanistan would be left to its own devices with limited American support since the White House was suspicious of taking on a nation-building role.[8] The other school of thought envisioned an American hand-off to the United Nations (UN) who would then handle reconstruction and political development, with OEF acting as a shield. This plan was rather vague. The UN, however, refused to become involved with such an exercise unless there was a non-U.S.-led military security force to protect it. At the same time, the victorious Afghan proxies were suspicious of the UN, the organization that abandoned them in the early 1990s. A compromise was reached in November 2001. The Bonn Agreement allowed for a limited non-UN, non-U.S. force that would be used to stabilize the capital, Kabul. Initially led by the United Kingdom, the International Security Assistance Force started to deploy in spring 2002.[9]

For the most part, however, ISAF was neutered. It was small (1500 'bayonets' and 3000 support troops), while the anti-Taliban factions boasted at least 26,000 troops equipped with the full range of conventional weapons. ISAF's purpose was symbolic and acted as a tool to get a reconstruction 'buy in' from the UN and non-governmental organizations. It was not a peacekeeping force; it was not neutral; rather, it protected the emergent Afghan Interim Administration and did what it could to provide an international, non-U.S. presence in Kabul.[10]

Around this time, enemy forces reverted to a relatively disorganized guerilla resistance in the southern provinces. By 2003, Taliban groups were incapable of operating even at the platoon level. At the same time, significant coalition operations were still tracking Al Qaeda and Taliban high-value leadership targets. An additional problem, however, lay in consolidating the areas that had been cleared of a Taliban presence. From these requirements, the Joint Regional Team (JRT) concept emerged in OEF planning circles. Initially conceived as small intelligence collection and aid liaison cells attached to friendly Afghan governors, the idea evolved into the Provincial Reconstruction Team (PRT) concept. The PRTs had more people (initially 100, versus 16 in the JRT concept) and included national development agencies. They were structured to coordinate the establishment of Afghan civilian government in each province with an eye to progressively linking provincial leaders with the emergent national government in Kabul. OEF PRTs deployed throughout the country in 2002-03.

The PRT situation reflected a continuity problem in the international effort in Afghanistan. Military forces have units to deal with the civilian population in areas where forces are manoeuvring. Called Civil Affairs (CA) by the Americans and Civil-Military Cooperation (CIMIC) by Canada and NATO, these units are not intended to be aid agencies nor to provide long-term development. In the Balkans, however, there had been coordination problems between CA and CIMIC, on the one hand, and aid from non-governmental organizations and governmental development agencies on the other hand. At what point did the hand-off take place? The non-governmental aid organizations, who generally view themselves as neutral, did not want to work with the PRTs in Afghanistan as they saw them as 'military' tools. Consequently, CA and CIMIC took on more and more responsibility for the development tasks that are vital in any counterinsurgency effort.

The PRTs, however, were there to support the Afghan government as well as to support OEF's ongoing need to have detailed information on the civil and security situations throughout Afghanistan. In the south, PRTs were part and parcel of military efforts to root out what remained of the Taliban. In the north, which was comparatively secure because of the ethnic makeup of the provinces, this function had a lower priority (at least outside of Konduz).[11]

It is important to note that the Afghan government was only embryonic in 2003. There was no bureaucracy capable of running the country. There were no central government organizations such as a ministry of the interior, an exchequer and so on. The governors were anti-Taliban leaders who had armies that paid allegiance to them, not to a central government. They were temporarily 'legitimized' by the Afghan Interim Administration, and with good reason. OEF was dependent on them for ongoing operations against the Taliban and Al Qaeda in that these commanders provided guides, linguists, protection forces for bases and vital logistics support.[12]

The degree of control exercised by coalition and Afghan forces throughout the country was extremely localized. For example, OEF exerted control of its bases in Kandahar province, while its Afghan Militia Force allies had a semblance of governance in Kandahar City where power came from the barrel of a gun and rough justice. There was little or no government presence in the region. The counterinsurgency operations in the south during 2003 involved the deployment of special forces to a network of forward operating bases. Civil Affairs units deployed into uncontrolled areas to assess the situation between those bases. These two webs were used to cue two types of forces: Tier I special operations forces in the event that a high-value target (HVT) was located; or a light infantry battalion if a significant number of Taliban were discovered.[13] Increasingly, however, there were fewer and fewer HVTs present in Afghanistan as most fled to Pakistan. Indeed, Tier II special operations forces working from the forward operating bases grabbed more HVTs than the specialized Tier I SOF did.[14]

Enemy forces, which included Taliban, Al Qaeda and HiG, then initiated a limited terrorist campaign that targeted ISAF in Kabul and OEF around Kandahar. IED attacks were used on a limited basis in both Kabul and Kandahar throughout 2003. A suicide attack against a German convoy in Kabul indicated that Al Qaeda and its affiliates were adopting new tactics even before the Americans entered and occupied Iraq, when we would see an even more dramatic evolution of these techniques.[15]

Police training started in Kabul but picked up in earnest in Kandahar at the PRT. (DND-Combat Camera)

2003-04: Preventing Civil War

There was increasing unease in European circles over the leadership of ISAF after these suicide attacks and it was difficult to get a European nation to accept leadership of the force. For a variety of national interest reasons, Canada agreed to command ISAF but only if it was transformed into a NATO force. By mid-2003, ISAF was 'NATO-ized' and Canada took command in 2004. Canadian commanders re-assessed the stabilization and reconstruction situation during this time and came to several conclusions. First, not enough was being done to assist the Afghan Interim Administration in capacity-building so it could actually govern the country. Secondly, there was no coherent national plan for reconstruction. The UN and the Europeans had failed to accomplish even the semblance of these critical tasks during their tenure while the Americans were now busy in Iraq. Thirdly, if something were not done to create national security structures, the heavily armed anti-Taliban factions might fight among themselves in a bid for political dominance. Progress was particularly slow in building up the police forces and a multi-ethnic Afghan National Army.[16]

The first two problems were initially addressed by assigning a small ISAF team to help the Afghan government plan and budget with an eye towards increasing governance capacity. The third problem became a focus of ISAF efforts for this period. Working with Canada, Japan, the United States and the UN, ISAF formulated a plan to demobilize and disarm regional military forces and then canton their heavy weapons for use by the emergent ANA, at first in Kabul, but with plans to move this program throughout the country. The ANA training function was handed off to OEF control since there had been no centralized body to coordinate numerous national efforts. ISAF forces in Kabul became increasingly involved with countering urban terrorism in conjunction with special operations forces from OEF.[17]

Unfortunately, when Canada relinquished ISAF command, the follow-on European commanders discarded the vital advisory and planning function. ISAF confined itself to administering the local disarmament and cantonment plans, protecting itself from urban terrorism, and other minor operations within the environs of Kabul. The coordination of Afghan National Army planning was in some disarray. This short-sighted approach significantly delayed capacity-building efforts and is, in retrospect, a major set-back.

Increased American involvement in Iraq during 2004 drove a plan to have NATO ISAF progressively take control of international efforts in certain parts of Afghanistan. In this scheme, NATO ISAF would take over a number of PRTs in northern Afghanistan. If that worked out, then 'Stage II expansion' would see NATO take over the PRTs in western Afghanistan. The mission would remain the same: assess and assist in governance capacity-building, defanging the AMF and assist with the introduction of Afghan National Army units and police into these areas. Germany, the United Kingdom, the Netherlands and New Zealand were the main players in what became known as Regional Command North. The fact that there was little or no insurgent activity in this region made it a fairly safe test-bed: the exception was Konduz where the Germans took casualties from terrorists embedded in the Pashtun population there.[18]

In the Pashtun-dominated provinces along the Pakistani border however, Al Qaeda and HiG particularly and then increasingly, the Taliban further south, mounted a border campaign. Military force, usually in the form of small raiding operations and rocket attacks, was mostly directed at OEF bases in border provinces, but the campaign also involved increasingly sophisticated political tactics designed to subvert the establishment of legitimate governance in these provinces.[19]

More and more enemy activity, usually of a political nature at first, was directed at interior provinces like Oruzgan to give the campaign depth, presumably in order to lay the groundwork for future operations. The enemy's political campaign coincided with the run-ups to the 2004 elections whereby the Afghan Interim Administration would become a fully-elected government. Widespread intimidation was employed in an attempt to coerce the populations in these provinces and, increasingly, in Kabul. A combination of ISAF and OEF counterterrorism operations in Kabul and the massive ISAF and OEF security presence thwarted enemy efforts to seriously interfere with the UN-led, and then certified, election. Afghanistan now had a legitimate, elected government supported by over 60 percent of the population.[20]

Another extremely important series of operations in the election run-up related to the disarmament, demobilization and cantonment programs. Afghan Militia Force leaders who wanted to be part of the political process had to relinquish control of their armed forces beforehand or be declared anti-government and, therefore, non-participants. In essence, these men were forced to choose between being players in the political power game within the new system or remaining outside the system and then being dealt with by coercive force. None of the major anti-Taliban commanders took up arms against the government. The combination of the election and the co-option of the commanders was a major victory for stabilization in Afghanistan and a significant defeat for the Taliban and its supporters who did not even attempt to participate in the elections in a non-violent fashion.[21]

The main security problem remained, however: the Afghan National Army was slow to build up and the expansion and professional training of the police was in an even worse state; all of which dictated the continued presence of OEF and ISAF. The policing 'pillar' of the international effort, held by Germany, was hampered by restrictions placed by the German government on how far the police trainers could mentor their students: German mentors were not permitted to accompany police outside of Kabul. The lack of a

Bosnian International Police Task Force (IPTF)-like structure meant that regional police training in the provinces was uneven, or even non-existent. In theory, there should have been IPTF-like police units in the provinces working with the PRTs to build police capacity right from the beginning.

And then there was the judiciary, the capacity-building pillar held by the Italians. Non-existent police could not turn over criminals to a non-existent judicial system. In some provinces, Sharia law continued to dominate the proceedings, while some Afghan judges training in Italy chose to stay in Italy as refugees and did not return.

Another drawback was the hesitance of NATO countries to accept responsibility for future PRT expansion which, in turn, should have been the basis for police and judiciary capacity-building. In most cases, NATO countries bickered over who would command 'safe' PRTs, that is, those not directly affected by the Taliban insurgency in the south and east. In this game of musical chairs, Canada hesitated and was the last to play. There were no 'safe' PRTs left. Consequently, Canada committed to the Kandahar PRT in the OEF operating area, the only country to commit to the reconstruction effort alongside the Americans in the 'front-line' provinces thus far. American PRTs were directed more towards supporting counterinsurgency operations with capacity-building, by necessity, taking a second-row seat.[22]

2005-06: The Southern Campaign

By 2005, OEF in the south had moved slowly away from the reactive air-mobile raiding operations that predominated in 2003. At some point in 2004 there was a loss of momentum in the American-led effort. Some have attributed this to the deployment of a divisional headquarters that had little or no coalition experience and which had trouble implementing an operational strategy for Afghanistan. PRTs were undermanned and were not, at least in Kandahar, pushing out into the hinterland to develop information and contacts with the rural population. When the command situation was rectified, American units moved away from a single big base and the PRTs to numerous firebases and forward-operating bases in the border provinces. Special operations forces changed focus: they moved to the interior provinces and worked with the new Afghan National Army units to counter the increased Taliban influence that emerged during the 2004 election campaign. Tier I SOF units remained on call but, since most high-value targets were in Pakistan, direct-action missions were more and more directed at medium-value targets inside Afghanistan.[23]

Al Qaeda and HiG raiding operations on the border became more sophisticated in both equipment and organization, leading some coalition observers to believe that this was all training for something larger in the future. For the most part, however, enemy forces were incapable of operating in any group larger than ten men; anything larger was targeted and destroyed by airpower.[24]

Although suicide bomb attacks directed against ISAF and OEF forces were not new in Afghanistan, enemy forces initiated a suicide-bombing campaign in Kandahar province during 2005. This campaign attracted a significant amount of media attention, as it was designed to do. The purpose of the campaign was to get the international audience to compare the international effort in Afghanistan to the apparently failing American effort in Iraq, and then exploit this to influence Western populations to pressure their governments to cease and desist operations in Afghanistan.

Operation ATHENA: Canada joined the NATO-led International Security Assistance Force in Kabul from 2003 to 2005. (DND-Combat Camera)

The proximity of the suicide campaign in Kandahar to the July 2005 London bombings, which in turn drew inspiration from the Madrid attacks, was not coincidental. As we will recall, the Madrid attacks influenced Spain's withdrawal from military operations in Iraq. This lesson was not lost on the opposing forces in Afghanistan and Pakistan.

The deadlock on the capacity-building front was finally broken in late 2005 when the Afghan government accepted the Afghan National Development Strategy (ANDS) as the central basis for reconstruction and security efforts. Initiated in 2003-04, then derailed by elements within ISAF who did not want NATO military elements engaged in strategic capacity-building, the ANDS gave the international community a strategy after four years of uncoordinated efforts. The ANDS had 'buy-in' from ISAF, OEF[24] and the UN.

Most importantly, the ANDS had buy-in from the International Monetary Fund (IMF), an organization reticent to invest in Afghanistan unless there was a clear plan. Only then could the necessary monies flow to fuel the reconstruction effort. It is in this way that 'tactical' considerations in the war in Afghanistan have 'strategic' implications: no stability plus no plan equals no money and no reconstruction. The level of stability established by ISAF and OEF over the proceeding years was high enough at this point to secure the resources needed for the first phases of reconstruction.[25]

It remains possible that the suicide campaign in the fall of 2005 was also designed to deter the IMF from investing in the reconstruction effort, with obvious benefits to the Taliban. If that is the case, the commitment of substantial forces to the south in preparation for the OEF-to-ISAF transition in 2006 had some part in muffling this attempt.

For the most part, there was comparatively little insurgent activity in Afghanistan outside of Kabul and the border provinces in the south and east. Media attention directed at the suicide campaign in the south, however, made it appear to the outside world as though Afghanistan had collapsed into complete anarchy. This in turn had a deterrent effect on NATO countries who had been asked to contribute to ISAF in its expansion into southern Afghanistan, or Regional Command South. OEF could not hand off to ISAF if there were no ISAF forces to hand off to. Canada, who had already accepted to lead the PRT in Kandahar province, committed to lead a multinational brigade under

OEF and then transition the region to ISAF command. The United Kingdom agreed to turn over its 'safe' PRT in Mazar-e-Sharif in the north and join the multinational brigade, while the Dutch decided to accept to lead the PRT in Oruzgan and then deploy forces to secure the province. No other nation would commit combat troops, so the multinational 'ABCD' (American-Britain-Canadian-Dutch) brigade, more properly known as Combined Task Force AEGIS, was established in early 2006 under the command of the American divisional headquarters for OEF forces responsible for Regional Command (RC) East and RC South. The Canadian-led Task Force AEGIS was the facilitating organization for the British and Dutch deployments.[26]

The pattern of enemy activity in the south throughout 2006 indicates a further evolution of methodology and objectives. As we will recall, OEF did not exert control over RC South, although it had selective control in certain areas and was pushing PRT and SOF patrols into uncontrolled areas to assess them. Some provinces, like Nimroz, remained *terra incognita* since 2001. Enemy forces had been using Pakistan as a base area in every sense: logistics, money, weapons, recruitment and training. Pakistani forces had sporadically cooperated with OEF in 2001-02 and again in 2004, but the Pakistani effort was focused mainly on Waziristan, from where it is believed Al Qaeda and HIG operate. Balochistan, which has been in the throes of insurgency for decades, is problematic for the Pakistani government. In the main, the Taliban are based in Quetta and has Al Qaeda and HiG advisors attached to it.[27]

The suicide campaign in Kandahar was undertaken for international effect, but it also reflected the Taliban's impotence in RC South. Whenever the Taliban deployed fighters in groups larger than ten, they were usually interdicted and pounded with airpower. Throughout 2005, however, individuals and small groups infiltrated Afghanistan along several remote trade routes to create facilitation cells. This 'magic carpet' was laid from Pakistan to Afghan districts on the border to certain areas inside Kandahar, Helmand and Oruzgan provinces. Weapons travelled separately from the personnel and mostly came in via the Spinboldak highway, concealed in trucks.[28]

A number of districts were selected by the Taliban to act as fortified areas, using terrain that would slow down coalition forces. Weapons and personnel were to converge and marry up in these areas in preparation for future operations. In effect, these fortified areas sat astride each of the four highways leading out of Kandahar City, with the obvious objectives of being able to cut off the city and launch attacks into it.

OEF operations, however, detected the build-up in some areas and conducted a series of operations to disrupt enemy forces before they could coalesce, particularly in Kandahar and Oruzgan. In most cases, the enemy dispersed when confronted but, throughout 2006, they kept coming back into these fortified areas and challenging OEF forces (and now ISAF forces) for control of the areas with operations that were nearly conventional in nature. OEF and ISAF responded with conventional operations using mechanized infantry and artillery. This prompted Western media commentators to draw a simplistic comparison of operations in Afghanistan to American operations in Vietnam and to criticize a supposed lack of resources deployed for reconstruction and aid. A dramatic suicide attack that assassinated the Canadian ambassador working with the PRT in Kandahar significantly interfered with aid and reconstruction operations, but to suggest that all activity stopped and only conventional warfare was underway was a gross exaggeration, leading to further confusion in Western media circles and electorates.

Enemy forces have not refrained from conducting suicide attacks in and around Kandahar City, nor have they abandoned political warfare in the rural areas of RC South, continuing to target schools, teachers, doctors and clinics. Practically every enemy action has a relationship both to the situation on the ground and to the international media and political arena. The enemy forces are adept at information operations and the willingness of Western media to assist in this effort needs further exploration.

The battle for the south is as psychological as it is material, a battle for the uncommitted portions of the population in RC South. As the past has demonstrated in Afghanistan, this uncommitted component will side with those who are perceived to be winning the fight; this is a reflection of Pashtun culture. Backing off on military operations and refocusing on aid and development will not succeed; the two components must work together.

This is a good place to introduce the narcotics issue as it cuts across all phases of the war in Afghanistan, but has particular relevance to the southern campaign. The schizophrenic approach to counter-narcotics by the international community in Afghanistan has had negative effects on the Afghan government's ability to stabilize the south and had particularly negative effects on the counterinsurgency campaign. Propelled by the United Kingdom's leadership of the counter-narcotics pillar, and supported by the U.S. State Department (but not the Department of Defense, nor the CIA), advocates insisted that ISAF and OEF be involved in supporting paramilitary operations against opium producers in Afghanistan. Both military organizations resisted involvement, but State Department-funded Afghan forces, supported by ISAF forces operating under national command, conducted counter-narcotics operations anyway.[29]

Narcotics producers are well organized and armed, particularly those in Helmand province. They also have the support of the population, who profit from opium harvesting. It was no surprise that they fought back. In some cases, they have formed alliances with enemy forces. The Taliban then used State Department- and U.K.-led counter-narcotics efforts as a recruitment tool, insisting to the population that this outside interference would destroy their livelihoods, which it does. This state of affairs led to severe problems in 2006. British forces encountered fierce resistance while deploying into Helmand province, prompting a significant diversion of Canadian and American military forces from Zabol and Kandahar provinces to rescue the situation. Indeed, the Taliban seized two districts in the south of the province and declared a liberated zone which was eventually crushed by Canadian and American OEF forces, but not before some Western media outlets declared that the war in Afghanistan was being lost.[30]

The spill-over effects of these reports have deterred most NATO countries from sending additional combat forces to ISAF in Afghanistan, leaving the ABCD countries (and now the Poles who had recently joined ISAF), already stretched thin, to counter the Taliban in the south. The enemy is succeeding on the international psychological plane while coalition forces are succeeding on the tactical, local military, aid and reconstruction fronts. Addressing that problem is, however, beyond the scope of this study.

On the positive side, international recognition that Pakistan's lack of control of Balochistan fuels the insurgency in southern Afghanistan is finally part of the public debate. Concealed out of concern for ongoing Pakistani cooperation in hunting down Al Qaeda cells and the remnants of AQ Khan's 'atomic Wal-mart', incremental steps have now been taken which at least indicates a willingness on the part of President Musharraf to disrupt the flow of resources into Afghanistan. We will see. NATO members can legitimately question the international effort if it seeks to limit its scrutiny to Afghanistan and not the region, especially when their soldiers are getting killed.

The public debate over how the campaign in the south should be approached reached its peak in the summer of 2006. Initially, simplistic media analysis applauded the hand-over from OEF to ISAF, asserting that the American-led OEF operations were too 'militarily-oriented' and believed that ISAF would bring a 'softer' approach to the situation, putting greater emphasis on developmental aid. The reality, as both OEF and ISAF commanders knew, was that the only things that were really going to change were the flags at headquarters and certain rules of engagement. It would have been a grave error to shift away from combat operations at the point where the Taliban were deploying larger, company-sized units equipped with heavy weapons, and were using more guerilla-oriented tactics, relying less on suicide terrorism.

This misunderstanding in the public debate regarding what should be the 'correct' balance between development and military force should be addressed more thoroughly by those who study counterinsurgency. Indeed, the simplistic analogies made between Afghanistan and Iraq, Afghanistan and Vietnam, and Afghanistan and Colombia continue to populate non-specialist discourse. This plays into the hands of the enemy's information operations campaign.

The nostalgia for Vietnam within the media leads us to the problem of the 'body-count'. Quantitative methodologies are simpler to understand: we lost X, they lost Y; they lost more, so we are winning. The difficulties of applying this paradigm in Afghanistan are obvious. Fragmentation of enemy personnel by modern weapons makes a body-count difficult.[31] It is easier for the media to count coalition casualties. Moreover, success in the southern campaign should be measured by what the enemy does not control; namely, the population and the districts. If the enemy does not control the population, he cannot succeed in controlling southern Afghanistan. The Taliban do have a semblance of a parallel government, but it is not extensive yet. It should be targeted before it can evolve and grow.

All the Taliban can do at this point is spread carnage which, in most cases, kills more civilians than coalition soldiers. The terrorist paradigms of the 1970s do not apply in this area, either. In theory, civilian deaths should be a tool used by the insurgents to undermine the trust between the state and the people, to demonstrate the limits of state power to protect the population and enhance the power of the insurgents. In Afghanistan, the level of violence between 1979 and 1996 far exceeded current levels. The population is used to it, in effect. They already know the limits of state protection. The audience, therefore, consists of the West's populations, with political success in the theatre of Afghanistan coming second. Indeed, almost all suicide attacks in the south from 2003 to 2006 have been levelled against coalition forces, not against large groups of civilians. Compare this to Iraq.

Operation ARCHER: The Canadian government chose to deploy a Canadian force to lead the Provincial Reconstruction Team in Kandahar in 2005. (DND-Combat Camera)

Operation APOLLO: The 3 PPCLI Battlegroup deployed in early 2002 as part of Operation ENDURING FREEDOM to protect Kandahar Air Field and project force into potential enemy sanctuary areas. (DND-Combat Camera)

The Prospects

The reality is that political violence does not permeate Afghanistan; it permeates parts of Afghanistan. So far, enemy forces do not control significant territory in the country as a whole. They do not have the allegiance of the majority of Afghans and the allegiance of other Afghans hangs in the balance. In parts of the south, enemy forces have challenged the Afghan government and its international supporters. Will this translate to an expanded influence throughout Afghanistan? Probably not. The Taliban are of Pashtun ethnicity, as is about 38 percent of the population of Afghanistan. It is unlikely that the Taliban, as a mass movement, could gain the allegiance of Afghani Tajiiks, Hazaras or Uzbecks. Nevertheless, the Taliban and its Al Qaeda and HiG supporters could take control of significant portions of southern Afghanistan if left unchecked. The ultimate result of such a situation would be the creation of a 'Pashtunistan statelet' which Al Qaeda and affiliates could once again use as a secure base area. It would destroy and discredit Western efforts to back a legitimate, progressive Afghan government. It would void the positive psychological benefits gained by the first clear-cut victory over the Al Qaeda movement in the wake of 9/11. In short, failure in the southern campaign in Afghanistan at this point would be disastrous in the 'Long War'.

Notes

1   The author has travelled to Afghanistan annually since early 2003 to observe coalition military operations and international capacity-building efforts. This article draws on this body of personal experience, numerous in-camera interviews and myriad briefings received over this four-year period, in addition to the growing secondary source literature.

2   See Gary Berntsen and Ralph Pezzullo, *Jawbreaker* (New York: Crown Publishers, 2005) Chapters 2-5; *The 9/11 Commission Report: The Final Report of the National Commission on Terrorist Attacks Upon the United States* (New York: W.W. Norton, 2004) Chapters 4-6.

3   See Berntsen and Pezzullo, Jawbreaker and Gray Schroen, *First In: An Insider's Account of How the CIA Spearheaded the War on Terror in Afghanistan* (New York: Ballentine Books, 2005) Parts 4, 5 and 6.

4   On U.S. Special Forces operations, see Robin Moore, *The Hunt for Bin Laden: On the Ground with Special Forces in Afghanistan* (New York: Random House, 2003). For the air campaign, see Chris Finn "The Employment of Airpower in Afghanistan and Beyond," *Air Power Review* Vol. 5 No. 4 Winter 2002 pp. 1-15; Anthony H. Cordesman, *The Air War Lessons in Afghanistan: Change and Continuity* (Washington DC: Center for Strategic and International Studies, 2002).

5   Sean M. Maloney, *Enduring the Freedom: A Rogue Historian in Afghanistan* (Dulles: Potomac Books, 2005) p. 50-51.

6   Berntsen and Pezzullo, *Jawbreaker* pp. 196, 294-95.

7   See Marc Sageman, *Understanding Terror Networks* (Philadelphia: University of Philadelphia Press, 2004).

8   Bob Woodward, *Bush at War* (New York: Simon and Shuster, 2002) pp. 233, 237, 241.

9   Sean M. Maloney, "ISAF: Origins of a Stabilization Force," *Canadian Military Journal* Vol. 4, No. 2 Summer 2003 pp. 3-11.

10   Ibid.

11   PRT briefing to the author

12   Author's observations of Task Force DEVIL operations in Kandahar Province, spring 2003.

13   Maloney, *Enduring the Freedom* pp. 219-223.

14   Anonymous, *Hunting Al Qaeda: A Take-No-Prisoners Account of Terror, Adventure, and Disillusionment* (St Paul: Zenith Books, 2005) p. 211.

15   Many assume that there has been a 'migration' of tactics from Iraq to Afghanistan. The situation is more complex; techniques used in Iraq were borrowed from those used in Sri Lanka, Lebanon, Palestine and Afghanistan, modified, and then re-adapted for use in Afghanistan later on.

16   Interview with Lieutenant-Colonel Ian Hope, Kandahar, June 2006.

17   ISAF headquarters briefing to the author, Kabul, December 2004.

18   ISAF PRT briefing to the author, Kabul, December 2004.

19   Combined Forces Command Afghanistan briefing to the author, Kabul, December 2004.

20   Task Force ATHENA briefing to the author, Kabul, December 2004.

21   Interview with Ambassador Chris Alexander, Kabul, December 2004.

22   Canadian Provincial Reconstruction Team briefing to the author, Kandahar, December 2005.

23   In-camera discussions with personnel from Task Force BAYONET, December 2005.

24   Combined Forces Command Afghanistan briefing to the author, Kabul, December 2004 and December 2005.

25   Technically, Combined Forces Command Afghanistan, which is the
      primary American headquarters commanding OEF operations in
      Afghanistan.

26   Strategic Advisory Team-Afghanistan briefing to the author, Kabul,
      December 2005; Strategic Advisory Team-Afghanistan briefing to the
      author, July 2006.

27   Combined Tak Force (CTF) AEGIS operations briefing to the author,
      June 2006.

28   Canadian Provincial Reconstruction Team briefing to the author,
      Kandahar, December 2005.

29   This is based on an in-camera discussion with personnel involved in
      supporting the Afghan Eradication Force, a U.S. State Department-
      funded force that took significant casualties in Helmand province in
      Spring 2006.

30   The author was present for these events at the brigade level while
      they were underway in June-July 2006.

31   Author's personal experience during the Battle of Pashmul in
      July 2006.

The use of Improvised Explosive Devices against Canadian troops and civilians seriously increased in late 2005. (DND-Combat Camera)

CHAPTER TWO
BLOOD ON THE GROUND:
CANADA AND THE SOUTHERN CAMPAIGN IN AFGHANISTAN.

"FOR THE AMERICANS, IT'S NO LONGER JUST 'BOOTS ON THE GROUND': IT'S BLOOD ON THE GROUND THAT COUNTS."   -JOEL J. SOKOLSKY

Once again, media portrayal of the war in Afghanistan has lazily fallen back on false historical analogies and predictions of doom. After a protracted suicide bomb campaign and the fierce back-and-forth battle over the Panjwayi and Zharey districts west of Kandahar, The Taliban are 'resurgent', it is Vietnam all over again and the United States and NATO are 'losing' the war.[1] Certain senior NATO commanders, seeking to draw attention to the need for more resources, have also engaged in hyperbole, thus fueling misperceptions that failure is on the horizon.[2] Alternately, we see continuing illogic in the bombardment of criticism that the international effort is too focused on military operations and not enough on 'reconstruction' and that this is the root cause of our 'failure'.[3] Yet, all is not well: there are significant problems and the enemy is succeeding in critical areas, particularly in information operations. The Taliban and their allies have also improved operationally, though not as dramatically as depicted in the media. There is, however, little or no American coverage of what is going on in southern Afghanistan, particularly the operations of Canada, the lead nation in southern Afghanistan, and of the other nations engaged in this fight. Totally overlooked by American and British professional military commentators, and generally ignored by American and British media outlets focused on their own national problems in-theatre, the combination of neglect has resulted in a distorted impression of what exactly is going on in southern Afghanistan and why.

49

But all is not lost. Combined Task Force AEGIS, a multinational brigade predominantly based on American, British, Canadian and Dutch forces and led by Canada, held the line during the vital transition from the U.S.-led Operation ENDURING FREEDOM control to the NATO International Security Assistance Force. The Taliban and their allies have not seized control of southern Afghanistan, let alone the rest of the country. They have, however, mounted a serious challenge to the Karzai government, its allies and those Afghans who do not desire a return to radical Islam.[4]

Canada in Afghanistan

Canada has been continuously engaged in military operations in Afghanistan since 2001, though this engagement has taken many forms as Canada has worked with both international coalitions, Operation ENDURING FREEDOM and the International Security Assistance Force. Canada first engaged with OEF in the fall of 2001 by sending a naval task force to the Indian Ocean to conduct leadership interdiction operations.[5] Subsequently, special operations forces deployed to Afghanistan, followed by a light infantry battalion that was integrated into an American airborne brigade in 2002. When the battalion was withdrawn, Canadians remained with OEF in a staff and training capacity, working to develop a plan for the future Afghan National Army.

In broad terms, the ISAF formed in 2002 was a 'fig leaf' to facilitate UN and non-governmental organizations (NGO) involvement in the stabilization effort: these organizations did not want to be under American military command or have any relationship to it.[6] When it became clear that OEF was not structured nor equipped to stabilize the bulk of the retaken countryside and that the United States was committing to Iraq *en masse*, a solution was needed. The Europeans who led ISAF, however, initially balked at expanding ISAF outside of Kabul. Canada agreed to lead ISAF, but only if the mission was 'NATO-ized'. In part, this move was designed to stave off domestic criticism regarding Canada's planned military commitment to Operation IRAQI FREEDOM, a commitment that was subsequently cancelled.

As a result, a Canadian brigade headquarters, a Battlegroup and special operations forces deployed to Kabul in 2003-04 to affect this changeover. Canadian trainers remained with OEF's Afghan National Army training program. While in ISAF lead, Canadian commanders formalized several important stabilization programs, including the disarmament and demobilization of factional armies and ISAF provincial reconstruction team expansion into northern Afghanistan.[7] Canadian commanders also identified a key problem: the new Afghan government lacked the capacity to govern. An ISAF team was established to assist with this area.

Working under a severe manpower shortage that was the result of imposed, shortsighted reductions to the forces in the mid-1990s, Canada could not sustain command of ISAF and relinquished it in 2004. Certain Canadian sub-units remained in Kabul, however, and were instrumental in working with American and British units to prevent interference with the 2004 elections. Canadian Embedded Training Teams were once again significant contributors to assisting the Afghan National Army.[8]

The stabilization effort in the country was attenuated by an unwillingness of Western European countries to commit to lead and support Provincial Reconstruction Teams in the wake of the controversy over the American decision to remove the Hussein regime in Iraq. A number of European countries scrambled to accept 'safe' PRTs outside of volatile southern and eastern Afghanistan to demonstrate to the Americans that they were still committed to Afghanistan, though they were not committed to Iraq. During the scramble, the Canadian policy establishment decided to take the Kandahar PRT, then in the OEF operating area, the least safe of the PRTs, in 2005. Working with Task Force BAYONET, an American brigade, it became clear to commanders that the situation in the south was deteriorating. Previous American commands had not been aggressive enough at pushing PRT operations throughout the vital province and critical monies needed for the stabilization effort were not making it south from Kabul.[9]

At the same time, the European-led ISAF had backed off on Canadian plans to assist the Afghan government when they took control of ISAF in 2004. When Canada deployed its PRT, another Canadian organization, the Strategic Advisory Team Afghanistan (SAT-A), stood up in Kabul in mid-2005. The SAT-A worked closely with the Afghan government to formulate the

Afghanistan National Development Strategy (ANDS). The ANDS was critical in that the IMF would not seriously invest in Afghanistan without a plan, and one that had accountability, at that.[10]

Information developed by the Kandahar PRT and the SAT-A highlighted a number of problems. First, the enemy forces altered their activities in Kandahar province. In mid-2005, the Taliban and Al Qaeda initiated a suicide bombing campaign. Suicide bombings were not new in Afghanistan; OEF and ISAF forces had been hit before. But the sharp increase in the number of attacks and their locality brought significant media and analytical attention to the international effort in Afghanistan and inevitably, Iraq comparisons were made. The possibility that a surge in Taliban and Al Qaeda violence might interfere with IMF investment became very real.

At the same time, OEF and NATO had been negotiating for an incremental handover of Afghan regions. RC North and RC West were at this point under ISAF control. Ostensibly, American troop requirements in Iraq were driving these handovers, but there may have been other reasons which remain

The coalition fight in southern Afghanistan in 2006 was hampered by a lack of Afghan security forces, particularly police but also the army, which placed a greater burden on Canadian units. (DND-Combat Camera)

unclear right now. The next region, RC South, became problematic. It was not 'safe' like RC North and RC West. Would NATO members commit forces to RC South, a sector that had an escalating insurgency? It was unclear. Delay in the ISAF expansion plan would be seen as a coalition failure and play into the hands of enemy information operations. The split command system in Afghanistan (ISAF and OEF) was inefficient in that there was no single plan for the country and each organization had its own distinct operating methods, a situation which the enemy exploited by hiding between the 'seams' of the two coalitions.[12]

As it had before in the pre-NATO ISAF to NATO ISAF transition, Canada decided to commit forces to command RC South in its OEF incarnation and then handle the transition to ISAF command. The objective was to facilitate the inclusion of other NATO countries into the RC South fight and to achieve, ultimately, a single command for coalition forces in Afghanistan, instead of two.[12] The Canadian commitment included a Canadian-led multinational brigade headquarters (HQ), a Battlegroup, special operations forces and the PRT. When the commitment was made in 2005, the only other partner was the United States. It took significant cajoling to get the United Kingdom and the Netherlands engaged. The U.K. was already deeply engaged in Iraq and had a 'safe' PRT in RC North. The Dutch initially committed to a PRT in Oruzgan province and decided to bring special operations forces and a Battlegroup, but domestic political debate nearly scuttled the whole deal, mostly because the Dutch were also committed to Iraq and because of the potential of casualties from the suicide bombing campaign. There was even concern in late 2005 that a negative Dutch decision would cascade and produce a negative British decision. In the end, however, both countries committed their forces to RC South under Canadian command.[13]

The Situation in Late 2005

When the Canadian PRT arrived in the summer of 2005, Combined Task Force BAYONET, based on the 173rd Airborne Brigade, had been at war for six months. CTF BAYONET consisted of two small American infantry battalions with Afghan National Army augmentation, an independent company group, a helicopter battalion, a Romanian battalion for air field protection, and PRTs in Helmand, Kandahar and Zabol provinces.

Enemy activity varied province by province. For the most part, there were small Taliban groups in north-west Helmand and across the mountainous northern portions of Kandahar and Zabol provinces. These groups conducted periodic harassment ambushes and laid IEDs. The level of political mobilization appears to have remained limited to these rural areas. There was significant enemy activity in and around Kandahar City, however. The built-up agricultural districts of Panjwayi and Zharey hosted a number of cells that regularly ambushed coalition forces along the east-west highway to Helmand, while a suicide IED network was particularly active in the city itself. Political mobilization was underway in the southern parts of the city and sporadic rocket attacks were conducted against the main OEF base at Kandahar Air Field to keep the coalition's heads down. Coalition special operations forces were working in operating areas in Oruzgan province and northern Helmand, as well as along the border with Pakistan; there were also significant engagements in southern Oruzgan in the interprovincial border region with the northern part of Kandahar province and northern Zabol.[14]

CTF BAYONET's operational focus was to keep the pressure on the fairly small number of Taliban groups operating in these northern areas and maintain a dispersed presence on infiltration routes leading from Pakistan through the eastern districts of Kandahar into Zabol while at the same time mentoring Afghan National Army units to replace American units in the holding role in Zabol province. It is clear that CTF BAYONET was stretched thin given the terrain it had to operate in and the formation's small size.

CTF BAYONET inherited what they described as a dysfunctional aid and reconstruction situation. The PRTs suffered from a number of deficiencies. Each PRT had limited protective resources and was unable to move into the rugged hinterland of the provinces without being escorted by the already limited number of manoeuvre units who were engaged in pinning down Taliban groups in the northern parts of the provinces. There was some tension in how to employ the PRT; was it there to support the brigade like a Civil Affairs unit? Was it there to coordinate aid and construction? What should the relationship be between the PRT and the provincial government? There was a lot of uncoordinated aid and construction activity going on in the region and it was not clear exactly what effect this was having – or supposed to have – on the counterinsurgency effort. It was possible the enemy was even benefiting from the aid effort in the areas they operated in.

The Canadian PRT immediately set to work in laying the ground for the fall 2005 provincial elections. CTF BAYONET and the PRT understood that the key to any aid and reconstruction effort was information. PRT operations focused on long-range patrols into the more remote districts to assess what exactly was going on. There were no indications that previous PRTs had even visited these areas. Special operations forces had, but the limited coordination between the CJSOTF and the conventional forces in Afghanistan blocked or filtered the passage of information. Information from the Canadian PRT, developed over months, indicated that the enemy was engaged in much more infiltration from Pakistan than had been believed – and not always in the areas the analysts predicted. Enemy religious/political mobilization was underway in the rural areas; it was not possible to tell whether this had dramatically increased or not because there was no real baseline.[16]

The Canadian PRT was extremely active in promoting capacity-building with the provincial government. It was critical that there be accountable government institutions before any NGO or IO would commit funds for aid and construction at the provincial level. Little had been done before 2005 in this area, thus the lack of focus for the disparate construction effort.

The enemy suicide bombing campaign was a significant distraction. It served to attract media attention to Kandahar City; it forced greater protective measures which, in turn, reduced the effectiveness of the assessment and capacity-building effort; it also distracted 'eyes and ears' that could have been out in the hinterland finding out what was going on. In January 2006, however, PRT work was further attenuated when a senior Canadian diplomat working in the capacity-building part of the PRT, was assassinated by a suicide Vehicle Borne Improvised Explosive Device (VBIED). Canadian aid organizations who were already skittish about working with the PRT used this event as an excuse not to continue work for a critical time. The suicide campaign continued, emboldened by this success.[17]

CTF AEGIS Deploys: 2006

CTF AEGIS replaced CTF BAYONET in January-February 2006. For a time, AEGIS commanded only two manoeuvre units: Task Force (TF) ORION, a Canadian Battlegroup equipped with LAV-III armoured vehicles, and a reduced American battalion group, TF WARRIOR, that was mounted in armoured Hummers. There was a mixed American helicopter battalion and there was a Romanian battalion protecting Kandahar Air Field. CTF AEGIS also took over command of the existing PRTs: Canada operated in Kandahar, while the Americans operated in Zabol. The British and Dutch contingents took several months to deploy, but would take over Helmand and Oruzgan provinces, respectively. Special operations forces continued to operate in northern Helmand and in Oruzgan, but withdrew from the Pakistan border regions by the summer of 2006.[18]

CTF AEGIS' concept of operation had a number of attributes. First, the PRTs were to be twinned with the manoeuvre battalions in each province. The PRTs would be in the lead, with the battalions in support of the aid and construction effort. Part of the plan involved assigning an Afghan National Army (ANA) battalion to each coalition battalion so that it could be mentored and ultimately become responsible for security. It is important to note that none of this precluded offensive operations against insurgents when they were discovered. It was, however, based on the assumption that the enemy was conducting operations as they had in 2005: dispersed rural operations, religious/political mobilization and urban suicide terrorism.[19]

As an OEF formation, CTF AEGIS was subject to command from Combined Joint Task Force (CJTF)-76, which was based on the divisional HQ from 10th Mountain Division. This relationship posed some problems. The American HQ was not used to commanding a Canadian-led formation and expected it to behave as any other American brigade would, that is, be responsive to higher direction and not think for itself. The compartmentalization within CJTF-76 between conventional and special operations forces also aggravated the relationship. The Canadian view of command is that a higher headquarters provides a general operational concept and the subordinate formation figures out how to use its resources to achieve the aim because it knows the terrain and the people better than the higher headquarters. In this case, CJTF-76 planners developed an overly-detailed division plan (Operation MOUNTAIN THRUST) in which the actions of CTF AEGIS were ostensibly orchestrated alongside operations over in RC East; air support for the entire theatre; Combined Joint Special Operations Task Force (CJSOTF) and other special operations capabilities; all without CTF AEGIS having visibility on many of these activities when conducted inside their battlespace.

There were detrimental effects on the conduct of the counterinsurgency campaign. Certain uncoordinated non-Canadian assets would conduct 'kinetic' operations in the CTF AEGIS Area of Responsibility (AOR) and then leave the area. CTF AEGIS would have to clean up afterward and suffer the wrath of upset locals who did not distinguish between those assets and CTF AEGIS units. Canada was unwilling to publicly take the blame for these incidents because of the potential for domestic political backlash, something the United States is used to but Canada is not.

The CTF AEGIS concept of operations was in conflict with what CJTF-76 wanted it to do. The CJTF-76 plan for 2006 was focused on reduction of what its staff referred to as 'Taliban sanctuaries' in the rural, northern parts of Helmand, Kandahar and Zabol provinces. This reflects, in general, a doctrinal disagreement on the nature of counterinsurgency. Is the threat best addressed by the reduction of enemy forces, or through shielded aid and construction efforts designed to get the population on side? The CJTF-76 plan seems to have focused on the former and paid lip service to the latter, instead of recognizing that both are important, so when the enemy shifted its approach in the summer of 2006, rapid unprogramed shifts had to be made.

It appears as though the CJTF-76 plan did not address a number of important variables, specifically the Dutch and British laydown that was underway throughout the spring and summer of 2006. The logistical process of getting the Dutch Task Force to Oruzgan and the British Task Force out to Helmand was dependent on controlling the main service routes from Kandahar Air Field, through Kandahar City, then north to Tarin Kowt in Oruzgan and west along Highway 1, past Zharey district and on to Helmand province. With only two battalions, and with each of them assigned to separate provinces, CTF AEGIS could not be everywhere at once.

TF ORION was particularly stretched thin: Kandahar province is nearly twice as large as Zabol, where the American battalion was operating. TF ORION also had to handle Kandahar, a major city, whereas Qalat is much smaller.

TF ORION was, through exceptional 'can-do' leadership, able to establish forward operating bases on the main service routes and facilitate the Dutch and British deployments while, at the same time, the force was under pressure from CJTF-76 to root out Taliban sanctuaries in the north. How? The enemy in the supposed sanctuaries dispersed whenever TF ORION deployed forces into the northern areas.[20] At the same time, a significant suicide IED network was rounded up which reduced, for a time, attacks in Kandahar City itself along the British and Dutch deployment routes. In time, TF ORION was forced to take over from an allied special operations force unit operating in and around the vital Spinboldak border area, which stretched the task force resources even further. Note that there was little time to focus on aid and construction efforts because the PRT was dependent on the TF ORION Battlegroup for protection and TF ORION was busy elsewhere.

It was, as usual, up to the infantry to close with and destroy the enemy in Zharey and Panjwayi districts. (DND-Combat Camera)

The Summer Battles

The enemy, of course, was not interested in adhering to any coalition plan or conceptualization dealing with counterinsurgency in RC South during the summer of 2006. While TF ORION was deployed in northern Kandahar in accordance with the CJTF-76 sanctuaries reduction plan, information was received that Taliban forces were building up in the Panjwayi and Zharey districts. This area was already a problem and had been during the CTF BAYONET days as ambush cells sporadically interfered with traffic on Highway 1. The new concern was related to the 'Tet Thesis' in which the Taliban were believed to be planning to infiltrate Kandahar City from Panjwayi and Zharey districts in order to conduct a series of 'spectaculars' against high-value government targets. TF ORION troops were withdrawn from the north in mid-June and went into Zharey district to disrupt the Taliban build-up. This effort collaterally assisted with the British deployment to Helmand by securing Highway 1. The British situation became problematic very quickly.

After the bulk of TF ORION re-deployed to northern Kandahar, British forces encountered significant resistance as they sought to exert a presence in Helmand province. Based on a parachute battalion with associated

The artillery's M-777's were called upon more and development less throughout 2006. This priority would change the following year – not always with success. (DND-Combat Camera)

helicopter support, the Helmand Task Force was supposed to deploy into dispersed operating locations and connect with the local population. These locations quickly came under attacks which were conducted with a level of tactical sophistication unseen in the other RC South provinces. A great deal of effort was spent trying to account for this state of affairs, but the sensitivities of the facts were unpalatable to some analysts because of the larger implications.

Helmand province is essentially one big poppy field. Poppy production touches practically every economic endeavour in Helmand. Up to the deployment of the Helmand Task Force in 2006, the only coalition presence was the American PRT and some special operations forces, who were not interested in narcotics-related issues. In Afghanistan, there are competing views of how to approach aid and reconstruction. The British policy, and U.S. State Department policy, is to support poppy eradication and 'alternative livelihood' crop programs. In this view, monies derived from poppy production support the Taliban war effort and enhance corruption in the emergent Afghan governance structures. The alternative view, held by the U.S. Department of Defense and Canada, is that narcotics reduction is not a military matter and that stability needs to exist in a region first, before policing can take place. And that policing has to be done by the Afghans and not by coalition forces. Poppy eradication attacks the economic basis of society in Helmand which, in turn, leads to more Taliban recruits and influence or other forms of resistance which are not necessarily Taliban-controlled but which can result in pinning down scarce coalition resources.

What the British encountered in Helmand was a combination of forces working against them. There were already Taliban cells operating there. There are narcotics producers that have infiltrated, and even control, portions of the Afghan security forces. There are family and tribal groupings that have relatives in the Taliban and in the security forces, and who produce poppy. Yet, there are narcotics producers who despise the Taliban and the government equally. The possibility that elements within the government are engaged in poppy production cannot be ruled out. The situation defies easy explanation. Indeed, part of the problem is that the U.S. State Department reneged on aid money for the region back in 2003 when they believed that it would go to the 'wrong people', and this in turn led to a loss of credibility for the coalition years ago; Afghans have long memories. To make matters even more interesting, Helmand serves as an alternative Taliban infiltration route from Pakistan all the way into Orugzan.

The British force structure for Helmand was not optimal. Equipped with unarmoured Land Rovers (and later semi-armoured Land Rovers) and dependent on helicopters that had operating restrictions imposed by British politicians and financial bureaucrats,[21] the Helmand Task Force was almost a static organization, vulnerable to IED attacks and to being pinned down in forward operating bases and platoon houses. Anti-coalition forces progressively tested the British throughout May and June.

TF ORION and TF WARRIOR were once again engaged in sweeping the empty northern sanctuaries. Though this may have had some benefit in that the sweeps distracted Taliban forces from conducting effective operations against the deploying Dutch, it was difficult to measure the effectiveness of these operations. Taliban forces once again re-infiltrated the Panjwayi and Zharey districts in July, while, at the same time, a number of British outposts came under attack in Helmand. Consequently, CTF AEGIS developed a plan to clean out Zharey and Panjwayi, and then relieve pressure on British forces in Helmand.

In Canada's most significant battlegroup action since the 1993 Medak Pocket operation in Croatia and possibly since Korea, TF ORION redeployed from the north and mounted a surprise night attack on Pashmul, the defended centre of Zharey district. Supported with U.S. airpower, TF ORION engaged a well-equipped Taliban force that included jihadis from foreign countries. This enemy force had a sophisticated defence system, was well-equipped, and was prepared to engage coalition forces, not just melt away in guerilla fashion when confronted with superior firepower. It succumbed to the TF ORION onslaught.[22]

The next phase of the AEGIS plan was to move to assist British forces. TF WARRIOR was positioned to enter Helmand province from the north, while TF ORION would perform a blocking action to the south and east. British forces would then air-assault into, and then sweep, an area which contained significant leadership targets with the aim of disrupting enemy command

and control province-wide. For a variety of reasons, this operation was less than successful and the enemy forces slipped away, particularly the leadership targets.

While the three CTF AEGIS battlegroups were engaged in this operation, the Taliban seized two districts in southern Helmand and burned the district centres. This action precipitated a political crisis in Kabul. The Karzai government demanded an immediate response from the coalition because of the repercussions of having the media describe the enemy as 'controlling' southern Helmand. At this point, the lack of British mobility, coupled with the fact that TF WARRIOR had been in the field continuously for over a month and was suffering a high VOR (vehicle off road) rate, meant that TF ORION, highly mobile and equipped with LAV-III, was the only force that could respond to retake the southern Helmand districts. TF ORION, augmented with an American Hummer-equipped infantry company from TF WARRIOR and supported with U.S. and British airpower, re-took the two district centres and re-established Afghan government control.[23]

Throughout the summer, Zabol province experienced less enemy activity than the other areas of RC South. Why? Some think that the combination of size (Zabol is smaller than the other provinces) and the continuity of the effort there brought about by American longevity is the key. Afghan forces have been successfully integrated into the effort. The other possibility is that the enemy chose to focus on the newcomers in Helmand and try them on. But what about Oruzgan? Why did the Dutch not run into the same problems as the British? Before the Dutch deployment, Australian and American special operations forces working with Afghan units were used to secure the main routes in and out of the provincial capital first, before the Dutch laydown took place. Again, size matters in that Oruzgan is smaller than Helmand and does not border Pakistan; this reduces the effectiveness of enemy operations since infiltration must pass through Zabol and Kandahar.

Effects

Let us examine the summer actions in light of the original counterinsurgency plan and the larger ramifications for Canadian-American cooperation in the war against the Al Qaeda movement and affiliates. The PRTs, by necessity, were pretty much left to fend for themselves throughout this period because their 'twinned' manoeuvre battalions were deployed outside of their assigned provinces. It is difficult to measure PRT effectiveness at the best of times but the need for protective assets to get PRT personnel into the field was attenuated. At this point, the Canadian PRT was receiving new leadership and was still processing a significant increase in funding but the capacity to absorb and distribute the funding took some time. Capacity-building efforts with the provincial government had been on hiatus since the January 2006 assassination and corrective action was still being sorted out in the summer.

The plan to twin and mentor an ANA battalion with each CTF AEGIS battlegroup worked in Zabol but did not bear as much fruit in Kandahar or Helmand. The reasons for this require more study, but it is important to note that, at the Battle of Pashmul, each Canadian infantry company had an Afghan National Army platoon working with it, with American ETTs advising. It seems that the ANA is not yet at the point of operating independently without coalition logistical and air support. Such dependency is dangerous in the long term if we ever want to leave Afghanistan.[24]

In essence, CTF AEGIS was forced to abandon CJTF-76's operational plan and react to what the enemy was doing elsewhere. CTF AEGIS had to adapt its own operational constructs to meet unanticipated threats and political pressures. The formation HQ and the Battlegroup were successful on both accounts. The ability of the TF ORION and TF WARRIOR commanders to effectively lead their troops and think creatively under arduous operational conditions was the critical factor in the success of the summer operations because those constructs had to be turned into action on the ground.

It is also important to note that TF ORION and its support battalion was subjected to near-constant suicide IED attacks throughout its operations. The only main service route for operations in Zharey and in Helmand provinces passes through Kandahar City. Though special operations forces and Afghan security forces were able to disrupt some cells, the importation of trained foreign jihadis from Pakistan to replenish their ranks could not be staunched. Canadian combat support personnel had never before been confronted with such a campaign, yet they adapted and met this particular challenge, as their American counterparts have in Iraq. The enemy was able to briefly interfere with, but never fully disrupt, support to operations in the field.

There are two areas that demand explanation when placing CTF AEGIS operations in the context of counterinsurgency. In addition to the 'military' fronts, this campaign was waged on two psychological fronts: the Afghan people in southern Afghanistan and the Canadian population, politicians and media.

International media outlets have been quick to brand operations in Afghanistan as a failure. They cite the combination of lack of 'reconstruction' progress, corruption and huge poppy growth as evidence. There are constant criticisms that there is too much coalition military activity and not enough aid and 'reconstruction'. In this view, large coalition military operations like those conducted in the summer of 2006 are indicators of failure, not success. Indeed, some commentators argue that, since the enemy has progressed in a Maoist fashion, moving from terrorism to guerilla operations to conventional operations, therefore they are succeeding.[25] This is simplistic. The enemy used a variety of techniques, indeed all three, at the same time. The real measurement should be in looking at what effects these are having on gaining the allegiance of the population. How well, for example, is enemy religious/political mobilization succeeding in the rural areas? Has it permeated into the urban areas? When the enemy conducts operations as he has this summer, does it distract the coalition from identifying and countering religious/political mobilization? We do not know; but the enemy's inability to actually hold ground for protracted periods, declare liberated zones and then govern and tax them in a widespread and systematic fashion, is a measure of coalition success, not failure. Even if the enemy is able to accomplish this in a limited fashion, he still has to contend with the rest of Afghanistan, not just the south.

Indeed, ignoring military action and focusing solely on aid and construction would be disastrous and negligent. At the same time, our existing aid and construction efforts do not address enemy mobilization in their primary transmission media, the mosques. Western powers recognize a separation of church and state; our enemy does not, and he exploits this ignorance.[26] In addition, some programs like gender equality are counterproductive in rural areas. Coupled with aggressive poppy eradication programs, we may be undermining our own efforts in critical parts of RC South to gain the allegiance of the population.

The proper tools to address these challenges are not supposed to be provided by CTF AEGIS and its Task Forces; they are supposed to be provided by the international community working with the Afghan government in Kabul. Where are the professional, trained police that are needed to hold cleared areas and assert law and order? Where is the judicial system that needs to accompany the police? Where is the Afghan National Army in battalion and brigade strength five years after the Taliban regime was removed? Where is the internal security and educational apparatus needed to address religious/political mobilization? CTF AEGIS is only a shield to allow these things to be put in place; its soldiers and PRT personnel cannot address these deficiencies.

And then there is the critical matter of maintaining support for the Afghanistan mission in Canada, something Americans and Britons should understand and pay attention to. After the CTF AEGIS commitment was made, there were federal elections that removed the Liberal government in Canada. The new Conservative government, a minority government, has continued with existing policy for Afghanistan and even enhanced it. Consequently, the Liberals, now in opposition, have used every perceived setback, particularly casualties, to call into question continuing with the commitment. The socialist New Democratic Party, which holds swing votes in the minority government, has demanded an immediate withdrawal and even wants to enter into negotiations with the Taliban.[27]

The Canadian population and the media were not prepared for casualties, particularly suicide IED casualties. Inoculated with decades of UN peacekeeping mythology and deceived by previous governments who sought to downplay Canadian combat operations in the Gulf and Kosovo, some see the current Canadian operations as something divergent from 'tradition'.[28] Indeed, there is still a mistaken belief that ISAF is a benign, non-lethal 'peacekeeping' mission, despite all protestations and evidence to the contrary. This misunderstanding also flies in the face of the facts, like the number of Canadians killed during supposed 'peacekeeping' operations in the Balkans in the 1990s and during ISAF operations in Kabul back in 2003-04.

By the fall of 2006, Canada has had 36 personnel killed in Afghanistan. The United States has lost 339 between 2001 and 2006. Canada has 10 percent of the American population, so the proportion of Canadian casualties to American casualties is about the same and is therefore significant in Canada. Most of these Canadian casualties were taken during the course of CTF AEGIS' operations in 2006. Though downplayed by internal Canadian analysis, it is clear the enemy sees Canada as a weak link, as Al Qaeda did with Spain and Iraq, and is trying to undermine support for the war in Canada with suicide IED attacks and the constant attempts to attrit CTF AEGIS in the Zharey and Panjwayi districts. Indeed, one successful and bloody suicide attack was conducted against Canadian troops on the eve of the opening of Parliament on 18 September 2006.[29]

The important thing for Americans and Britons to understand is that every single Canadian combat death becomes politically sensitive in ways that it does not in the United States or in the U.K. Why? The combination of the novelty of being at war, the small size of the Canadian Forces and the intense media scrutiny brought to bear are all factors. When American aircraft miss and kill Canadians, as they have in Afghanistan on a number of occasions, each incident becomes a major political event (in Canada and not the United States) that can destabilize Canada-U.S. relations, regardless of who was to blame; not because of the deaths particularly, but the perceived lack of sensitivity or outright dismissal by Americans that the event is significant to Canadians, which is in turn understandable because of the comparatively large numbers of American dead in Iraq and elsewhere.

The lack of Canadian visibility in the American and British media and lack of recognition of Canada's efforts in statements by senior American and British military and political leaders on the war in Afghanistan, coupled with the overbearing behaviour of some American commanders in Afghanistan and American overreaction to criticism from their 'lessers',[30] becomes magnified in Canada. This state of affairs has the potential to undermine support for the mission in Afghanistan as much as enemy suicide IEDs. The only people who profit from this state of affairs is the enemy.

The southern campaign will continue in various forms, but now under ISAF command. The reality is that American, British, Canadian and Dutch forces will continue to serve together in the pursuit of a stable Afghanistan. The Canadian contribution to this effort in the spring and summer of 2006 was critical to the continued success of the mission in the face of significant opposition. Canada's soldiers do not deserve to be taken for granted, particularly after the summer of 2006.

Notes

1 "Afghanistan: Are the Taliban Winning?" Newsweek
http://www.msnbc.msn.com/id/14975282/site/newsweek/; Argued
de Borchgrave, "Of Afghanistan, Iraq, and Wars Unwinnable",
Pittsburgh Tribune Review 19 September 2006.

2 "UK General Warns of Afghan Threat",
http://news.bbc.co.uk/2/hi/uk_news/politics/4779321.stm

3 Jim Lobe, "US Losing the Peace in Afghanistan", *Asia Times*
21 June 2003.

4 The author was present with CTF AEGIS and TF ORION for the summer
of 2006 and closely observed planning and operations conducted over
this time frame.

5 Richard Gimblett, *Operation APOLLO: The Golden Age of the Navy in
the War Against Terrorism* (Ottawa: Department of National Defence,
2004).

6 Sean M. Maloney, "ISAF: Origins of a Stabilization Force", *Canadian
Military Journal* Vol. 4 No. 2 pp. 3-11.

7 ISAF HQ briefing to the author, Kabul, December 2004.

8 Task Force ATHENA briefing to the author, Kabul, December 2004.

9 Provincial Reconstruction Team briefing to the author, Kandahar, December 2005.

10 Strategic Advisory Team-Afghanistan briefings to the author, December
2005 and July 2006.

11 Task Force AFGHANISTAN briefing to the author, Kandahar,
December 2005.

12 Task Force AEGIS briefing to the author, Kandahar, June 2006.

13 Hans de Vriej, "Dutch Under Pressure Over Doubts About Afghan Mission", http://www.radionetherlands.nl/currentaffairs/region/nether-
lands/ned060113; Judy Dempsey, "Dutch Pressed Over Afghanistan",
International Herald Tribune 30 January 2006.

14   Task Force AFGHANISTAN briefing to the author, Kandahar, December 2005; Provincial Reconstruction Team briefing to the author, Kandahar, December 2005.

15   Provincial Reconstruction Team briefing to the author, Kandahar, December 2005.

16   Provincial Reconstruction Team briefing to the author, Kandahar, December 2005.

17   Provincial Reconstruction Team briefing to the author, Kandahar, July 2006.

18   Combined Task Force AEGIS briefing to the author, Kandahar, June 2006.

19   The author observed CTF AEGIS and TF ORION planning and operations throughout the summer of 2006. This discussion is based on those observations and in-camera discussions with the CTF HQ personnel.

20   The author participated in these operations.

21   Sean Rayment, "Helicopter Shortage Puts Our Troops at Risk", *Daily Telegraph* 16 July 2006.

22   The author participated in this action at the company level, after having observed the Battlegroup-level planning cycle leading up to it.

23   The author observed the brigade planning cycle and execution of these operations.

24   National Training Centre briefing to the author, Kabul, July 2006.

25   The author has continuously encountered this perception in dealing with media outlets and Canadian parliamentarians on the Standing Committee on Defence. It clearly reflects a 1960s generational understanding of insurgency that the Baby Boom generation would be familiar with from the Vietnam era, but has been imposed as a template on today's operations.

26   I am indebted to Padre Captain Sulyman Demiray, the Canadian Forces' mullah, for bringing this vital aspect to my attention while we were at a Forward Operating Base in Kandahar.

27   "Layton Suggests Talks with the Taliban", *Globe and Mail* 1 September 2006.

28   To understand this debate, see Sean M. Maloney, "From Myth to Reality Check", *Policy Options* September 2005 http://www.irpp.org/po

29   "Suicide bomber kills four Canadian Soldiers", 18 September 2006. http://www.cbc.ca/world/story/2006/09/18/bombing-canadians.html

30   The author observed and experienced this behaviour in Afghanistan.

PART 2:
THE ENEMY

The use of suicide terrorism became a mainstay of insurgent operations in the south after some debate. (DND-Combat Camera)

Chapter Three
A Violent Impediment:
The Evolution of Insurgent
Operations in Kandahar province
2003-2007

"God as our witness, if you do not follow our instructions, you will die by the bullets of the mujahedeen. Your death will be your responsibility." Taliban 'night letter'

There has been little public-domain analysis of insurgent operations in Afghanistan in the years following the collapse of the Taliban regime in 2001-02. This is most likely due to a disproportionate focus by the analytic community on the more complex insurgency(ies) in Iraq. When it comes to Afghanistan, most discussion revolves around 'big hand-small map' approaches.[1] What is the 'correct' balance between kinetic and non-kinetic activities at the strategic level? What do we do about Pakistan? Should the constitution be changed? Is the 'lack' of aid producing a 'resurgent' Taliban? What do we do about the narcotics issue? Because of the complexity of the local, district and provincial environments, existing studies do not help us understand how the Taliban operate on the ground and therefore cannot provide us with insight into how the insurgent should be fought in his environment. Any successful approach to the insurgency in Afghanistan must address local conditions and the provincial makeup of the insurgent forces, especially in Kandahar. Overly centralized and Kabul-centric strategies may not be able to do so.

Indeed, gathering first-hand information on insurgent operations in Afghanistan is a dangerous prospect apt to deter most analysts who are not part of NGOs, or military or intelligence organizations. The importance of understanding how the insurgency conducts its affairs is obvious: those practising counterinsurgency in Afghanistan need to know their enemy and how he adapts to counterinsurgent strategy and operations so he can be defeated, or at least contained. For historical purposes, examining insurgent operations in Afghanistan reveals unique aspects of the case at hand and can be one of several inputs into the body of knowledge that supports more general insurgency/counterinsurgency analysis.[2]

Consequently, this study will focus on Taliban operations in Kandahar province and how they have evolved. In southern Afghanistan, Kandahar is the key province. All roads lead to Kandahar City, be they from Kabul, Herat or Quetta in Pakistan. Kandahar province has the largest population in the south and Kandahar City is the largest concentration of that population. Control of Kandahar province, therefore, is the *sine qua non* for insurgent success in the south. The insurgency in Kandahar province has specific attributes and any counterinsurgency effort must take into account the unique evolution of Taliban operations there.

Who Are the Insurgents?

The answer to this question depends on what year and where in the province itself. The insurgency has evolved year to year with different players playing greater or lesser roles. In the early days, there were the remnants of Al Qaeda's conventional formations and Al Qaeda-supported jihadists. There were the defeated leaders and the remnants of the Taliban regime's conventional formations as well as local opponents to the Karzai government who have dubbed themselves Taliban. There were the professional killers from Gulbiddin Hekmatyar's HiG organization as well as the highly motivated fighters from the Haqqani Tribal Network (or Organization). Between 2003 and 2005, an organization called the Quetta Shura emerged to act as a mechanism for these diverse groups to discuss and coordinate policy, strategy and operations. Between 2006 and 2008, the Quetta Shura evolved further and has developed an even more sophisticated approach to the insurgency in southern Afghanistan.

There are other well-armed entities in Kandahar province that are not part of the Quetta Shura yet they pose problems for the security forces and the counterinsurgents. The first of these are the various police groups in the province, especially when they are not being paid regularly. The second are the so-called 'drug barons' and their private armies. These narco groups tend to be tribe- and family-based, are devoted to making money from the poppy crop, and will align themselves against anybody interfering with their activities.

Similarly, the Pashtun tribal code of Pashtunwalli affords various forms of blood revenge between aggrieved parties over the course of generations. Blood feuds involving RPGs and AK-47s are not necessarily Taliban violence, nor are they necessarily insurgent violence.

Consequently, not all violence in Kandahar province is Taliban violence. Every possible permutation of alliances between these groups – Taliban, Al Qaeda, HiG, HTO, Narcos, Police, tribal groupings – exists throughout southern Afghanistan. Every incident, every action, has to be carefully examined to see what the motives were behind the specific use of violence by a particular entity or entities. Some Taliban violence may even serve multiple purposes for different groups. This state of affairs poses significant challenges to any attempt to generalize about the insurgency in Afghanistan.

In terms of tactics, techniques and procedures, there are numerous traditional and non-traditional methods employed by the insurgency array. There are clear patterns and there are distinct emphases that change year to year. Some of these methods are designed for tactical military effect while at the same time serving a strategic psychological purpose. Other methods are extremely subtle and are not visible to analysts who have not visited the region. The employment of combinations of these techniques reached a fairly sophisticated level by 2006.

Early Days: 2002-03

The ejection of Taliban regime control of Kandahar City by 2002 brought with it a re-definition as to what constituted the Taliban. Many Afghans who had joined the Taliban in a bandwagon effect in 1996 when the Pakistan-supported movement rolled in to establish order, had, by 2001, become dis-illusioned with the regime. We should take 2002 as our breakpoint with the past. By May 2002, Mullah Omar, the leader of the Taliban regime, had established what amounted to small stay-behind groups in Oruzgan and Zabol provinces. At this time, weapons were distributed to some small groups in northern Kandahar province in the Shah Wali Kot district. Instructions had gone out in Pashtun-dominated areas to resist Operation ENDURING FREE-DOM forces as the American-led coalition and their Afghan allies from the Northern Alliance and other disaffected, but loosely-organized, anti-regime forces blitzkrieged over the Taliban 'shell', looking to get at the Al Qaeda 'meat' beneath it. By the summer of 2002 however, Taliban regime forces were completely defeated and the Al Qaeda structure put to flight. Radio propaganda emanating from Pakistan exhorted the remnants of the regime to conduct guerilla action throughout late 2002.

For the most part, insurgent action in the country, as distinct from operations conducted by retreating units like those in the Shah-I Kot Valley and Tora Bora region, was limited to the border regions with Pakistan roughly from Zabol to Nuristan, with sporadic incidents in Pashtun ethnic areas. The state of the insurgency in Kandahar province in 2003 is best described as undeveloped and uncoordinated. OEF forces and their associated Afghan Militia Forces (AMF) allies did not exert overall control of the province; they did not have the forces for outright occupation of all districts. OEF controlled Kandahar Air Field and used it as a large Forward Operating Base (FOB) from which air-mobile forces sortied against Taliban and Al Qaeda remnants, based on intelligence hits. The AMF occupied Kandahar City and set about establishing a rudimentary local governance with little opposition from inside the city. Many districts in the province, however, had no OEF, AMF or other Afghan Interim Administration presence. The lack of apparent enemy activity may have been the product of a lack of contact and not a true measurement of actual government or coalition control.

The next evolutionary steps regarding the Taliban insurgency occurred in February-March 2003. Taliban officials initiated an email and fax campaign to inform the international media that they existed as a formed body and that their intent was to regain power in Afghanistan. A prominent Taliban military leader, Mullah Dadullah Lang, then announced to the BBC that Mullah Omar was the supreme leader of the effort.[3]

In 2003, the pattern of enemy activity in Kandahar province, at least in terms of active measures against OEF and AMF forces, included: sporadic 107mm rocket attacks against KAF or other FOBs; very rare and small improvised explosive device attacks; and infrequent ambushes involving less than ten Taliban insurgents usually equipped with automatic weapons and RPGs. Notably, the movement employed 'non-insurgent insurgent' tactics as a force multiplier. Operatives would pay citizens to lay mines on well-travelled OEF and AMF routes and essentially walk away. They would not be contacted again; there was no organization to target, *per se*. The emergent IED specialists, of which there were very few, used primitive detonation mechanisms attached to leftover or scavenged ordnance. Uncoordinated and extremely rare attacks against NGO personnel started in early 2003 when mob action, stimulated by *agents provocateurs*, resulted in the death of a UN water treatment engineer.

Maintaining weapons stocks for future operations was another insurgent priority in Kandahar province in 2003. The remote Maruf district, not serviced by paved roads and contiguous with the Pakistan border, served as a weapons depot protected by what appeared to be Afghan government forces but who were in fact sympathetic to the Taliban. These stockpiles included everything from assault rifles to crew-served weapons and even a small number of thermobaric munitions. Similarly, remote valleys in Helmand and Oruzgan provinces hosted similar stockpiles and small guard forces. Almost all were raided and destroyed by OEF sorties throughout 2003.

The establishment of Taliban base and support structures in Pakistan of course pre-dates the 2001 intervention, but these structures were reactivated in late 2002. By 2003, the Taliban were able to mount the first cross-border foray into southern Kandahar province west of Spinboldak. At least one cross-border operation involved a company-sized group of insurgents, but the comparatively large size of the force rendered it vulnerable to OEF air-power. Such operations remained rare in Kandahar province and were more likely to occur in the Khost region.

The Taliban Lose the Initiative: 2003-04

Strategically, the period running from late 2003 to late 2005 marked three significant strategic defeats for the insurgency. Any counterinsurgency effort is dependent on securing the legitimacy of the government and its forces, particularly in terms of international legitimacy as well as with the population. The establishment of a political process in Afghanistan accredited by the United Nations and supported by the international community pro-vided the basis for this legitimacy.[4] The Constitutional Loya Jirga (CLJ), in which all Afghan factions, including the Taliban movement, were invited to participate, was held in fall 2003. The CLJ established the future direction of Afghanistan as a state and established what the national legitimacy mech-anisms would be elections and the constitution. In the fall of 2004, the pres-idential elections were held, followed a year later by provincial elections. Again, the Taliban movement was invited to participate.

The Taliban leadership rejected participation in all three activities, thus ensuring their label as an illegitimate insurgent force in the eyes of the in-ternational community as well as illegitimate in relationship to the elected government. That was their largest defeat since the collapse of the regime. The Taliban movement's failure to seriously interfere with the CLJ or presi-dential elections was their next mistake. There were ample opportunities to use violence to disrupt the CLJ and the presidential elections, but successful security measures, Afghan and coalition, played no small part in limiting these actions, particularly in Kabul. There were, however, Taliban attempts to use violence in Kandahar and Oruzgan provinces in 2004 to intimidate and kill election registration workers. OEF forces were augmented to stave this off as much as possible.[5]

Parenthetically, the Taliban movement appears to have been operationally successful in Kandahar province and also in Zabol, Oruzgan and Helmand provinces adjacent to Kandahar over the course of the following year. These provinces marked the lowest registered voter turnout rate for the 2005 provincial elections in the country: Helmand 36.8%; Kandahar 25.3%; Oruzgan 23.4%; and Zabol 20% versus 60-70% in the rest of the country.[6] Why this was the case is a matter of some dispute. Did citizens stay home on their own because of the potential for violence, or were they deliberately or systematically intimidated? Or did they boycott the elections because they sided with the Taliban? Or did they not have confidence in the government candidates? There may be some correlation between increasing levels of violence in 2005 and voter turnout in Kandahar province, which we will address later.

Successes in establishing a government and solidifying it in 2003-04 now paved the way for a further Taliban strategic defeat. If the insurgents had disrupted the establishment of the federal political process, the government of Afghanistan would not have had legitimacy in the international community and there would have been no aid money flow from the IMF, World Bank and other institutions. If there was no 'funnel' to put monies in in the first place, then aid monies needed by counterinsurgency forces to undermine the Taliban's attempts to shift the allegiance of the population at the provincial and district level could not flow. With a federal political process and an emergent bureaucracy the 'funnel' was put into place, though it would take some time for the process to be activated. This state of affairs related to the lack of capacity, at the provincial and district levels, to use the reconstruction monies as well as the interference of insurgent operations.

The Taliban movement re-focused on southern Afghanistan where the Pashtun confederations are the strongest and where they could exploit the comparatively low support for the government. HiG, Al Qaeda and HTO tended to focus on the eastern provinces of Paktika, Paktia, Khost, Nangahar and Nuristan in 2004-06, though there would be increased cross-pollination between the insurgent groups over time, depending on operational capabilities.[7] For the most part, however, Taliban forces dominated in Kandahar province.

It took some time for the Taliban movement to build up forces that could pose a serious threat to coalition and Afghan forces in the southern provinces. In 2004, Taliban operatives slowly worked on establishing facilitation networks in Kandahar City and the surrounding districts. One of their primary concerns was that they would lose any residual coercive hold over the rural populations. A campaign designed to manage the perceptions of those populations was implemented. Its purpose was to give the perception that the Taliban were more powerful than they actually were and to keep the rural populations from embracing aid and government or coalition organization. This campaign took two forms. The Taliban, like the coalition forces, could not be everywhere, but they could appear to be omnipotent to an uneducated population. Taliban mullahs moved into the rural areas on an individual basis. These 'wandering mullahs' could proselytize at will and make contact with the lesser-educated local mullahs and manipulate them. Wandering mullahs were and remain next to impossible to target. Related to the 'wandering mullahs' were their urban counterparts. Infiltrating the mosques in Kandahar City, Taliban-sympathetic mullahs conducted similar activities. Taken together, this amounts to a 'Battle for the Mosques'.

Secondly, the small number of Taliban operational groups that did exist on the run in the province employed 'night letters' to intimidate officials at the village level. These missives threatened retaliation for 'collaboration' with the government and implied that there were spies operating in all rural areas so 'transgressors' would be brought to account some day in the future. The combination of the two methods appears to have had a disruptive effect, particularly in the 2003-04 period before the Provincial Reconstruction Team started to enter rural districts to assess them. It most likely had a detrimental effect on the 2005 elections in Kandahar province.

By the end of 2004, the Taliban insurgency in Kandahar province was still limited to what it could accomplish using violence. It was able to intimidate in some rural areas, it could conduct sporadic demonstrative attacks on coalition forces, but it did not have the features necessary for a successful insurgency. For example, for the Taliban to regain control, a parallel government structure was needed, even in shadow form, so that government legitimacy could be challenged; ie, there needed to be Taliban shadow leaders for the districts and a shadow governor should have been proclaimed, along with shadow apparatus, to tax the population and provide an alternative legal system. Some of these attributes existed in crude form; the 'wandering mullahs' were key here, but the structure was not advanced enough in 2004 to decisively shift the allegiance of the population. Indeed, the lack of government control and lack of structures to translate national policy and aid to the local level were threats to stability equal to the Taliban movement in the province.

Initiative Regained: 2005

2005 is a crucial year in the insurgency. At some point in the spring there was a Quetta Shura reassessment of what could be accomplished in Kandahar province and what tools should be used. The existing measures – wandering mullahs, intimidation, sporadic attacks – all continued, as did efforts to contact Taliban regime remnants and sympathizers to build a fighting structure. A number of new ingredients were now added to the operational stew. The interesting aspect about all this is that the main Taliban spokesman to the media, Abdul Latif Hakimi, announced this in April 2005, stating that new targets would include government officials, aid workers and foreign forces. The Taliban effort, he said, would now be a war of attrition.[8] Mullah Dadullah Lang started to emerge in the western media as a public face of the Taliban around this time, particularly on Al-Jazeera, and he confirmed that there was a stronger link between Al Qaeda and the Taliban.[9]

As noted earlier, OEF forces in Kandahar did not occupy the entire province; nor could they. The AMF was disarmed and part of it was converted into the Afghan National Army, but the deployment of these new forces took some time and they were not ready in 2005. In 2005, there was only one OEF manoeuvre battalion assigned to Kandahar province – and it was a re-roled U.S. airborne artillery battalion. A U.S. Provincial Reconstruction Team åexisted and it was trying to assess the entire province, but it was too small and lacked protective capabilities. NGOs and national aid organizations were active in the province but their efforts were not effectively coordinated. That said, there was a school construction program underway. Education was and remains critical to the counterinsurgency effort over the long term as even basic education is several cuts above the constrained, backwards religious education offered by the Taliban regime during its tenure. Indeed, the biggest long-term threat to the Taliban is an educated, politically active population.

A country-wide Taliban campaign against the education system – what I call 'The War of the Schools' – started in 2005, though there had been uncoordinated attacks against schools in the Kabul area in the previous year. The initial focus was on girls' schools but the repertoire rapidly expanded to all educational facilities. In time, teachers themselves were also singled out for assassination. In Shah Wali Kot district in northern Kandahar, a Taliban group even beheaded a teacher in front of his class. By the end of 2005, the media reported that 200 schools in the southern provinces had been shut down, with an estimated 20 schools destroyed between September 2005 and December 2005.[10]

At the same time, the first transmissions from the Voice of Sharia, a pro-Taliban propaganda radio station, were received in April 2005. This led to an interesting debate in the media as to who actually controlled Voice of Sharia. One view was that this was a Taliban-controlled operation; another that it was a black propaganda device of the coalition. A third view was that the coalition 'leaked' that the Voice of Sharia was a black propaganda tool employed to discredit and disrupt a Taliban-controlled Voice of Sharia![11]

OEF forces in Kandahar were confronted in 2005 with an increasingly militant network operating in Shah Wali Kot district. A series of coalition operations in Zabol and Oruzgan provinces were 'backstopped' by the Kandahar-based U.S. battalion; that is, the battalion deployed as a net to catch any enemy trying to escape from those other operations. When the battalion deployed, they encountered small but well-armed groups of insurgents operating in this district and understood that the locals had some allegiance to them. The situation deteriorated with the establishment of a government district centre in Shah Wali Kot that year. Consequently, more and more resources were focused on this area to determine what was going on and to deal with the emerging problem.

At the same time, another network operating from the Zharey district west of Kandahar City initiated a series of ambushes on Highway 1. Initially, these ambushes were not well organized but they evolved significantly throughout 2005. Then the ambush parties started to attack road-building crews and their security forces along the highway when there were no coalition forces present. U.S. forces discovered a 'rat line' from Zharey District into southwestern Kandahar City and also discovered that the police districts there had been compromised by an urban insurgent network. At the same time, there were sporadic attacks against aid workers; later on came the outright assassination of unarmed doctors and healthcare workers from the Afghan government.

PRT operations in Kandahar province expanded when the Canadians took control in July 2005. This particular PRT had a robust protective capability and consequently was able to get into remote districts that their predecessors had not been to. Important discoveries were made: there was a significant facilitation network in Maruf district backed up with a fighting unit in the hills; Zharey district was essentially a no-go area for coalition forces and an intimidation campaign was emanating outwards in all directions from it; there was an IED cell operating in Ghorak district against Afghan police forces; and schools were being burned in Khakriz district.

We must not forget that Kandahar Air Field, the primary operating base for OEF in southern Afghanistan, was under rocket attack from cells or individuals who would set up a 107mm rocket with a timing device which, in turn, would launch the weapon some time later. This technique had been in play since 2003 but increased in frequency in 2005.

How coordinated was the Taliban effort in Kandahar province in 2005? It is easy to see a symbiotic relationship between Shah Wali Kot and Zharey operations in that OEF could not be in both places at once. Then to what extent were the other insurgent methods coordinated with the more military activity in those districts? At this time, there was no notion in coalition circles that there was a specific Taliban provincial command, or even a provincial commander; there were several. Given the increased availability of the cell phone network in the province, however, and the availability of satellite telephones, it is possible that there did not need to be a provincial commander and that the insurgent organization did not necessarily correspond to Western organizational constructs. The Soviets had made this sort of mistake in their analysis in the 1980s.[12]

By mid-2005, then, there appeared to be several insurgent networks in the province. The big questions at the time were: how specialized were those networks or cells? How much of the violence was undertaken by Taliban, 'non-insurgent insurgents' or local 'pinch hitters'? How did they coordinate? Some analysts believed that there were specialized cells and specialized individuals: ambush cells, intimidation cells, religious/political mobilization cells, facilitation networks, financiers, IED specialists and so forth. Others thought district networks were composed of several specialized cell types. Another school of thought was that certain cells could multitask: intimidate, ambush and proselytize all at once. What was clear to everybody was that there was an extremely effective observation and reporting system in each district of the province and that Taliban elements operating from district to district could plug into it.

This thinking evolved yet again with the introduction of the most spectacular Taliban development yet: the urban suicide bombing campaign.[13] Inaugurated in the fall of 2005, the Taliban facilitation networks in Kandahar City worked with Al Qaeda-trained, madrassa-recruited jihadist or other suicide bombers to their mutual advantage. The suicide bomber was the 'ammo' brought into the city, 'loaded' into a 'gun' (suicide vest or car) and 'fired' at the coalition forces. The suicide bombing campaign had a fitful start. The first attacks accomplished little in terms of material damage except to the bombers themselves but, as 2005 waned, the attackers were getting better.

The improvement of improvised explosive device attacks was a parallel development. In 2003, the rare IED attack took place but it was usually ineffective once vehicles were up-armoured, By 2005, sophisticated IEDs were being employed by insurgents in Kandahar province, particularly in Ghorak district and in Kandahar City. In some cases, detonation components produced on an assembly line were used, though they were mixed with scavenged ordnance. More importantly, trained insurgent IED specialists were now present in the province and were building the devices there. They believe that these specialist IED cells gained credence, particularly after a number of attacks in the Spinboldak area. In most cases, these attacks were not backed up with ambushes or other activities.

The importance of suicide and IED attacks was not merely limited to the tactical degradation of coalition forces; it was also strategic. The spectacular nature of the attacks attracted substantial Western media attention, particularly when media outlets started to compare coalition efforts in Afghanistan with the supposedly 'failing' American-led effort in Iraq where similar enemy IED tactics were employed. This 'guilt by association' generated by Western media between the two conflicts was, and remains, a major strategic victory for the Taliban and they would exploit it to greater effect in subsequent years. The linkage tool for that was the IED and the suicide IED coupled with growing Western concern over casualties.

There was a debate inside the Taliban, as to the Koranic legality of suicide attacks and attacks that result in civilian casualties. Mullah Omar was wavering, but in Kandahar province there were strong advocates for their use, particularly from the Mullah Baqi network operating in Zharey district and inside Kandahar City. These networks were associated with Mullah Dadullah Lang. Baqi won out and the campaign continued.

The most important development for the Taliban in Kandahar province occurred in January 2006. A Canadian diplomat of ambassador rank, working for the PRT on provincial government capacity-building, was assassinated by a suicide car bomb. Though some believe this was a lucky hit, there are others that do not. Regardless, the effects of this killing were profound. Elements within the PRT suspended capacity-building and aid operations right when they were needed most and this generated a nearly six-month suspension of the reconstruction efforts in some critical areas. This may have given the Taliban breathing space in rural districts since the PRT did not deploy to those districts for months.

Another spin-off effect of the suicide and IED campaign was to generate a perception in the international aid community that Kandahar was not safe and, therefore, that Afghanistan was not a safe place to invest money and aid resources. It was at this time that the Afghanistan Compact was under discussion, an agreement which would provide some ten billion dollars to Afghanistan for reconstruction and development. The linkage between the suicide and IED campaign, the generated perception of lack of security, and a desire by Quetta Shura to disrupt the Afghanistan Compact, cannot be conclusively proven but is highly, highly likely. For the first time in Kandahar province, we see cooperation between Taliban forces on the ground, HiG terrorists, Al Qaeda training facilities and Al Qaeda strategic information operations.

The cumulative effects of IED attacks benefited the Taliban in that Western media focused solely on casualties generated by the attacks and not on reconstruction and development progress. This still has long-term effects on coalition populations, particularly in the academic/analytic community. The question was; how sophisticated was the Taliban's understanding of information operations? Some analysts downplay this and claim that it was a bumbling, crude approach and that the Taliban 'exhibit a general lack of strategic planning and activity, particularly in the area of communications'.[14] If this is the case, how were the Taliban able to generate the perception in the Western media, throughout the 2005-2006 period, that the war in Afghanistan was a lost cause?

The answer is the relationship between the Taliban and Al Qaeda via the Quetta Shura. The Al Qaeda movement does indeed exhibit a sophisticated understanding of information operations and, in 2006, it became more and more evident that the techniques were being employed to support the Taliban's efforts to promote their activity in ways that they had not done even two years before. Taliban leaders in Kandahar province, for example, know whom to call in the Pakistani media to get their version of events out before coalition forces can even react. Their contacts are a cell phone call away, whereas coalition forces have to practically form a committee to respond to anything.

In time, the Taliban developed their own pool of media 'fixers' who became adept at 'spinning' the more naive Western reporters flocking to Kandahar. Any analysis of Canadian media from late 2005 on, for example, (the American media tended to focus on Iraq and stayed away from southern Afghanistan) will encounter a breathlessly sensationalistic, even alarmist, tone along with the uncritical reprinting of bold statements by shadowy Taliban commanders; but with little analysis.[15]

Escalation: 2006-07

In early 2006, Afghan analysts concluded a study of the insurgency in the south that, in their view, confirmed that the Taliban threat was much more developed than had been previously understood and that it had a three-phased strategy: strategic survival and re-organization; establishment of foothold bases in remote areas; and mass mobilization using tribal and religious elements. The Taliban were estimated to be in the second phase and trying to transition to the third. Their inability to establish a parallel government at the district level was inhibiting their progression to phase three and the coalition and Afghan effort, no matter how flawed it was, was a serious impediment. Yes, the Taliban could mobilize in the rural areas; but could they control all of them all of the time? Could they eventually take the urban areas and consolidate them?

The suicide and IED campaign continued throughout Kandahar in the spring and summer of 2006 drawing most of the media's attention away from important developments in the insurgency. As before, the geographical enemy grouping tended to be in Shah Wali Kot and Zharey districts, with Maruf playing a supporting role. Taliban activities were, at this point, expanding in Helmand province as British forces deployed into it. Canadian forces were tasked to keep the main service routes to Helmand and Oruzgan open to facilitate deployment of British and Dutch forces. A series of operations conducted by the Canadian Battlegroup discovered that Taliban forces were discreetly infiltrating Zharey district, using sporadic operations in Shah Wali Kot as a distraction. The intent behind this summer build-up was interpreted by Afghan government sources as preparations to strike multiple targets inside the city itself, with the express purpose of generating a Tet-offensive-like effect. This planning went beyond the conduct of IED attacks and ambushes in the hills and indicates that the enemy outlook was more sophisticated than was previously understood.

The Canadian view was that the insurgents were positioning themselves to dominate the green areas on the three highways surrounding the city so they could blockade it, or otherwise interfere with the commerce flowing on those routes, with obvious detrimental consequences for the people. There was a concern that, along with the strikes inside the city, the perception that the Taliban were on the verge of regaining control might tip the allegiance of the population, as it had back in 1996.

Disruptive Canadian operations into Zharey district confirmed a number of things. First, the insurgents stood and fought from prepared defensive positions in a coordinated fashion. Secondly, the presence of foreign fighters (Punjabis and Chechens) was confirmed. Thirdly, the insurgents understood the decreasing propaganda value of using the people as human shields; thereafter, they depopulated certain potential battle areas by insisting that the civilian population leave. Again, this went far beyond what the previous American battalion had encountered back in 2005.

Further north, the enemy melted away in the face of coalition forces and laid IEDs and mines instead. They still had significant pull in the Shah Wali Kot district and the Ghorak IED cell remained active, but as Canadian forces moved into forward operating bases, enemy tactics changed. Mortars were now employed. In time, Canadian forces even captured a Pakistani mortar fire-control specialist trained by the Pakistani Army.

IED and suicide IED attacks against coalition forces in and around Kandahar City also increased in number and sophistication throughout 2006. As before, jihadis were 'facilitated' into Kandahar City, provided with information and the weapon and unleashed. In the main, these were foreign jihadis, some from Pakistan, some from Saudi Arabia.[16]

Mullah Dadullah Lang (MDL) became a Western media darling around this time. The media was finally able to put a 'face' on the Taliban that was not merely some shadowy Pakistani cutout spokesman and they flocked to report on the muscular and personally violent 'MDL'. The Taliban exploited this and created what amounted to a personality cult around MDL which included the distribution of extremely violent and explicit CDs in Kandahar province and throughout western Pakistan. MDL's importance, however, was that he was internally advocating a more conventional approach to the insurgency. This advocacy was apparently the impetus behind the operations in Zharey district and around Kandahar City. Did the media attention permit MDL to gain more influence with the Quetta Shura? Nobody knows for sure. What is known is that some form of green light was given since, in the fall of 2006, coalition forces encountered Taliban forces that had massively infiltrated Zharey district. In the resulting battle, Operation MEDUSA, both sides fought using nearly conventional tactics, including tanks, artillery and airpower by the coalition, and anti-tank, mortar and positional defence by the Taliban. This was a far cry from the days of 2003.

Yet another Taliban operational form emerged, concurrent with operations in Zharey. Knowing that coalition and Afghan forces could not be everywhere at once, Taliban cells started attacking the district centres in outlying rural areas. The importance of the district centre requires explanation. Generally, the centres are the headquarters of the local and provincial government representatives, the police and administration. They are practical, as well as symbolic, representations of government control or influence.

In 2006, a Taliban campaign was directed against a small number of outlying district centres in Helmand, Oruzgan and Zabol provinces. In each operation, Taliban forces moved into these towns, occupied and then burned the district centre and then withdrew, sometimes after fighting coalition forces were sent to re-take the centres. The objective, in all cases, appears to have been to draw off coalition and Afghan forces conducting operations against other insurgent forces, as much as it was to destroy the facility. In all cases, the Karzai government insisted that the loss of such centres, even in outlying districts, amounted to strategic losses. They demanded that coalition forces be redeployed, even in the middle of other operations, to retake them. This technique was repeated in Kandahar in 2007 when the Ghorak district centre was seized in the summer while operations were ongoing in Zharey and Shah Wali Kot. The multiple and concurrent effects of district centre seizures are clearly understood by the Taliban and, once again, this is an indicator of operational sophistication that was not there in previous years.

Another example of Taliban operational sophistication revolves around the issue of deployment and use of coalition armoured vehicles. Canada was the first coalition member to start using armoured fighting vehicles on a protracted basis in Kandahar province in 2006. These Canadian-designed and built LAV-III Kodiak vehicles are eight-wheeled MICVs equipped with 25mm guns. Taliban fighters referred to them as Green Monsters That Spit Fire and Shit White People Out The Back and the ability of these vehicles to drive into areas that the insurgents believed to be unnavigable seriously unnerved them. Similarly, when Canada deployed Leopard C-2 medium tanks to support operations in Zharey district, they were called Super Monsters by Taliban fighters who were unused to the presence of tanks on the battlefield.

To counteract the psychological shock produced by the presence of these vehicles, instructions went out to various Taliban commanders in Kandahar province to catastrophically kill a Canadian armoured vehicle and, if possible, film or photograph such an attack. This would be used in two ways: to bolster the morale of Taliban fighters and to ignite a wave of media criticism back in Canada as they did over the tank deployment. Previous to that time, there was no interest in conducting such an attack; the Taliban already knew they could kill American up-armoured Hummers and Canadian G-Wagon vehicles with car bombs. Indeed, when the Canadian media announced that Canada would replace the 'vulnerable' G-Wagon with the supposedly 'mine-proof' RG-31 Nyala, purchased by the Canadian Government partly in response to severe media criticism about the lack of protection for Canadian soldiers, a Taliban cell catastrophically killed one with an anti-tank mine, just to prove they could do so.

In time, the Taliban learned, with some difficulty and personnel loss, that they could destroy Canadian armoured vehicles; however, measures taken by Canadian forces to deny enemy forces access to strike sites, together with preventive measures to restrict any dissemination of images by the media, has had a countervailing effect on the enemy's Information Operations (I/O) war. Taliban procurers then tried, in 2006, to acquire Anti-Tank Guided Missiles but failed, apparently, to deploy any in Kandahar province. In time, machine-milled Explosively Formed Projectiles (EFP) made in Iran have made their way into an adjacent province, but none have been employed against coalition forces in Kandahar province. The game continues.

This leads us to another extremely important point. The Taliban are able to use the Internet to gather battle-damage assessment data about coalition forces. The hyper-specific media reporting of coalition operations in Kandahar province, particularly of combat deaths and their associated ramp ceremonies, provides the Taliban with ready-made images of weeping Canadian soldiers carrying coffins; they can use these images in many contexts and in many forums, such as Web sites and uploadable film clips. This 'reach back' capability should be assumed. Indeed, it is being employed by Iraqi insurgents. Raids against Al Qaeda sympathizers in Germany have found Web sites with substantial Google Earth imagery that is used to conduct reconnaissance of American forces in Iraq and then target them.[17] It is also relatively easy for the Quetta Shura to request vulnerability studies from its Al Qaeda allies, who have tentacles in Western universities. Even a crude analysis of media on the Internet can inform Taliban and Al Qaeda operations.

This leads us to the controversial idea that the Taliban and Al Qaeda can generate strategic psychological effects on coalition populations using a tactical attack against coalition forces in Kandahar province; this is a level of sophistication that some analysts and observers do not want to see.

In the plethora of IED and suicide IED attacks against Canadian forces operating in Kandahar in 2006-07, two attacks stand out. The first occurred on 18 September 2006, the day Parliament opened in Canada after its summer recess to debate the continuance of Canada's combat role in Afghanistan. In this incident, a suicide bomber attempted a mass casualty attack against Canadian forces that killed four and wounded ten Canadians and over twenty Afghans in Bazaar-e-Panjwayi, which abuts Zharey district. The debate in Canada over Afghanistan was already picking up steam and this incident accelerated it. Many analysts wrote this attack off as a coincidence, even as the Opposition in Canada's Parliament demanded Canada's immediate withdrawal and that Canada open negotiations with the Taliban to surrender the country.

Then there was a mass casualty IED attack that catastrophically killed a LAV-III vehicle and six Canadian soldiers. This attack took place on Easter Sunday 2007. This was the 90th anniversary of the Battle of Vimy Ridge, an event that has been elevated in recent years in Canada to a second independence day. The entire country and its media was focused on Vimy Ridge ceremonies as it had been for weeks in the run-up to the anniversary. After the attack, the Opposition again demanded the Canadian withdrawal from Afghanistan, though tactical commanders and analysts insisted this attack was also a coincidence. We will recall that some also believed that the killing of the Canadian Foreign Affairs PRT representative in January 2006 was also a coincidence. That makes three coincidences in just over one year. Spain, by way of comparison, only needed one 'coincidence' to pull its forces out of Iraq. Some wish to debate whether the Taliban suicide and IED campaign is specifically designed for 'strategic' effect or 'operational/tactical' effect. Many forget that Taliban leaders and their networks are merely a cell phone call away from Quetta and do not really care about categorizing in the Western fashion; they are interested in effects.

The most overlooked Taliban 'front' remains, however, the mosques. Western analysts completely missed or misunderstood the role of the mosques in the Taliban mobilization effort. This, in part, shows an ethnocentric bias: Westerners recognize the separation of church and state while Islam does not. While the battle waged on in Zharey district in 2006-07, the first tentative steps were taken by the coalition to assess the religious framework of Kandahar City and its relationship to the Taliban effort.

The National Ulema Shura is a body of religious leaders separate from the government of Afghanistan, yet wielding tremendous influence in religious affairs throughout the country. The Kandahar Ulema Shura (KUS) is the provincial equivalent. The KUS is a mixture of appointed and self-appointed Mullahs and in theory can influence district and community Mullahs. The Taliban recognized that the KUS was a moderate institution and that it was mildly pro-government and, from 2005 into 2006, they sought to manipulate the KUS' makeup through selective assassination. Why? Canadian information operations staff realized that independent KUS condemnation of Taliban suicide and IED attacks that resulted in civilian casualties had a detrimental effect on Taliban operations, reducing their influence in critical areas. The KUS issued fatwa after fatwa condemning the Taliban and those fatwas somehow reached a broader audience than television or radio outlets could.[18] The Battle for the Mosques reached new heights in 2006-07 when the Taliban overreacted to a series of new fatwas and successively assassinated three popular Mullahs in Kandahar City. There public backlash, unfortunately, was not exploited effectively by coalition and Afghan forces and promises of funding and salaries, which the government reneged on, were taken up by the Taliban.

Another development in 2006 involved the use of intimidation against civilian personnel employed by coalition forces. This took two forms. Direct attacks started in the summer of 2006, including the bombing of a bus carrying interpreters to Kandahar Air Field for work (killing ten and wounding a dozen more) and the attempted assassination of interpreters working for the Provincial Reconstruction Team. The second was a campaign of intimidation directed at truck drivers in the Kandahar City region. Coalition forces and, particularly, the Afghan National Army extensively use local trucking to support operations throughout the province. Indeed, a small number of trucks were destroyed, but it was unclear whether some of those attacks related to commercial and tribal rivalry over contracting disputes. It is possible that tribal rivals and the Taliban have overlapping interests; this plays itself out with a Taliban cell conducting attacks on behalf of another entity. Interpreters, however, still interpret for the PRT and truck drivers still support coalition operations and facilities.

De-escalation in 2007-08: Temporary or Enduring?

There were significant changes to the Taliban's approach to operations in Kandahar province throughout 2007. The most important was the elimination of Mullah Dadullah Lang in the course of an extensive special operations forces mission. MDL's killing had multiple effects. He had been set up by the media, his followers and his own ego into being the 'General Patton' of the Taliban, so his killing generated a psychological shock throughout the movement. Additionally, there was already internal criticism of his attempts at near-conventional operations in Kandahar province and their thwarting by coalition operations in Zharey district in 2006. Indeed, no new leader with MDL's experience or stature has emerged on the public stage. Increasingly effective coalition efforts at all levels seriously reduced the Taliban's capacity throughout the province during this time, although this was not noted by the Western media who continued their hypercritical mantra that the coalition effort in Afghanistan was failing.

The Taliban were forced to adopt a new posture. The War of the Schools evolved away from outright killing and burning towards a madrassa-like policy that included the distribution of Taliban-approved school books, in some rural districts, in an effort to counter government efforts. The educational battle is on. Indeed, the leaders of Panjwayi district independently sent an emissary to Quetta to insist that the Taliban stop attacking their schools. The Taliban relented. The government polio vaccine campaign, implemented in 2006-07, was not opposed by the Taliban, who publicly announced that they would not interfere with it. That campaign has virtually eliminated polio in the province. Despite their information operation stunts, the Taliban still do not possess an effective shadow government capable of meeting the needs of the people, though they tried in Maywand district which straddles the vital Highway 1 corridor to Helmand province. Those needs are increasing as more and more contact is made between the urbanized population and the rural population, especially among women from urban and rural districts, and as coalition soldiers demonstrate by their actions that they are not merely some *kafir* occupation force.

Do these developments mean an end to violence? No. Successful coalition operations against IED cells have seriously reduced the Taliban's capacity in this area, albeit temporarily. The 'A' team suicide bomber cells have been reduced to the 'D' and 'E' teams and there appear to be fewer willing recruits for the process. Indeed, one Taliban cell was reduced to manipulating mentally retarded people into wearing wire-filled vests with no explosives in order to entice coalition forces into overreacting and killing them. In many cases, IED specialists have been attritted which in turn has forced many Taliban cells to resort to the good old dumb land mine laid by the 'non-insurgent insurgent'. Ominously though, Taliban IED cells are increasingly resorting to extremely large, obliterative explosions which completely, or nearly completely, fragment the target. This new type of attack emerged on four occasions in the summer of 2007. That said, subsequent efforts to regenerate networks in Zharey district are frustrated by coalition operations, and attempts by the Taliban to expand similar operations to Arghandab district in the fall of 2007 have met with failure.

In early 2008, the enemy resorted to mass casualty-producing IED attacks against the security forces and the civilian population. This has resulted in a backlash from the community; so much so, that the Taliban refused to take credit for one particularly violent attack in February 2008 that resulted in over 100 dead and at least 80 injured. The extremely negative public response to a second attack the day following the first one may have had a role in forcing the Taliban leadership to curtail further operations of this type. Indeed, the split between Mullah Omar and Mullah Dadullah Lang in 2005 over the use of suicide terrorism may be repeating itself; the proponents of suicide terrorism are now at odds with Mullah Omar again and further fragmentation within the movement appears to be developing. At least three senior Taliban commanders in Kandahar and Helmand provinces have expressed an interest in the Afghan government amnesty program. This is in part due to a drop off in the enthusiasm of the personnel commanded by these leaders for continued operations in the face of improved operational techniques by the coalition forces, especially in Kandahar province.

Among these techniques was the implementation of a 9/11-type reporting system that takes advantage of the geometrically expanded cell phone network in southern Afghanistan and has produced substantial information on enemy activity, information subsequently exploited by the Afghan national security forces. Taliban groups in Zharey district have even burned down cell towers out of frustration, even though they need the system to communicate among themselves.

Indeed, rocket attacks against Kandahar Air Field and Canadian forward operating bases in the province are at an all-time low. The peak year was 2006, with a substantial drop off throughout 2007. In 2006, there were attacks nearly every second night for most of the year, with multiple rockets used in each attack. During the first three months of 2008, there has been only a single attack against Kandahar Air Field (KAF) with a rocket, with the previous one occurring on Christmas Eve in 2007, again with a single rocket.

One Taliban response has been an attempt to open new fronts in the province. An active network in Arghistan district emerged but was suppressed by coalition forces more or less immediately before it could evolve. There was a move by the Taliban to infiltrate and seize a softer target, Shorabak District, in 2007. Shorabak is a remote district right on the Pakistan-Afghan border south-west of the primary border entry area at Spinboldak. It is far away from Kandahar City, is close to Taliban support areas in Pakistan and should have been an easy win. A Taliban operational commander infiltrated the district and intimidated the local mullahs in an attempt to build a facilitation network. Three madrassas controlled by the operational commander inside Pakistan generated an armed force to use the facilitation network and open up operations against the pro-government district leadership. The Taliban effort failed by the summer of 2007. Importantly, there was no coalition military support for the government forces; this was a purely Afghan affair. A powerful pro-government leader in Spinboldak deployed forces to assist the district leadership and police, while moderate mullahs from Shorabak proselytized the population to try to counter the pro-Taliban message. In this desolate terrain, the Taliban forces had nowhere to run and had no support among the people, even with Pashtunwali operating in the background. They were forced to retreat back into Pakistan.

We are now seeing an expanded intimidation campaign in certain districts, as well as in Kandahar City. If all the enemy can do is intimidate through night letters and blow things up, he has reached the limits of his influence. Engaging only in these two activities is not enough. The Quetta Shura must have Kandahar City in order to achieve its objectives in southern Afghanistan. It has been thwarted from doing so thus far. If the Quetta Shura is incapable of mounting operations similar in scope and scale to those of 2006, the movement will lose ground in Kandahar province in the face of dramatically expanded construction and governance activities, activities they cannot compete with.

One mystery that has emerged in southern Afghanistan revolves around the Taliban's weapons. On the whole, Taliban fighters are equipped with AK-47 assault rifles, PKM machine-guns, 82mm recoilless rifles, and RPG rocket launchers. Mortars have been used too, as have 107mm rockets. Explosively formed projectiles started to make an appearance in 2007. However, between 2005 and 2007 there has been no confirmed use of advanced weapons by the Taliban. They have sought ATGMs and continuously claim to have MAN-PADs. Al Qaeda fighters possessed a handful of thermobaric munitions back in 2002-03. No coalition armoured vehicles have been engaged with ATGMs, nor have coalition aircraft been engaged with MANPADS.

The amount of money available to the movement, including the supposedly massive amounts ascribed to them from those who unrelentingly emphasize the narco-Taliban nexus, has produced no influx of advanced weapons throughout the course of the war. The most advanced weapons appear to be IED detonation components, mass produced and provided to the Taliban by elements operating within a neighbouring power.

One possibility is that those supporting and sponsoring the Taliban movement have deliberately chosen to limit access to advanced weapons for reasons of their own. The one clue to the answer is a historical one. In the 1980s jihad against the Soviet Union, General Mohommad Yousaf of the Inter-Services Inteligence (ISI) noted:

"For the Majahedeen, the possession of heavy weapons and plentiful ammunition was a common goal for which they were willing to show their flexibility, some inclination to listen, or to follow instructions. My giving assurances that a certain operation would be backed up with extra weapons or more missiles, and that success would lead to further supplies, was sometimes the only way I could obtain cooperation. I had a carrot to offer. My stick was to withhold the weapons. Had the ISI not retained this prerogative my task would have been hopeless."[19]

If this scenario is operative, there is no Taliban success to reinforce and, therefore, it is possible that they have been denied access to advanced weapons for use in Kandahar province because of their failures.

Ammunition to fuel the insurgency came from many sources: China, Iran and Pakistan.

Conclusions

The war in Kandahar province will continue and the Taliban's operational methodology will evolve. The pattern of operations is unique and does not follow existing models like the Maoist or Focoist approaches. It would be disingenuous to attribute a linear progressive, terrorism-guerilla, action-conventional, operations-victory structure to the insurgency. The Taliban and its allies are less systematic in their approach and appear to have tailored it to the specific requirements of a given province.

Thus far, the Taliban have not achieved their objectives in Kandahar province short of mere survival. Despite the simplistic rhetoric on insurgency in the western public domain, survival is not enough. Time is no longer on the side of the insurgents. The development effort in Kandahar, though slow to start and problematic in areas, is gathering momentum. In time, the educational system will produce a generation that is not interested in living a mediaeval version of Islamic life. That generation will have high expectations from the society they are growing up in; this places an immense responsibility on the emergent government of Afghanistan's leaders and structures. The future fuel for the insurgency can be shut off with effective development and governance, particularly at the provincial level. It is equally crucial for the Western partners in the coalition effort to provide a more robust defence against the perception of failure. This is the only way to counter the only real weapon the Taliban have left: our short attention span coupled with our Western cultural fear of death.

Notes

1   See for example Thomas H. Johnson's "On the Edge of the Big Muddy: The Taliban Resurgence in Afghanistan" http://www.silkroad-studies.org/new/docs/CEF/Quarterly/May_2007/Johnson.pdf

2   This study is based on the author's annual participation in coalition operations in Kandahar province, starting in 2003. In the main, it is derived from personal observations and discussions with local people as well as with counterinsurgency practitioners. The paucity of documentation derived from what is actually occurring on the ground is the primary motive for the production of this paper.

3   BBC, 28 March 2003, Rahimullah Yusufzai, "Taliban aims to regain power."

4   The external academic reviewer of this article snidely referred to this depiction of the situation as 'naive' and implied in his review that federal government legitimacy is not relevant in the Pashtun areas of Afghanistan. That is a gross generalization not borne out during my travels in Kandahar province. The reality is that any international effort in stabilizing Afghanistan has to be seen by domestic audiences in Western countries to be supporting a legitimate government. International aid money on the scale necessary to rehabilitate Afghanistan will not flow without a legitimate government. The legitimacy of the federal and the provincial governments is indeed important to people in Kandahar province and the perceived lack of legitimacy in 2005-06 was deliberately exploited by the Taliban for their purposes.

5   RFE/RL 6 July 2004 "Afghan Voter-Registration Site Attacked"; 27 June 2004, "Taliban Targeting Would-be Afghan Voters."

6   Strategic Advisory Team-Afghanistan, 3 November 2005, "An Assessment of the 18 September Election Results."

7   For example, HiG deployed specialist personnel to assist Taliban efforts in Kandahar's Zharey district, while Chechens affiliated with Al Qaeda acted as a close protection party to a Taliban leader operating in western Kandahar province.

8   A summation, "Desperate Taliban," is available at www.longwarjournal.org written by Bill Roggio.

9   Jonathan Landay, "A New Taliban has Re-Emerged in Afghanistan," Knight Ridder news agency, 19 August 2005.

10   30 January 2006, "Militants begin targeting Afghan schools parallel to soldiers," www.AfghaNews.net

11   For these evolutions, see RFE/RL 22 April 2005, "Taliban Says US Forces Won't Find Radio Station"; 9 May 2005, "Afghanistan: Taliban Radio Back on the Air."

12   See Lester W. Grau and Michael Gress (ed) *The Soviet-Afghan War: How a Superpower Fought and Lost* (Lawrence: University Press of Kansas, 2002) p. 72.

13   Suicide attacks had taken place elsewhere in Afghanistan, particularly in Kabul in 2003-04, but there does not appear to have been this type of activity in Kandahar province until 2005.

14   Tim Foxley, "The Taliban's Propaganda Activities: How Well is the Afghan Insurgency Communicating and What is it Saying?" June 2007, SIPIRI Research Paper. This paper is worth reading, though there are some problems with its discussion of the tactical aspects of Taliban information operations when it comes to the local rural populations.

15   One such 'fixer' who 'assisted' one of Canada's major television networks and several prominent print journalists was arrested in 2007 by American forces, declared an enemy combatant, and placed in American custody at Bagram Air Field. Back in 2006, this individual allegedly filmed a lethal suicide attack against a convoy I was travelling in, demonstrating that he knew in advance about the attack. That television network insisted publicly that the Americans were 'mistaken' and 'wrong' to apprehend this fixer and refused to publicly entertain the idea that the fixer was working for the Taliban and that they had been bamboozled by him.

16 The suicide car bomber that attacked and destroyed my vehicle was a Pakistani, for example.

17 As discussed at www.mypetjawa.mu.nu, "For those who say the Internet Jihad is No Big Deal...." 16 October 2007.

18 I am indebted to Padre Captain Suleyman Demiray for his insights into religious operations in Kandahar province.

19 Mohommad Yousaf and Mark Adkin, *Afghanistan: The Bear Trap* (Havertown: Casemate, 1992) p. 103.

The Target and the Prize: The Afghan people. (DND-Combat Camera)

CHAPITRE 4
TALIBAN GOVERNANCE:
CAN CANADA COMPETE?

I first met Sitara Achakzai in December 2005. We were both present for a Confidence in Government presentation by Canadian International Development Agency's (CIDA) Michael Callan at the Governor's Guest House in Kandahar City, at the start of the Taliban suicide IED campaign. Sitara was one of three women on the Provincial Council, a body that was new and tentative as to where it fit into the provincial power structure. At the end of the presentation, I heard her speaking German, so I said "Hello" and introduced myself in German. We had a productive discussion on the events of the day. Over the course of the next three years we met from time to time whenever I was sitting in on council meetings and we talked about the evolution of the situation in the province. In April 2009 Sitara was gunned down in an act of Taliban governance.

Sitara represented many things to many people. Canadian women's rights proponents saw her as a fighter for women's place in the halls of Afghanistan's misogynistic socio-political system. For her Kandahar City constituents she was there to represent their grievances and mediate to improve their community. For the Achekzai tribe she was a tribal voice on the Council ready to be activated when tribal influence was threatened. For the Karzai government Sitara was there to prove to the Western aid donors that they were 'doing something' about women's rights.

For the Taliban, however, Sitara represented something else. She was the perfect target. By assassinating Sitara, the Taliban could hit the Afghan and coalition effort on several planes at once. All of the aforementioned attributes became vulnerabilities when concentrated in one person. Killing Sitara would send the message 'do not get involved in politics' to other Afghan women and those pushing a women's agenda in Afghanistan. It could then be turned into an information operations weapon in the rural areas designed to cater to those illiterate, male, community power brokers who fear the infidel will impose a loss of power to women. The tribe would lose a voice on the Council, cause infighting as other tribes sought to fill the vacancy and improve their influence base at others' expense. The Karzai government would look impotent if the media attacked them with false logic ('If only the security forces had been better/less corrupt, this would not have happened.'). Western donors, particularly non-governmental organizations, now have an excuse not to participate in provincial reconstruction, citing how bad the security situation is ('Even the Provincial Council is not safe in the capital!').

The coalition effort in southern Afghanistan has no retaliatory capability to balance out the death of Sitara Achakzai. There is no single target that ISAF or OEF forces can strike that would have the same impact on the Taliban's ability to govern the areas in districts that are in dispute. Yes, coalition forces can take out enemy military leadership – and do so frequently – with measurable effect on enemy operations. We do not have the ability to do the same in order to attenuate Taliban governance efforts. Why is that the case? How does the Taliban govern the disputed areas in Kandahar and in Afghanistan? What can we do about it?

During the Cold War, numerous theories emerged to explain the revolutionary insurgency phenomenon that emerged in the 1950s and 1960s. The basis of any insurgency during those years was the need to shift the population's perception of the legitimacy of the state to the insurgent apparatus which then achieved power and went about consolidating control of the country. For counter-insurgents, their job was to maintain the legitimacy of the state in the eyes of the population using a variety of lethal and non-lethal means while, at the same time, discrediting the insurgent forces so that the population then assisted them in hunting down the insurgents, thus eliminating the threat to the state. Let's call this tension 'competitive governance'.

In Afghanistan, this model does not completely hold true, but it is a good basis for discussion. When the Taliban took control over portions of Afghanistan between 1994 and 1996, they used what insurgency theorists call a 'foco' approach, so named after a Latin-American method employed by Fidel Castro in Cuba and elsewhere. A small group of heavily armed and well-organized men gathered local support, declared that the regional leadership was corrupt and marched on the city (in this case, it was Kandahar City). As the 'foco' moved closer to the city, more and more people joined it, swelling the ranks of the insurgent force and creating a physical and psychological momentum that continued to build and apply pressure. In time, commanders of various tribal factions inside the city were at odds with each other. Some opportunistically chose to side with the insurgent force and turned on their tribal rivals, thus handing over the city to the Taliban with little violence. This pattern repeated itself during the Taliban's 2004-05 drive north through Ghazni and Logar towards Kabul and, in the west, from Helmand to Herat.

In time, the Taliban and its allies controlled a significant portion of Afghanistan. The Taliban was created and funded by merchants in Quetta who were having problems moving goods up Highway 4 and into central Asia. The Taliban were not intended by their original patrons to lead a revolution, *per se*. This changed, however, as elements in Pakistan saw how the Taliban could be used to further their strategic and commercial purposes in Afghanistan. Still others, like Al Qaeda, saw the Taliban as a shield for their global activities which were related to the Salafist Wahhabist jihad, so they poured into the country to train.

Still, Mullah Omar and his leaders had to govern the areas they controlled. They chose to turn the calendar back to the 7th Century as much as they could while retaining the military technology needed to fight their enemies. The methods used to control the population were just like those employed by a mediaeval theocracy. Sharia law became the only law and it was enforced by randomly appointed 'religious police' who utilized extreme violence. There were rudimentary shuras for larger issues in Kandahar and Kabul, but very little 'middle management'. Fear of retribution legitimized by a fundamentalist interpretation of a 6th Century text was the basis of Taliban governance.

Did the subjugated civilian population view the Taliban as legitimate at this point? In some cases, yes. The Taliban appeared to establish order during the War of the Commanders where it had been circumspect. They appeared to have a rudimentary legal system based on the Hanafi school of jurisprudence which appealed to the rural communities and to certain tribal leaders. They definitely had a monopoly on the use of force. However, the population, particularly those in the cities, did not appear to be represented in any governance structure higher than the community shura. The existing bureaucracy, damaged after years of war, collapsed and was replaced with the fatalistic doctrine "Allah will provide". Tribal chieftains who had been co-opted by the Taliban retained their tribal affiliations and allegiances. Tribal chieftains who had not done so were on the run, but they still retained the allegiance of their members.

It is important to note here that prior to the Soviet intervention there was an extensive and functional governance system in Afghanistan. Twenty-five years of war destroyed it. There was a basis of political legitimacy in the memory of the aging survivors of that period, but less so with younger people. The young all grew up in an environment where tribe and community had achieved ascendence in the wake of the collapse of the governance system. Recall that Afghanistan was relatively peaceful and free of tribal and ethnic violence from the 1920s to the 1970s. It was not Bosnia and it was not Cambodia.

Fast-forward to 2001-05. When the Taliban regime was removed from power in the south, it was through another 'foco'. A Durrani tribal confederation, supported by U.S. Special Forces and airpower, moved up Highway 4 from Tahtapol and Spin Boldak to the gates of Kandahar City. Tribal elements inside the city, previously co-opted by the Taliban, changed sides when they saw that the tide was turning and the city fell to the coalition forces and their tribal allies. The Taliban fled and dispersed. The 2001 Bonn Agreement and Canadian-led ISAF operations in Kabul in 2003 prevented another

War of the Commanders. This gave the emergent federal government the legitimacy it needed to start reconstruction money flowing from international sources. In 2004, the country overwhelmingly supported the Karzai government and in 2005 provincial elections were held without significant Taliban interference. The Taliban, incidentally, were invited to join the political process in 2004, but chose not to.

These victories were then challenged, starting in 2005. In 2006, the Taliban and their allies attempted their version of the 'foco' against Kandahar City, this time from and through the Zharey and Panjwayi districts. Canadian and allied forces repeatedly defeated the Taliban's attempt to gain momentum with the rural population and gain allies within the city.

It would be simplistic to suggest that the Taliban and their allies shifted from terrorism to guerilla action in 2003-05, then to near-conventional operations in 2006-7 and then back to guerilla operations by 2008. The Taliban approach has always had a 'political' dimension to it which has evolved over time. While the Taliban and their foreign jihadi augmentees were throwing themselves against Canadian forces in Zharey and Panjwayi and blowing themselves up in cars in Kandahar City, the Taliban constantly had measures in play designed to influence the rural population since at least 2005, and probably before that. What we are seeing over the past year are much more systematic attempts to develop a governance system with the intent of shifting the allegiance of the population away from the Afghan government.

How has this state of affairs evolved? It is important to understand that many methods are employed simultaneously by the insurgency, but in varying degrees and sometimes without consistency. It is difficult to detect exactly what a shift in approach looks like. The methods by which the insurgents seek to influence the civilian population are evolutionary. Some have been emphasized at certain times more than others. Some techniques even have multiple audiences and this produces some confusion. For example, IEDs were employed against coalition forces in 2003, but they were essentially nuisance devices, randomly detonated. By 2007, IEDs were used as part of a strategic information operations campaign designed to undermine Canada's national will by causing casualties. However, many other detonations would continue to be nuisance devices or weapons designed to generate tactical effects.

So it goes with Taliban governance. The 2002-05 period is best characterized by survival. The Taliban as a movement struggled to exist throughout this period. The movement had to demonstrate to its constituent audiences that it was viable. Those audiences included pro-jihadists from the Gulf states and elements in Pakistan who provided weapons and safe haven. The other audience was the Afghan people, particularly in the south and east. Most Taliban activity during this period was demonstrative; essentially, the message was 'We continue to exist and fight the infidels'.

The movement had to exaggerate its capabilities. The best way to do this was to generate an omnipotent milieu in the rural areas. 'Night letters' (messages nailed to mosque doors) coupled with selective acts of nocturnal violent intimidation, followed by withdrawal during the daytime, kept many rural areas in a state of agitation. With the lack of government presence in those areas, let alone police, it was essentially a form of control. The fear that the Taliban might show up at night was enough to keep elements of the rural population from actively siding with the government and from accepting government aid and reconstruction programs. On occasion, an NGO or aid worker would be killed or kidnapped to thwart the reconstruction effort, but this was not yet systematic. In effect, this state of affairs existed for several years. At the same time, Taliban allies like HiG and the Haqqani Tribal Network conducted increasingly violent and sophisticated suicide attacks in the cities, mostly Kabul. Again, this was demonstrative in nature. 'We're still in the game' was the message.

The shift from survival mode to more active engagement occurred in 2005. 'Negative governance' is one way we can describe these activities. During that year, the intimidation methodology employed by the Taliban became slightly more integrated and systematic. These new methods, however, were overlooked by Western coalition forces because they did not understand that, in Islam, religion and politics are the same thing. Many Westerners viewed the mosque as a church and the mullah as just a religious figure. The reality was that the mosque and mullah were integral aspects of the rural and urban populations' lives in ways incomprehensible to the secular and atheist Westerners involved in the Afghanistan reconstruction.

Taliban religious engagement took several forms. The first was the 'wandering mullah'. Unarmed proselytizers trained in Pakistani madrassas infiltrated Afghanistan and moved about the rural areas living with local illiterate mullahs and passing on an 'educated' but Talibanized version of Islam. In other areas, 'wandering mullahs' paid cash to unpaid local mullahs to pass on the Taliban message to their constituent populations. They played on xenophobic and misogynistic fears of loss of control.

These activities had their urban counterparts, but when the moderate Kandahar Ulema Shura (a scholarly religious body) actively disagreed with this 'messaging', their members were targeted by Taliban operatives and killed or intimidated into silence; this amounted to an assassination campaign that continues today. In 2005-06 alone, twelve prominent members of the KUS were assassinated, including the highly respected Mawlawi Abdullah Fayaz in June 2005 and Mullah Mulavi in April 2006. The effect on the rural mullahs, who looked to the KUS for educated guidance, was profound, unmeasured and un-noticed by coalition forces.

The War of the Schools was another important tactic employed throughout 2005. The destruction of schools and the killing and intimidation of teachers teaching a secular curriculum were clearly designed to prevent the rural populations from achieving a level of education that would permit the people to question the Taliban's mediaeval belief system over the long term. The short-term benefits included the discrediting of the government at the local level, amounting, essentially, to more negative governance.

It also was apparent in 2005 that the Taliban were systematically targeting the Afghan healthcare system as it struggled to expand into the rural areas. The Taliban's approach to this was much more sophisticated and insidious than it was with the education and religious authorities. The Taliban were able to employ two methods alongside each other. One was to force the medical system to declare itself to the coalition as a neutral entity; they were supported in this by neutral NGOs like the Red Cross who did not support the government. The other was to kill medical professionals, burn clinics and ambush ambulances. The Afghan healthcare system, paid for with Western aid money and administered by the Afghan government, was in some areas co-opted by the Taliban and used to repair and evacuate their wounded fighters. The population still got medical care, but at the sufferance of the Taliban, and government workers disavowed their own government in the disputed rural areas.

Without a viable Afghan National Police or an Afghan National Army, the ability of the pro-government forces to project power in these rural areas was limited, particularly in 2005 and into 2006. The fledgling ANA and the unprofessional ANP, which had barely transitioned from the disarmed chieftains' militias, were in no position to move out and create a secure environment where students could learn, medical problems could be taken care of and moderate religion practised free of a climate of fear.

The new Taliban methodology, however, was put to use to support the increased emphasis on conventional and near-conventional actions that were being prepared for 2006. Exerting control over portions of the rural population was geared more towards exerting control over key geographical areas that could act as support bases for operations against Kandahar City. This is quite different from mounting a broad-based campaign to control the population in every rural district and then shifting legitimacy to some new governance structure. In this case, there was no governance structure to shift to.

Why was that the case? There are two possible answers. First, if the Taliban were following an "Allah will provide" doctrine, a formal hierarchical apparatus for the village- and district-level control is not necessary; it is enough to intimidate the population, or use what I will call 'negative governance' to gain compliance. Secondly, it is possible that the Taliban were still banking on the 'foco' method in taking Kandahar City, that would result in the withdrawal of coalition forces and collapse of the government effort in the south. They could then go about governing the population as they had in the 1990s, using the same methods. In this scenario, a formal structure was not really needed either. It is possible that both reasons co-existed.

Once the Taliban failed to gain momentum in 2006-07, however, the movement had to re-assess its approach to the war in the south. From that period to today we have seen a progressive shift from 'negative governance' to 'competitive governance' in certain rural areas. It is important to understand that this shift has occurred because of coalition and Afghan successes. For a change, the enemy has been forced to respond to our initiatives and not the other way around.

In Kandahar province in 2007 and early 2008 the situation in Zharey and Panjwayi districts became a competitive system between the coalition and the Taliban and its allies. That stasis resulted in enemy attempts to seize control of Arghandab district to outflank the stalemated area and generate yet another 'foco' momentum in a bid to seize Kandahar City. That assault was thwarted by coalition and Afghan forces under Canadian command not once, but twice (October 2007 and June 2008). Stasis then set in on the Arghandab front. The insurgency had been constantly frustrated. Whether this contributed to a new approach, or if that existed earlier in a systematic fashion, is hard to determine.

What is clear is that from early 2007 on Kandahar province (and elsewhere) has been subjected to a systematic assassination and intimidation campaign designed to kill the mullahs and educated Afghans in the police and the bureaucracy. This campaign is also deliberately designed to attenuate the aid and reconstruction community's efforts to support government initiatives in the rural areas. The purpose of the campaign is not only to reduce the ability of the government to connect with the people, but also to generate space for the Taliban's fledgling efforts at competitive governance. The elements of that campaign include: co-opting aid and development; counter-police; counter-governance; counter-development; a Taliban 'Hitler Youth'; and a parallel legal system.

Co-opting Aid and Development

Kidnapping tends to be a criminal enterprise, but the insurgents sometimes 'buy' victims and, at the very least, imply through their information operations methods that they were behind the events. The kidnapping of American NGO worker Cyd Mizell in January 2008 is instructive. Originally a criminal kidnapping, Ms. Mizell was apparently transferred to Taliban custody and later killed. The effect of this singular event in the NGO and UN aid community in Kandahar was profound and even affected CIDA activities at the Provincial Reconstruction Team. The kidnapping shocked the aid community to the point where they did not want to go 'outside the wire', with obvious effects on program delivery and validation.

Like the healthcare delivery situation, however, the insurgents generally have changed their views since 2005-06 and rarely assassinate aid workers. They co-opt them instead. Where aid workers are carrying out activities in disputed areas, Taliban-inspired mullahs and other agitators take credit for aid and development. The government, which has no presence in those areas and has no direct connection to the supposedly 'neutral' aid groups, cannot take any credit for the projects. The Taliban get what amounts to 'free' development and this assists them in building rapport with the rural populations. Aid activities are portrayed to the locals either as Taliban aid activities, or activities that the Taliban 'permits' to continue at their sufferance. Note that the insurgents have not targeted the polio eradication program. Why not? They benefit from it because it is not seen by the population as linked to the Afghan government (or to Canada for that matter).

Terrorism was effective at distracting Canada from its development operations. (DND-Combat Camera)

Counter-police

The police are normally a target during any insurgency, but the pattern of activity directed at the emergent Afghan National Police is more than the sporadic raiding of police stations to acquire arms (as depicted in the movie Michael Collins) or the overrunning of small rural police posts for local information operations effect, which occurs with some frequency. Starting in 2008, however, the police commander in charge of the administration of police in Kandahar province was shot and killed after getting a haircut. A number of other mid-level police officers in Kandahar City were also killed and an attempt was made on Matulla Achakzai, the Chief of Police, with a donkey-borne IED. Then in September 2008, the Afghan National Police Headquarters in Kandahar was attacked by suicide bombers, killing two and injuring 30. One interpretation is that this last event was designed to kill a senior police figure from Spinboldak, or it may have been intended to be a 'spectacular' like the Sarposa prison attack, or something akin to the series of Kabul attacks that occurred in January 2009. The number of wounded and their particular administrative positions, however, indicate the attack may have been designed to cripple the fledgling administrative and logistics staff and to kill or wound the best-educated police officers on the force. (Note that the vast majority of police officers are illiterate.)

The assassination of the Afghan National Police 'poster girl', Lieutenant-Colonel Malalal Kakar in September 2008 was, like Sitara Achakzai, an attack on several planes: intimidating women; directing "to hell with you" messages from the Taliban; and deterring women from joining the police. Out in Panjwayi district, the Canadian police mentors have been deliberately targeted by insurgent cells there in order to kill the teacher so the students will not learn. All of these enemy efforts are designed specifically to undermine the Afghan government's ability to provide security and extend governance.

The assassinations of moderate mullahs from the Kandahar Ulema Shura also spiked again in late 2008 and early 2009, and has started to reach 2005-06 levels. Five members were killed, plus another moderate mullah from Spinboldak. This can only be interpreted as an insurgent method to shape the religious environment in southern Afghanistan and possibly even the

National Ulema Shura in Kabul, which draws members from the Kandahar Ulema Shura. These assassinations stave off attempts by the government and the religious authorities to expand into the rural areas and urban mosques in an attempt to maintain government legitimacy and counter the insurgents' messaging.

Counter-governance

There has also been a notable upsurge in direct attacks against the provincial bureaucracy and governance structures since the September 2006 killing of Safia Ama Jan from the Ministry of Women's Affairs. Again, we are not interested in high-profile targeting of the Governor here; rather, it is the Provincial Council and other organs of power that have received increased insurgent scrutiny. In October 2008, Dost Mohommad Arghestani, the head of the Labour and Social Affairs Department, was gunned down. An insurgent suicide 'spectacular' attack was directed at the Provincial Council itself on 1 April 2009, killing 17 people, including the director of Health Services and the director of Education. Zahir Jan, the official in charge of the transportation system in southern Afghanistan, was also murdered in April 2009.

Counter-development

Examples of enemy 'counter-development' have also occurred. This takes two forms. First, there is direct military action against Canadian projects. An example of this is the Construction Management Organization's CMT-1 road-paving project in Panjwayi district. It has been subjected to mortar fire, small arms fire and IED attack. Secondly, there are Taliban attempts to provide projects in areas they influence. In a reversal from the War of Schools, the Taliban have taken control of government-built schools in certain areas and are using them to promulgate their own curriculum, partly by providing text books. The Taliban have even initiated a road-construction project of their own in Zharey district, using conscripted labour. In Mushan, the Taliban constructed a bazaar and convinced the population to use it instead of the traditional bazaar in the area. The Taliban provided security checkpoints and presumably took a slice of the financial actions as 'taxes'.

The Taliban 'Hitler Youth'

A disturbing development that has emerged is the expanded use of youths in the insurgent effort. As the insurgents gained knowledge of coalition rules of engagement, they started to use unarmed youths for spotting, reconnaissance and early-warning tasks on the peripheries of disputed areas where they had a presence. Clearly, the insurgency was also exploiting the unwillingness of Western forces to kill children, even if they were engaged in military activity. There is some evidence that co-opted youth are being used as part of the Taliban's governance apparatus. Pairs of youths attend local shuras conducted by manoeuvring coalition troops and local elders. These youths are not local and the elders are intimidated by them. It is evident that these teams are being used as the Taliban's 'social' eyes and ears to identify and intimidate people who are pro-government, and not just in a military reconnaissance and observation capacity.

Slightly older youths, operating in gangs, are being used by some Taliban commanders as the primary intimidation units in rural areas. Unarmed and travelling on motorcycles, these teams let local people know they represent the Taliban and move around at night committing acts of violence against pro-government people. Locals are warned that if they are not compliant, armed Taliban groups will arrive and coerce them. Without the ability to contact Afghan government security forces or protect themselves, the rural populations are at the mercy of such activity.

Parallel Legal System

One of the most important Taliban evolutions is their expansion into the realm of dispute resolution. In most rural areas, and even urban areas in Afghanistan, the matter of who owns water access rights and cultivatable land is contentious at best. The destruction of land registry papers, the reliance in some areas on oral tribal traditions and similar means of determining ownership have produced significant local grievances, even at the district level. When the Afghan government cannot or will not mediate those grievances, somebody else will. In this case, the insurgents have started to employ their own judges to mediate in areas they influence. This is a relatively new phenomenon, though rumours that the Taliban were engaged in these activities have been around for about two years. This activity usurps one of the prime functions of government. There are numerous anecdotal stories of Taliban 'kangaroo courts', but more recent rumours, that the local mullahs are co-opted into the so-called process, are disturbing.

A number of attributes of the insurgent campaign fall out of this discussion. The population-control strategy is based on manipulating the population's perceptions as to who is in charge by playing to illiteracy and religious ignorance and backing it up with several varieties of coercion. Locals are now increasingly co-opted into the Taliban program as much as they are coerced. Measures taken by the Afghan government to extend programs to the rural (and even to the urban) population are countered on a number of levels through direct targeting, both locally and, increasingly, at the heart of the governance process in Kandahar City. The insurgents especially see the police as a primary target in this effort. It appears as though the enemy is attempting 'competitive governance' and has abandoned 'negative governance'.

This particular enemy campaign generally remains unrecognized by the coalition for a number of reasons. On the whole, these events are not seen as a comprehensive enemy approach but only as data points that do not have a discernable pattern, just something the insurgency 'does' rather than something that is profoundly dangerous to the overall coalition effort in the long term. One problem is the military/tactical focus on the 'main force' insurgents, the 'red icons' and the counter-leadership campaign. These organizations and individuals are easier to target and show more productive results than do all the competitive governance efforts.

Similarly, the emphasis on the Cabinet-mandated 'signature projects' is a distraction from the real nature of the insurgent threat in the rural approaches to Kandahar City. Building schools does not counter these threats, nor does polio eradication, let alone the Kajaki Dam project. Those are long-term projects and dependent on a positive security environment. Indeed, the Department of Foreign Affairs and International Trade (DFAIT) and CIDA have insisted that development and governance are in their bailiwick and they jealously guard their turf. However, CIDA and DFAIT are conceptually disabled from understanding the nature of this threat and are apparently incapable of harnessing Canadian or coalition military power in order to confront enemy development and governance when it is appropriate to do so. Projects alone will not counter Taliban governance. They have to be linked to Afghan governance. A concerted and specialized campaign to target the emergent insurgent 'competitive governance' capacity, something like the existing counter-IED campaign, needs to be established and it must be a 'Whole of Government' approach. Canada needs to stifle enemy efforts in this realm as quickly as possible. Destruction of this enemy program at its source, before it goes further, may have a lasting effect on the stability of Kandahar province and southern Afghanistan. The security and Afghan National Security Forces (ANSF) capacity-building lines of operations remain the critical tasks in Kandahar province, not development. No security, no development.

PART 3:
INTO BATTLE

The Leopard C-2 medium tank is employed by "A" Squadron, Lord Strathcona's Horse (Royal Canadians) [LdSH(RC)], in operations in Zharey District. The Leopard C-2 shown here is equipped with a mine plough not unlike those developed during the Second World War.

CHAPTER FIVE
OPERATION SEASONS:
INCURSION AT HOWZ-E MADAD
JUNE 2007

On 20 June 2007, Canadian and Afghan National Army forces, supported by Dutch and American air forces, conducted one of a series of incursions into the Zharey district west of Kandahar City. This incursion, called Operation SEASONS, was representative of operations undertaken in the summer of 2007 by ISAF forces in this area and is an evolution from how Canadian ground forces had been employed since they were re-introduced to the region in 2005. This account is based on the personal experiences of the author who observed these combat operations while they were in progress. In the interests of operational security, certain aspects of the action have been blurred and the names of code-named geographical locations have been changed. The exception is Route SUMMIT which has appeared regularly in the media.

The Terrain

It has become a media *cliché* to use the phrase "the volatile Zharey district", but it is fairly accurate. Zharey district occupies what amounts to a triangle of well-cultivated land north of the Arghandab river, west of Kandahar City. The top of the triangle parallels Highway 1, the main and only paved east-west highway from Kandahar City, Helmand province and then to Herat. Highway 1 meets Highway 4 east of Kandahar City, which in turn links the entire southern part of Afghanistan with Spinboldak and then on to Quetta in Pakistan. Insurgent forces occupying Zharey can theoretically interfere with commerce on Highway 1 and this can have detrimental economic effects on the entire region, not just the province.

South of Highway 1 can only be described, in military terms, as complex terrain. Though Zharey district is fairly small compared to other provincial districts, it consists of a densely packed array of grape-growing ditches, walled compounds, walled fields, irrigation streams covered with foliage, and narrow tracks. Grape-drying huts, in the middle of the trench-like rows of grape ditches, are made of mud that has dried into concrete effectively turning them into ready-made bunkers with firing ports.

South of the Arghandab River lies Panjwayi district which, for the most part, resembles Zharey district in its complex terrain. A steep hill-line separates most of Panjwayi from the Arghandab River which, together with the huts, present a significant obstacle to north-south traffic, with the exceptions of two fords: one at Bazaar-e Panjwayi, a significant town and marketplace; and another to the west. The terrain north of Highway 1 and to the west of Zharey is open and arid. The Reg Desert lies to the south and south-west of Panjwayi district.

What of the human terrain? Zharey district is the product of a 'redistricting process' conducted in 2003 to rationalize the physical conformation of the land to provincial administration districts. Consequently, Zharey was carved out of several other districts: Panjwayi, Arghandab and Maywand. The tribal overlay, of course, does not conform to the artificial administrative overlay. Zharey district is completely dominated by Pashtuns, though they come from both Pashtun confederations: the Durrani and Ghilzai, who have competed for dominance of the area for centuries. At least six tribal groups are present in Zharey district.

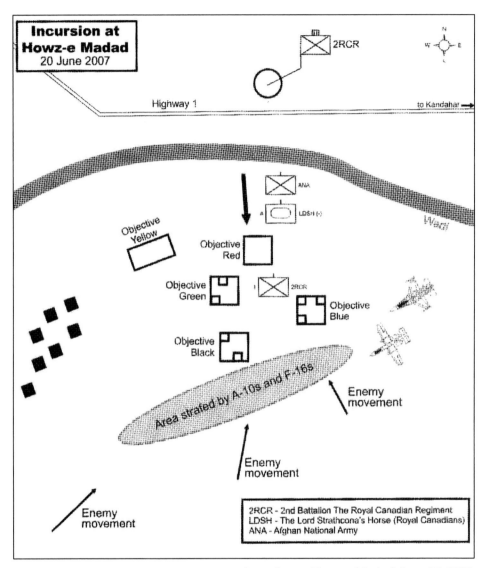

Incursion at Howz-e Madad, June 20, 2007.

125

Canada's involvement with Zharey district dates from 2005-06 when the Canadian-led Provincial Reconstruction Team working with the US 173rd Airborne Brigade attempted to assess the area for aid and reconstruction purposes. At that time, American forces were attacked along Highway 1 on a regular basis by small numbers of Taliban forces operating from Zharey. Task Force BAYONET, which was under-strength, focused on the Shah Wali Kot district of Kandahar province and did not have the resources to deal with Zharey. At this time, most of the action was in Oruzgan province north of Kandahar and Zabol province to the north-east. The Shah Wali Kot district operations were supporting this effort. In effect, Zharey was a no-go area for the PRT which instead focused its efforts on Panjwayi district and elsewhere. These contacts led to better information on activities in Zharey and when the Canadians took over Regional Command South in January-February 2006, there was increased interest in the district.

Throughout the spring of 2006, it was more and more apparent that the Quetta Shura, the council leading the anti-Afghanistan and anti-coalition effort out of Pakistan, had shifted its operational approach to RC South. A steady increase in infiltration of both personnel and weapons was detected and by the summer several pre-emptive actions were conducted by Task Force ORION, the Canadian Battlegroup based on 1st Battalion Princess Patricia's Canadian Light Infantry (PPCLI). One of these operations was the first full battalion-sized combat operation since Korea. The enemy was forced to either reinforce Zharey or pull out and leave a small presence. The Quetta Shura decided to make a stand and massively re-infiltrated Zharey in August 2006. This led to Operation MEDUSA, a Canadian-led, brigade-sized multinational operation that inflicted significant damage on the enemy forces in Zahrey and Panjwayi districts. There were, however, insufficient resources to garrison Zharey with Afghan police or with paramilitary forces.

The follow-on operation, BAAZ TSUKA, was mounted in December 2006. This was a Dutch-led multinational operation (RC South had changed from Canadian to Dutch command) designed in part to sweep through Zharey again and then leave an Afghan security force behind to facilitate development and aid activities. For the most part, enemy forces melted away in the face of the ISAF onslaught and they reverted to pre-2006 tactics. Again, there were simply not enough police or paramilitary forces to maintain their presence and control over the entire district so the development effort stalled in the western parts of the district. The decision was made to focus the police and aid effort on the quieter Panjwayi district and to contain Zharey as much as possible.

This effort was called Operation BAAZ TSUKA Phase III. NATO ISAF forces established an enduring presence in the area in the form of several fire-bases to supplement existing ones. Forward Operating Base Masum Ghar (called FOB MSG by the troops) was constructed on the hills south of the river overseeing Zharey district. Along Highway 1 to the north was Patrol Base Wilson (PBW) which had been established by TF ORION the previous year to assist with route control activities to facilitate the British deployment to Helmand province. Other ISAF forces operated along Highway 1 from Maywand district west of Zharey.

The Plan

In the spring of 2007, the Canadian Battlegroup, based on 2nd Battalion, The Royal Canadian Regiment (2 RCR), deployed to Zharey and Panjwayi districts. India Company, 2 RCR and "A" Squadron, The Lord Strathcona's Horse [LdSH(RC)] based out of MSG, while "C" Company, 3 PPCLI and a detachment of M-777 guns from "D" Battery, 2 Royal Canadian Horse Artillery (RCHA) operated from the Sperwan Ghar (SWG) FOB located in Panjwayi. At this time, the Canadian Operational Mentoring and Liaison Team, led by Lieutenant-Colonel (LCol) Ken Eyre, worked closely with elements from the Afghan National Army 205 Corps based out of MSG. LCol Rob Walker, Commanding Officer of the Battlegroup, knew that neither he nor the Afghan security forces had the resources to occupy Zharey and that those forces would not be available in the near future; there were barely enough to handle the vital parts of Panjwayi. Working with Major (Maj) David Quick, Officer Commanding (OC) India Company, the Battlegroup developed a concept of operations to keep enemy forces off-balance in Zharey, in effect: denying them the ability to rebuild infrastructure that could later serve as a mounting-base; preventing any substantial build-up of conventional or near-conventional forces along the lines of what occurred in 2006; and reducing the enemy's ability to interfere with commerce and any ISAF re-supplying traffic on Highway 1.

The issue of what constituted enemy activity in the district caused some problems. When Canadian forces built a combat road (Route SUMMIT) from Bazaar-e Panjwayi to Highway 1, there were unintended consequences. The construction of this road diverted water in the east end of Zharey. Age-old and intricate tribal agreements over water use were now disrupted. Certain communities now potentially had the upper hand over others and resentments built up and bordered on violence. A Canadian solution was to put in culverts to restore the water-use patterns … but then the culverts made ideal locations for IED attacks against forces using Route SUMMIT. When culverts were blown up, was this Taliban activity or not? If one community resorted to AK-47 use over a diverted stream, was this Taliban action? What if Canadian troops were caught in the crossfire? Or, what if Afghan police from one area were conducting activities on behalf of someone else for pay because they had not received money from their own chain of command for months? These factors complicated any Canadian response to activity in Zharey district. That said, there were organized Taliban teams and sub-units operating in the area in significant, but not overwhelming, numbers. Their intent was to resuscitate the severely damaged Taliban structure in the district.

Indeed, the use of intelligence-driven operations placed a premium on the need for multiple information sources that could be rapidly cross-checked. Such operations demanded substantial understanding of personalities, Afghan tribal culture, local grievances, historical relationships and how all of this had evolved over the past 20 years. In all cases, the Battlegroup and company commanders would have to operate with incomplete information and rely to a certain extent on their hard-won experience with Zharey district, something not easily transferable in any handover between units. Gut instinct became as important, possibly even more important, than any super-secret signals intelligence (SIGINT) intercept scooped up from something orbiting in space.

In effect, the Battlegroup did not have a single linear plan like Operations MEDUSA or BAAZ TSUKA. The overall plan was to mount a series of short-term sorties into Zharey as targets presented themselves, or to conduct sorties to flush-out the enemy in a particular area forcing them into fight or flight mode. This approach meant that the limited number of ISAF and ANA forces did not need to garrison Zharey. It was denial, not occupation, that was key. Randomness was crucial. There was to be no pattern to coalition operations and the maximal use of night cover and deception operations was critical, given that the enemy had significant observation assets, knew exactly what the Battlegroup consisted of, and what it was capable of doing. MSG is a fairly exposed FOB on the side of a hill and an enemy scout with binoculars in Zharey does not have to leave home to see what is there.

A previous India Company operation had rattled enemy leadership in Zharey. Information came into Battlegroup HQ that some 50 enemy fighters had narrowly avoided this previous sweep operation and were moving to link up with another cell, estimated to have 30 fighters. These forces were equipped with AK-47 and PKM automatic weapons, RPGs and 82mm recoilless rifles. An enemy commander killed during a parallel operation involving coalition special operations forces (SOF) was about to be replaced and the new leader was on his way. They would all be in the vicinity of the Howz-e Madad bazaar and compound complex. The planning cycle for Operation SEASONS had begun.

The geographical position of Howz-e Madad explains why this cluster of dun-coloured compounds is important. As Highway 1 traverses Zharey from east to west, it curves off from the Zharey green belt and heads north-west to Maywand district. The point where it curves off is the point where Zahrey's greenbelt ends and arid open terrain starts. It is the last opportunity for insurgent forces to attack traffic on Highway 1 and retreat into the complex terrain of the greenbelt. Ambushes west of the greenbelt are potentially suicidal. There is nowhere to run and a 25mm round from a LAV-III vehicle or a 30mm round from an AH-64 Apache gunship is faster, in any event. Ambush operations conducted from the west end of Zharey have a better chance of success than those conducted from the east end. At the east end, Zharey tapers into a point and there is less depth to retreat into before hitting the river and the hill-line.

In addition, enemy infiltration routes and 'rat lines' come into Zharey from the west and south-west, from Helmand province. Enemy personnel usually rest in the western part of the district after their long journey and before deploying to sites east. In addition, larger weapons caches are broken down and then dispersed east. When truck traffic is used by the enemy, Howz-e Madad is the first stop along Highway 1, making it a convenient location. The police in the area are unreliable as the Taliban pay them more money with greater frequency than the government does.

The scheme of manoeuvre that Maj Quick, LCol Walker and Lieutenant Colonel Shereen Shah agree on is to move India Company by LAV-III to a drop-off point to conduct a night march into a blocking position south of Howz-e Madad. The LAVs were to continue along the highway to draw enemy eyes away. Then two troops of the Strathcona's Leopard C-2 tanks (call-sign T-1A) led by Captain (Capt) Craig Volstead, accompanied by an Afghan infantry company from 2-1-205 kandak (with the OMLT attached) mounted in armed pickup trucks, and the Battlegroup command post (call-sign 9er TAC) would sortie from MSG, move along Highway 1 and then swing south to catch the enemy, like a hammer striking an anvil.

The Action

At 0337 hours on 20 June, there was a slight delay in the departure of the tank/Afghan infantry force when a key member of the command post severely cut himself by accident and this had to be attended to. This was just as well, as not all of the Intelligence Surveillance and Targeting Systems (ISTAR) resources[1] were in place; it took the Tactical Unmanned Aerial Vehicle (or TUAV; the Canadian Sperwer system) a.k.a. SKIDOO (so named because the machine has a Bombardier Skidoo engine) time to fly from its base to Zharey. At 0353 hours, LCol Walker took the lead with his LAV-III and the force moved out along Route SUMMIT. India company had already deployed and was in position. At 0430 9er TAC, accompanied by an artillery forward-observation officer/forward air controller (FOO/FAC) LAV-III and a security element, moved into a position north of Highway 1 opposite Howz-e Madad. The area was carefully checked on arrival for mines and IEDs. The first contact with the enemy was at 0435 hours, just at dawn. Red tracer fire arced across the sky from west to east and a forward air controller immediately called for air support. The two USAF A-10 Warthogs that were on call were now on the way.

The battle area requires some description. In effect, there were several compound complexes (see map) and a wadi system, all surrounded by grape trenches. Each walled compound and its associated outbuildings formed natural defensive positions and usually held several extended families; in this case, the enemy had temporarily depopulated part of the area. The complexes were connected by narrow roads and tracks, most of them lines with high mud walls on either side.

India Company, called Objective RED, deployed to its blocking position during the night and without incident. When the Leopard/Afghan National Army 'hammer' came down south from Highway 1 to meet the 'anvil' (Objective RED), there was no contact. Then the enemy started firing from Objective BLUE at the forces moving around Objective RED. But BLUE was south-east of RED, not north. India Company engaged BLUE … then the enemy opened up from BLACK to the south of RED. Then, from another location to the west, a single shooter wounded an ANA soldier from some distance. A 'nine liner' MEDEVAC request went out and a U.S. Army UH-60 Blackhawk was dispatched to collect the wounded. A variety of ISTAR assets were now orbiting the battle and the information was continuously fed to LCol Walker. One of these detected a pickup truck with an enemy RPG team moving in from the west. A fire mission was called in to suppress the shooter and the RPG team. At this point, there was a detachment of Canadian M-777 155mm guns at another fire-base, commanded by Lieutenant (Lt) Eric Ross. Only one gun was operational, but the volume of fire made it look as if a half-battery was in action.

On-call artillery employed during the Howz-e Madad action included one M-777 155mm gun fireing from FOB Sperwan Ghar in Panjwayi district. The M-777 is highly accurate and is airportable when slung under CH-47 Chinook helicopters.

The Afghan company and OMLT started to conduct a detailed search of several compounds while the Leopard tanks moved to form a cordon. At this point, at 0506 hours, a Canadian soldier was wounded and moved to a casualty collection point. India Company held Objective RED, the tanks were observing to the west, and the plan was now to move a platoon from India company to Objective GREEN. ISTAR resources then detected what they suspected was a significant, dismounted enemy force south of Objective BLACK. As the platoon was breaking contact from RED to move to GREEN, another Canadian was wounded.

The FOO/FAC, co-located with India Company, call-sign G 12, was engaged with RPG and small arms fire and they saw the enemy was reinforcing from the south-west. The question for LCol Walker was this: was the enemy bringing in forces to cover an extraction of their engaged forces, or was the enemy reinforcing the fight? ISTAR resources were tasked to find out and their 'eyes and ears' were directed further south. India Company was at this time engaged by 14 enemy personnel equipped with RPGs firing from positions directly south of BLACK; it looked like a pickup truck was moving in from the west to assist them. An A-10 was brought in to engage and opened up with its GAU-8 30mm gun on these enemy forces.

The situation as it stood at 0517 hours, had: a Canadian platoon with the Leopards on Objective GREEN preparing to move to Objective BLACK; a Canadian platoon on Objective RED; and the ANA company consolidating compounds behind the Canadian screen. Suddenly, fifteen enemy were engaged north-east of GREEN. LCol Walker instructed the force to assume an all-round defensive posture, consolidate the interior of the 'goose egg' and prepare to meet several attacks. The ANA company was to move to BLACK

A U.S. Army UH-60 Blackhawk MEDVAC stands off while the dust generated by an artillery strike abates. It will then fly in and extract coalition casualties.

and sweep it east to west.

Three close air-support missions were flown by United States Air Force (USAF) A-10s and the Dutch F-16s that showed up to replace them to the south of BLACK to suppress enemy fire. The three coalition wounded were by this time in an armoured TLAV ambulance (a modified and completely rebuilt M-113 APC) and were moving to a helicopter landing-site for evacuation by the UH-60 Blackhawk. Significantly, the UH-60 came in alone without its usual AH-64 Apache escort. There were simply not enough AHs available that morning as other coalition operations were going on elsewhere.

Enemy survivors from the A-10 and F-16 sorties tried to break contact and headed west. At the same time, five enemy with RPGs moved north to replace them and fired at Canadians in the vicinity of BLACK. Then enemy in a grape-drying hut south-east of BLACK opened up with small arms. The TUAV also located three 'squirters', survivors of the A-10 strafing, hiding in a tree-line. G 12, the artillery FOO/FAC, tried to acquire them when the TUAV then picked up what looked like 50 persons moving to the west of the battle. When queried, the operators noted that none appeared to be carrying weapons. Call-sign 66B, a sniper detachment, then engaged enemy targets occupying rooftops to the west. Were the 50 people reinforcements? Were they civilians fleeing? Snipers observed individuals, not part of the group, that were equipped with RPGs and they looked like they were a separate entity. But nobody could be sure. Maj Quick instructed that no action be taken until a positive identification could be made.

In effect, the combined Canadian-Afghan force was in a hedgehog posture at 0550 hours. LCol Walker's intention was to let the enemy come to him and then kill them. It appeared as though there were enemy standing and fighting in small groups all around the hedgehog; some enemy were withdrawing but, at the same time, there appeared to be two large enemy groups approaching from the south and south-west. At 0610 hours, the wounded were flown out by helicopter.

The snipers require some mention. Sniper information flowed into the command post with TUAV information forming a notable proportion of the information picture. At the same time, 66B snipers killed an enemy RPG team with shots at ranges of 700m.

At this time, the ANA encountered some insurgents hiding in the Objective BLACK compounds and set about clearing them. Searches continued for information as much as insurgents. LCol Walker took stock of the situation at 0605 hours. The enemy was taken by surprise by the incursion; ISTAR information indicated this as did their behaviour on the ground. It appeared as though the 50 persons to the west were civilians, not reinforcements, though the enemy was still present to the west in small numbers and firing sporadically. The TUAV then spotted organized enemy on Objective YELLOW to the west. The Leopards traversed and opened fire. The situation at BLACK, however, was confused. As the Afghan company cleared the site, an RPG opened up on them from behind, i.e., to the north, and wounded two Afghan soldiers. A Leopard was brought in and the RPG team was killed by main armament fire.

The enemy again attempted to introduce two-man RPG teams into the interior of the hedgehog using grape-trenches and wadi systems. There also appeared to be more enemy hiding in Objective BLACK. The Afghan company engaged in close combat in the compounds to ensure, once and for all, that they were cleared. Then the TUAV operators reported that the enemy was hiding RPG teams among the civilian population and moving south of BLACK. LCol Walker concluded they were using the civilians as shields and held fire. Then the Afghan company struck gold: as they moved slightly east of BLACK, they uncovered a cache. They were immediately engaged and then covered by Leopard HESH rounds and coaxial machine-gun fire as they exploited this site.

New information arrived in the command post. The enemy was trying to introduce 82mm recoilless rifle teams into the battle. Their intent was most likely to engage and catastrophically kill a Canadian Leopard, or other armoured vehicle, if possible. This would have significant spin-off effects. It would be a morale victory for enemy forces in that they could prove to their personnel that tanks could be engaged and destroyed. It would have an I/O effect in the Canadian media and tie up Canada's military leadership, forced to explain to the vociferous critics why they deployed tanks to Afghanistan in the first place and why Canada needed tanks at all. Instructions were therefore issued to prioritize the destruction of anything resembling an 82mm recoilless rifle team.

As another UH-60 arrived around 0644 to evacuate the wounded, the battle entered a lull. It was already getting stiflingly hot and, in a matter of hours, it would reach the point where Leopard crews in their non-air-conditioned vehicles would be increasingly incapacitated. The crews joked that the 'mechs' should have welded mounts onto the turret ceilings so that IV solution bags could be hung from them for re-hydration purposes.

A Canadian platoon and combat engineers from 42 Field Squadron consolidated Objective BLACK. There they found Taliban graffiti and weapons all over the complex. Sensitive Site Exploitation (SSE) and Battle Damage Assessment (BDA) activities commenced on several locations. SSEs are designed to produce intelligence on enemy structures, operations and intentions, while BDA is designed to assist with improving operational effectiveness. The engineers uncovered a significant cache at BLACK. Initial reports were that there were RPGs, artillery shells and a variety of other explosives stockpiled there. The assessments continued when more reports came in that there was significant civilian movement to the west and southwest. At this point LCol Walker and Maj Quick were considering a move onto Objective YELLOW to clean it out. Then, at 0703 hours a Canadian platoon and its accompanying Leopards were engaged with small arms fire. Simultaneously, back north of Highway 1, the Battlegroup command post LAV-III suddenly traversed its turret onto a white car that was moving at speed towards 9er TAC, thereby dissuading the car from coming closer and it sped off in the direction it came from. There is no classic 'rear area', and all coalition forces must be capable of defending themselves at all times, no matter what activity they are engaged in. There was a series of explosions to the west which sounded like RPGs but remain unexplained as there was no damage to friendly forces. It is possible that the enemy's poor ammunition handling resulted in the detonation of reinforcement stocks.

After 0700 the enemy renewed his activities to the south-east of BLACK. There were three groupings of Taliban firing onto BLACK but they were using the cover of buildings, walls and grape-trenches making target identification difficult for the Leopards and the platoon on BLACK. The Leopards tried to get coaxial machine-gun fire to suppress enemy fire while the infantry picked out individual insurgents and killed them with aimed shots. Fire resumed against BLACK from the south as well, which brought with it an A-10 strafing run (the terrain south of BLACK is much more open and conducive to this). The two A-10s rolled in, popped flares and fired extended bursts of 30mm from their GAU-8s, sounding as though heaven itself was being ripped open.

Elements of the Afghan company were in positions north-west of BLACK. They started taking sporadic fire and a Badger armoured engineer vehicle was moved in to breach a high wall so the Afghans could deal with this threat. There was another significant lull that lasted until 0726 hours. Another SSE, this one conducted by the Afghans, discovered a Taliban command post containing significant information. Then, enemy ammo cached in a grape-drying hut exploded without warning and everyone took cover. Other SSE activities uncovered RPG launchers and RPG rounds. Most importantly, a stock of artillery rounds that were in the process of being converted to IEDs was discovered, as were IED detonators and other components critically necessary for their manufacture. This, it turned out, was a significant find. BLACK was the base of a Taliban IED cell and it afforded significant insight into current IED techniques and procedures. More and more ammo was found throughout the battle area.

ISTAR resources then detected 30 enemy moving west on a route south of the battle area; they appeared to be fleeing. At 0745, the Provincial Operations Centre reported that an IED attack in Panjwayi district to the south had killed two people. It was not clear whether they were coalition forces, civilians or police. One interpretation was that it was designed to draw attention away from the Howz-e Madad battle.

The next contact was at 0750. Four Taliban, equipped with an RPG and a PKM machin-gun, were running away from the battle area. Inexplicably, two pickup trucks, with four Taliban equipped with anti-tank weapons, followed by a motorcycle team, approached the battle area from south-east of Objective BLACK. A Leopard opened fire with HESH and coaxial machine-gun fire and took them out at 200m range.

These two Leopards slowly advanced south of BLACK when they were engaged with enemy anti-tank weapons. One of the Leopards was equipped with a plough; the plough was hit but the vehicle remained operational. As this position was slightly south of the limit of exploitation established for the operation, they were ordered back to BLACK.

More information came in about the IED strike in Panjwayi district. It turned out that a Canadian vehicle was hit, but the situation was developing. While 9r TAC was dealing with this new incident, an A-10 on a strafing run fired on the road next to an Afghan platoon, narrowly missing them. This resulted in a temporary check-fire. Another IED strike was reported in Panjwayi district, but it was unclear if this was follow-on reportage of the first incident or if it was another incident altogether.

As LCol Walker and Maj Quick planned the withdrawal from Howz-e Madad, "C" Company 3 PPCLI in Panjwayi reported that three Canadians on a re-supply run on a Gator vehicle had been blown up by a massive IED. This was a stunning development. It was likely that this attack was related to the morning's operations; probably, it was designed to draw off resources from the Howz-e Madad operation. Indeed, ISTAR, medical, engineering and investigative resources would have to be moved and employed in another district. They would have to be protected. They might be ambushed. They might require extraction. The Battlegroup was not finished with Howz-e Madad yet. Sporadic engagements were occurring around the perimeter.

One of these engagements involved an insurgent equipped with a Dragunov sniper rifle. This individual, firing at 300m range from a rooftop and then from a grape-drying hut west of Objective RED, was bracketing his Canadian and Afghan targets without actually hitting them; this indicated that he lacked experience but was trying to make up for it with determination. There was talk about using airpower to get him, in part to boost the morale of the Afghan troops he was shooting at. He was mobile, however. One of the tank crew commanders reported hearing the 'crack-thump' of the Dragunov within 10 metres of his vehicle. The tank was instructed to pop smoke and then pull away from the building so that a 500-pound bomb could be used against the sniper.

The exfiltration of India Company, the Afghans and the tanks was not simply a matter of driving away. As with every incursion operation, the danger was that the force would be ambushed on the way back to the MSG FOB. The routes were predictable: Highway 1 to SUMMIT with its culverts, across the Arghandab and into the FOB. It was always possible that suicide vehicle IED specialists from Kandahar City could be requested by Zharey district insurgents to attack along Highway 1. Another cell could use its anti-tank weapons, and so on. A variety of deceptive means were employed to reduce this possibility, but the ace in the hole was a pair of AH-64 Apache attack helicopters that suddenly arrived overhead, each sporting a white "E" on its underside. Afghan police would form a cordon between Howz-e Madad and the exfiltrating force, while the AH-64s provided top-cover all the way back to MSG. There were no further contacts on the way back to the FOB so attention then shifted to dealing with the aftermath of the Gator attack.

This IED incident completely overshadowed the Howz-e Madad operation (which received no Canadian media coverage) and dominated public discourse for several weeks while pundits debated the relative merits of using Gators in Afghanistan and who was to blame.

The Results

Operation SEASONS was only one of several similar incursions into Zharey district in the summer of 2007. The cumulative effects of the Battlegroup plan are difficult to measure this close to the action, but a tentative assessment can be attempted. First, at no time during the entire battle did commercial truck traffic on Highway 1 abate, even when there were air-strikes in progress and prodigious amounts of tracer-arced over the road. Civilian car traffic did not stop either, though it tended to route itself north of the action into the desert and then back on to the highway. Thus far, the enemy has been unable to seriously interfere with the movement of coalition or commercial traffic on this route. The Howz-e Madad IED cell was forcibly dismantled and it will take months to replace it.

The enemy has not been able to use Zharey district as a mounting base for conventional operations against Kandahar City. He has not been able to attrit coalition or Afghan forces by using the district as a trap, as he has attempted to do in the past. This key terrain remains disputed and is dominated by coalition and Afghan forces. The enemy has only been able to export terrorist violence from Zharey into adjacent districts with limited effect and he certainly does not exert control over the population of the adjacent districts.

He has been unable to inflict mass casualties during these operations and has chosen to use massive IED attacks to do so, with the intent of generating strategic effects on the population and on political leadership in Canada.

In sum, Operation SEASONS successfully built on the base established during previous actions in Zharey district conducted throughout 2006. It demonstrates that, for key terrain, denial can be as important as occupation, but only temporarily. In order to succeed in Zharey district, the population needs to shift its allegiance to the government side. Until effective governance capacity can be implemented in Zharey district, denial will have to suffice. The enemy's decision to focus on Zharey ultimately benefits the coalition forces and the Afghan government as it permits reconstruction and aid activities to continue elsewhere in the province to the detriment of the Taliban cause. ISAF is happy to oblige them.

NOTES

1   ISTAR or Intelligence Surveillance and Targeting systems is a term used to represent the intelligence community and the various surveillance platforms available to collect the information. Unmanned Aerial Vehicles are ISTAR assets but not all ISTAR assets are UAVs.

Members of the Operational Mentor and Liaison Team and the Provincial Recon-struction Team working with 2nd kandak on the northern axis of advance on Ob-jective J. (DND-Combat Camera)

CHAPTER SIX
OPERATION INTIZAAR ZMAREY:
THE BATTLE OF ARGHANDAB
30 OCTOBER - 1 NOVEMBER, 2007

Canada's war in Afghanistan has produced numerous company- and battalion-level fights but, without a historical framework, it can be difficult to assess their relative importance. The Battle of Arghandab, however, is a clear-cut case of success in a war fraught with the normally high level of ambiguity endemic to any counterinsurgency campaign. Conducted over a three-day period, a Canadian-led multinational effort blocked a major Taliban move to dominate key physical and, more importantly, psychological terrain in Kandahar City. The enemy bid for control of Arghandab district could have had catastrophic operational consequences for NATO's International Security Assistance Force in the fight against the Taliban, not to mention long-term ramifications for the alliance efforts in the region.

At the tactical level, the brunt of the battle was fought in complex terrain and borne by a dismounted Canadian infantry company, "B" Company from the 3rd Battalion, The Royal 22nd Regiment (R22eR), working alongside an Afghan National Army infantry company and supported on a number of levels by other coalition and Canadian forces.

The perceived political problems with employing Quebec troops in combat, the potential for casualties and the potential loss of political support for the Canadian government all loomed large in the background during this particular deployment. Paradoxically, this added strategic (and unnecessary) pressure makes the Battle of Arghandab even more historically important for Canada. The objectives of Operation INTIZAAR ZMAREY were achieved without a single Canadian death.

Setting the Stage: Arghandab District

'Christening the ground' is a time-honoured tradition in Canadian battle procedure. An observer must have an accurate idea, in the mind's eye, of where a battle is fought in order to understand why it was fought. In this case, Arghandab is a rural district north-west of Kandahar City. It is one of several 'green zones' surrounding the city, areas that have access to irrigation along the rivers and areas that are agriculturally, and thus economically, prosperous. All of these green zones are significant to any military commander, insurgent and counterinsurgent alike. They provide cover in an otherwise arid, desert-like and mountainous environment. They sit astride or adjacent to the four major roads leading into Kandahar City. Domination of all or some of the green zones permits a force to control the city or, at the very least, interfere with commercial, civilian and military movements throughout the region. Kandahar City is the primary commercial, transport, governance and religious hub of southern Afghanistan. Its seizure is *sine qua non* for control of the region.

Any traveller in Arghandab, especially one moving along route GREEN LIGHT, the main south-west-north-east road north of the river, would notice that the terrain is different from the vineyard trenches of the more familiar Zharey and Panjwayi districts in which Canadians have fought since 2006. A Coyote crew commander taking a patrol down GREEN LIGHT would see brown, dusty hills with virtually no cover off to his left, at about 10 kilometres. The contested district of Khakriz lies over those hills. To his right, there is flat but cluttered ground populated with orchards and scrub and interspersed with several hundred family compounds. Each house is a rabbit warren of irregular rooms and appears to be a natural fortress surrounded with a wall, or walls, and linked by trails which only a motorcycle can go down. The crew commander might glimpse the Arghandab River three kilometres away. If the river is not in full flood, it is strewn with rocks with channels of water flowing down the river; it can be classed as a wadi acting as a highway of sorts, albeit one that is seasonally dependent. The wadi is about 500m wide and completely open.

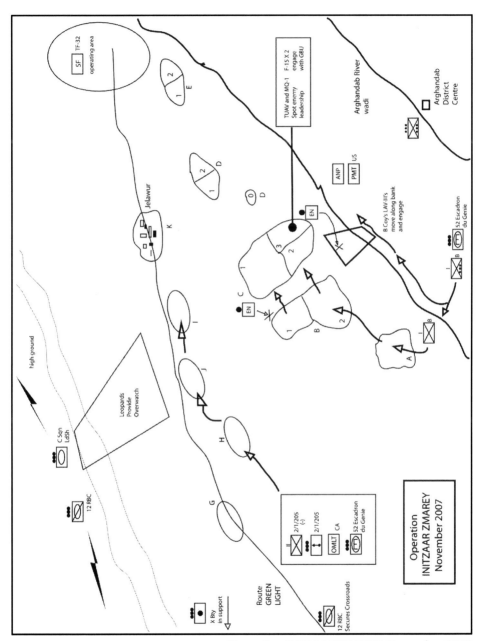

Operation INTZAARZMAREY, November 2007.

Along the road, a traveller would pass by family compounds and walled fields, some right up to the road itself forming significant built-up defiles. Five kilometres down the road from Highway 1, are the towns of Jelawuhr, Hajji Kodayraham and Tabin, commercial centres with markets and services. Stopping at a checkpoint in Adihira, a gunner traversing his 25mm turret can make out the district centre four kilometres away to the east, across the river; it has an incongruous cylindrical building, with cell-phone advertising, perched on the side of the hill next to an elaborate shrine. To the north about 20 kilometres away is the Dala Dam, built in the 1950s. It commands the flow of water to Arghandab and the districts to the south-west. North of Dala Dam is Shah Wali Kot district which, like its neighbour Khakriz, is contested by the enemy. Kandahar City, itself, is less than five kilometres from Arghandab over the hills, as the crow flies.

Arghandab is also key ethnic, and therefore political, terrain. All counterinsurgency campaigns emphasize the role of the population and that influence with the population is, itself, a battleground as much as a geographic location. Arghandab is dominated by the Alokozai tribe and, up to early 2007, was led by the charismatic and respected leader Mullah Naqib. As long as Mullah Naqib was in charge of Arghandab the coalition forces did not have to divert scarce resources to garrison it. Mullah Naqib's militia and police were capable of handling any Taliban threat and were generally able to keep the enemy at bay on their own.

On 9 March 2007, Mullah Naqib was the object of an assassination attempt. Badly wounded, he withdrew from Afghanistan to recuperate, but his sons were killed and the possibility of a power vacuum, or even internecine tribal conflict, loomed large. Militias and police in Afghanistan are leadership-dependent and the possibility that the Taliban were deliberately trying to destabilize Arghandab district was discussed among the Task Force Kandahar staff as early as June 2007. When Mullah Naqib died on 12 October, rumours circulated that it was only a matter of time before the Taliban arrived to exploit the situation. Coyotes from 12 Régiment Blindé du Canada Recce Squadron were sent to patrol in Arghandab district as a precautionary measure.

144

Indicators and Plans: 12 October – 29 October 2007

Contrary to assertions from individual observers and aid agencies in Kandahar,[1] Canada's Task Force Kandahar (TFK) was closely monitoring the situation after Naquib's death. The All-Source Intelligence Centre (ASIC) went to heightened alert status on 12 October and established a number of indicators in and around Arghandab district. If a sequence or combination of them were triggered by enemy movements or actions, the planning staff would swing into action and develop a contingency plan to counter the enemy move. Brigadier-General Guy Laroche, TFK Commander, and LCol Alain Gauthier, the Battlegroup commander, and their staffs agreed by 20 October on a number of decision points that linked the indicators with specific responses.

If the enemy massed outside Arghandab district, this would be detected and dealt with using a combination of special operations forces, UAVs and airpower before they moved in. However, a more complicated scenario was the possibility of infiltration, either singly or in small groups, over a protracted period. Such a move could not be pre-empted using the other tools and could only be dealt with once the enemy embarked on a detectable course of action. Brigadier-General Laroche determined that the primary trigger-point would centre on a enemy threat to the Arghandab district centre, the symbolic seat of power in the area and located next to the main road leading over the hills into Kandahar City.

The Taliban were not exactly subtle in their approach. One of the commanders selected to carry out operations against Arghandab initiated a cell-phone intimidation campaign against the district chief of police telling him and his men to get out, that the Taliban were coming and that they would be slaughtered. The police chief taunted them back: "If you come as friends, don't come. If you come as enemies we'll kick you out."

Another key monitoring tool was the Kandahar Provincial Reconstruction Team led by LCol Bob Chamberlain. The PRT regularly deployed a Civil Military Cooperation representative, SMaj Michel Pelletier, to Arghandab district. Other development and aid contacts, established through DFAIT and CIDA representatives at the PRT, were additional venues for situational awareness.

Until the enemy made an overt move, however, there could be no effective response.

The situation changed drastically on 28 October. The PRT was made aware of a significant exodus of civilians from Charlog village who reported that Taliban had entered the area, but it was not clear how many. Subsequently, a small number of enemy held a shura[2] near Jelawur and claimed they were now in charge. Other Taliban were seen to take over Mullah Naqib's compound, a clear attempt to attain psychological ascendancy over the population. Then the cell phones started to ring.

The cell phone network in Kandahar province had expanded geometrically since the fall of the anti-technology Taliban in 2001-02. People with little or no apparent means, in the most remote locations imaginable, seemed to all have cell phones by 2007. When the Taliban entered Arghandab district, a wave of panic not only ran through the population in the area, but it spread rapidly among the half-million citizens of Kandahar City. This cascading wave of panicky cell phone calls, coupled with the sight of carloads of Arghandabians fleeing the district, panicked NGO and UN aid workers who then reported to superiors in Kabul through their communications systems that the enemy was at the gates. The media also contributed to the panic. Families with relatives in Pakistan received calls telling them to get out of Kandahar City before it fell. One family on the east side of the city even cancelled an elaborate wedding on the strength of a couple of cell phone calls.

The situation within the district itself was confused. The police checkpoint at Jelawur was attacked and its forces scattered. The locals called several police agencies in Kandahar City to report enemy movements; these agencies in turn informed the Governor, Asadullah Khalid, who was pressuring ISAF to intervene. The commander of the Afghan National Auxiliary Police (ANAP)[3] in the district, Abdul Hakim Jan, was in Kabul at the time. He phoned his militia and ordered them to engage the Taliban as soon as possible. The subsequent abortive attack resulted in three wounded police who retreated in the face of significant firepower. Two RAF Harrier GR-7 ground support aircraft were brought in and conducted a low-level show of force. These moves may have forced the Taliban commanders to delay their assault on the district centre.

The problem for Task Force Kandahar was the possibility that the Arghandab move might have been designed to distract the coalition forces' attention away from the Zharey and Panjwayi districts to the south-west, districts where substantial ground was being made in retaking key communities from Taliban control. The clincher came on the morning of 29 October when a delegation of leaders from Arghandab presented themselves to BGen Laroche and formally requested help in ejecting the Taliban.

By 1200 hours, BGen Laroche, part of his staff and the district elders deployed to the district centre on a recce. An hour later, battle procedure started for the 3 R22eR Battlegroup. Radio orders were given at 1700 hours and, in time, the Battlegroup quick reaction force – which amounted to a LAV-III platoon and some surveillance assets – arrived at the district centre. An American Police Mentoring Team, in its armoured Hummer vehicles, was accompanying 120 Afghan National Police and their leader, General Saquib, and they deployed around the district centre and along the east bank of the river in a screen at around 1800. The 12 Régiment Blindé du Canada Recce Squadron sent a Coyote troop to secure the road junction of Highway 1 and route GREEN LIGHT as a possible staging area.

Two hours later, a coordination meeting was held at Forward Operating Base Wilson, over in Zharey district, with all of the principle Canadian and Afghan commanders, including Lt Col Shareen Shah of the 2nd kandak, an Afghan National Army infantry battalion operating in Zharey district. Analysis of the enemy's strength concluded that there were between 100 and 300 Taliban in what became called 'The Box' (see map). The general plan was to establish blocks to the north and east, screen the west and then drive an Afghan infantry company and a Canadian infantry company along route GREEN LIGHT – Afghans to the left of the road, Canadians to the right – like a plunger into a syringe. At the same time, the Battlegroup still had to be able to control Zharey and Panjwayi districts, so the whole infantry battalion could not be available.

Indeed, it appears in retrospect that the Taliban sought to coordinate their actions in Arghandab district with supporting operations in Zharey district. A Taliban unit operating near Howze-e Madad prepared to block the vital Highway 1 east-west route to draw off reinforcements. Pre-emptive manoeuvring by the OMLT and 2nd kandak deterred this action for the duration of Operation INTIZAAR ZMAREY; therefore, this and other enemy operations were not mounted in Zharey district.

The ANP were already to the east of the river with the PMT, so the issue revolved around establishing blocks to the north and the screen to the west. Part of an American Special Forces task force, TF-32, was available but, since it did not belong to ISAF, it took some time to sort out where and how it could be used. Ideally, TF-32 elements would handle the northern block. LCol Gauthier decided to handle the western screen by using a combination of Recce Squadron Coyotes and Leopard 2 A6M tanks from "C" Squadron, a composite tank squadron led by The Lord Strathcona's Horse (Royal Horse). This force would watch in both directions; first to support the infantry company as it advanced, but also to prevent any enemy reinforcements from coming down from Khakriz district. The Afghan infantry company, transported in Ford Ranger pickups and working closely with a Canadian Operational Mentor and Liaison Team, was bolstered with an engineer troop mounted in LAV-III. Orders went out at 2200 hours. "X" Battery, 5e Régiment Artillerie Légère du Canada (5 RALC), prepared a M-777 155mm gun detachment to support the operation from a forward RMA.

LCol Gauthier's scheme of manoeuvre, dictated by the terrain, meant that the mechanized infantry company would have to operate dismounted. Maj David Abboud, OC "B" Company, assessed his forces. A combination of the rotating leave policy and static protection tasks meant that "B" Company could muster 58 personnel, or three platoons with two sections each. Two of these platoons were led by Warrant Officers St-Germain and Royer because the platoon leaders were on leave. When the crews of the LAV-III vehicles were subtracted, the number of dismounts dropped to 52. A small number of combat engineers from 53 Escadron de Campagne were added but "B" Company would have to mount the operation at reduced strength. Maj Abboud decided to use his company headquarters, 15 soldiers, as a small manoeuvre group.

The size of the Taliban force remained sketchy, though better information was coming in. The ISTAR apparatus identified three Taliban commanders and each was thought to control between 30 and 50 insurgents plus support augmentees, making around 200 enemy in all.

The Battlegroup's initial planners, using 1:50,000 maps, which did not provide a lot of detail (one maze-like area was simply labelled 'numerous ditches'), hastily identified compound areas called A, B, C and so on, essentially as blobs on the map. Two hours before the company deployed from FOB Wilson, however, Abboud received more detailed imagery. The generalized blobs became sharper clusters of compounds and were re-labelled A-1, B-1, B-2 and so forth. His team had less than an hour to rename and learn all of the control measures before departing.

Day 1: 30 October 2007

Preliminary moves took place, starting around 0200 hours. With the 2nd kandak and the OMLT massing at the road junction, at around 0530 "B" Company passed through into Kandahar City and made its way to the Arghandab district centre, down the hill and into the wadi opposite Objective A (see map). The troops dismounted from the LAV-IIIs. The intent was to use the Zulu vehicles to move along the wadi, parallel with the advance, and provide fire support, if possible. There was substantial gunfire to the north as the police and their American mentors engaged the Taliban with harassing fire.

The Afghan infantry company and the OMLT mentors arrived at Objective H around 0730 where the retreating population warned them that the enemy was in a compound complex up the road (designated Objective J). The Afghans even snagged a lone, unaware Taliban and detained him for questioning.

The first troops from "B" Company into Objective A found fleeing civilians, shocked people moving south-west in groups of 15-20. A detailed clearance of Objective A, completed at 1100, produced nothing. The next objectives, B-1 and B-2, were approached tactically and quietly, with the company TAC and 3 Platoon to B-1 and 1 and 4 Platoon to B-2. Abboud was surprised to find a lone man in B-1; he was happy to see the Canadians and told them the enemy was 300m away. He was even willing to show "B" Company where they were located.

That compound complex, designated C-2, was located across a 200m open field. Abboud had the company's C-6 and C-9 machine-guns set up to cover the approach, but when the company TAC turned a corner in a maze of compounds in B-1, they surprised an insurgent. He was wearing a black tactical vest, had dark brown uniform pants and top, a long black beard and an AK-47. The enemy had observation posts, but their men were languid in the heat of the day. Shots were fired and the fight was on.

The company TAC and 3 Platoon were then engaged from the compounds in C-2, mostly with PKM machine-gun fire, but soon after, the Taliban fired RPG round after RPG round at B-1 (about 25 shots) with their distinctive two bangs – the first when fired and the second when detonated. The enemy lofted the RPG rounds in an arc in an attempt to use plunging fire.

2 and 3 Platoons, hearing the firing, pushed hard into and through the B-2 compounds emerging south of objective B-1. Royer and St-Germain had clear shots and good fields of fire, so they engaged the C-2 objective from their direction.

This firefight lasted about two hours, with the Van Doos moving back and forth along walls and on compound roofs, getting better firing positions under a rain of RPG rounds; they returned fire with C-7A1 assault rifles, 203mm grenade-launchers and C-6 and C-9 machine-guns. The volume of enemy fire was heavy and it was clear that C-2 was a major Taliban position.

The Taliban then tried to manoeuvre to flank objective B-1 to the north with a 12-man group. The company TAC and 4 Platoon caught the movement through the orchards and walls and put down a high volume of fire. The forward observation officer was by now in contact with the two M-777 artillery pieces. Two fire missions blasted the Taliban group, the rounds crashing down, permanently eliminating it from the order of battle.

Not long after, the Taliban commander in C-2 tried another flanking move, this time to the south, to the right side of the compounds in B-2. Unfortunately for this group of insurgents, the Zulu LAV-IIIs in the wadi detected the move. The 25mm guns, with their distinctive "Boom-boom-boom" three-round bursts, forced the enemy to take cover. The forward observation officer with the LAV-IIIs then called in another fire-mission from "X" Battery, again eliminating the flanking force as a threat.

This enemy was no rag-tag force of Jezail-wielding farmers from the hills, as some commentators in the Canadian media portray them. They had distinctive uniforms, heavy weapons and a command-and-control hierarchy. When surprised on their flank, they manoeuvred. They fought in place and did not want to withdraw. This was not hit-and-run warfare in the hills, but a classic Fighting in Built Up Areas (FIBUA) battle. Experienced and probably professionally trained, they were also not ageing Mujahideen from the 1980s. It is possible some were foreign fighters, but this remains unclear.

Under normal conditions, airpower would have been called in to obliterate the compounds in Objective C-2, using several 1000-pound Guided Bomb Units (GBUs) dropped from Harrier, A-10 or Mirage aircraft. The fact that Arghandab was a friendly district and had very little battle damage throughout the course of the war, played a role in deliberately employing coalition firepower with the objective of reducing collateral damage.

The fact that the enemy was not withdrawing from C-2 piqued the interest of the planning and intelligence staff back in the Provincial Operations Centre (POC) at Kandahar Air Field. They directed a Sperwer Tactical Unmanned Aerial Vehicle, and later an MQ-1 Predator, to take an in-depth look at what was going on behind the C-2 compound complexes. Much maligned, loud, unarmed and not as sexy as the MQ-1 Predator or the MQ-9 Reaper UAVs, the Sperwer still carried a respectable sensor package. One eye was better than none. In due course, observers located what looked like a meeting of enemy personnel, about a platoon's worth, clustered around a commander who was giving them instructions. Two USAF F-15 Eagles were orbiting the battlefield and, once the airspace was deconflicted by the POC staff, one plane was cleared to engage the concentration with a 500-pound GBU. At least fifteen Taliban were fragmented by the blast. The only collateral damage was to the mud wall they were leaning against.

"B" Company had contact for the rest of the day in the vicinity of Objective C-2. Two soldiers were wounded with RPG fragments to the face and legs but continued to fight nonetheless. Meanwhile, on the second axis of advance, the Afghan National Army company made good time and cleared the compound complexes in Objectives G and H without incident. A troop of Leopard 2A6Ms and a troop of Coyote surveillance and recce vehicles moved along the western flank in parallel fashion, turrets traversed in all directions, when a forward observation officer confirmed that a section of

Taliban with anti-tank weapons was manoeuvring to engage the tanks. A fire mission from the M-777s finished off that group.

When the Afghan force tried to move into Objective J, however, the Taliban opened up with a high volume of small arms fire. The Afghan lieutenant leading the attack was killed outright. The attack stalled and became an exchange of fire, with the Afghans engaging in an RPG duel with the Taliban. 53 Escadron's LAV-IIIs provided fire support but, throughout the afternoon, it proved difficult to extract the enemy from Objective J without employing tank fire or air support. The ANA finally brought up mortars and lobbed several rounds at the enemy positions in the compounds.

LCol Gauthier was confronted with a problem as the sun waned. "B" Company's advance and the 2nd kandak's advance were asymmetrical. His concern was that the enemy, having demonstrated a level of tactical sophistication, might try to exploit the widening gap at night; they might harass or assault either company or they might exfiltrate through the gap and get away into Zharey district. LCol Gauthier ordered Maj Abboud to halt and establish observation posts for the night.

Soldiers from "B" Company, 3 R22eR engage the enemy in Objective C. (DND-Combat Camera)

At the same time, LCol Shareen Shah from 2nd kandak was deploying another infantry company to back up the one at Objective J and he was figuring out how to bring in his third company. The Afghan National Police also wanted to be involved in the next day's operations. By this time, the U.S. Police Mentoring Team had moved north on the east side of the river, in part because there were delays in getting TF-32 into position up near Dala Dam. Eager to get into the action, the PMT engaged the Taliban with 203mm grenade fire along the river but several ANP officers were wounded during the night.

"B" Company did not get much sleep. The temperature, usually 25 degrees during the day, dropped to 0 degrees at night. Each soldier was already loaded down with personal protection gear, weapons, ammo, water, ammo, food and more ammo; some were carrying 100 pounds and had been sweating all day. At night, however, some became nearly hypothermic. At this point, the medics treated six orthopedic injuries – turned ankles and strained backs – plus two wounded by shrapnel.

Recce Squadron Coyotes secured advance routes, provided long-range surveillance, and patrolled Arghandab District once it was secured. (DND-Combat Camera)

Re-supply was complicated by the lack of navigable roads, so the Zulu LAV-IIIs moved as close as they could along the wadi. Fifty percent of each platoon moved through 800m of uncleared complex terrain (the possibility of mines was very real) down to the wadi and back to the positions to re-supply depleted stocks – particularly ammo and water. Maj Abboud also decided to move a LAV-III platoon back to the Arghandab district centre, park the vehicles and bring those nine crewmen back to fight dismounted.

A variety of ISTAR resources were deployed that night to watch for enemy movement, but nothing was seen. By 2007, the enemy understood how capable the coalition forces were in this realm, so they limited their movements to covered routes.

The Taliban commanders, however, were stunned by the rapidity of the coalition forces' response and by their own losses on the first day, estimated to be 15 dead and 50 wounded (many of whom would later die). Their command and control was breaking down and fear was palpable in the enemy camp. It was possible that leaders were killed in the air strike and the remaining leaders were unsure what to do; stay and fight or withdraw. They contacted their higher commanders and asked for reinforcements. Those men subsequently tried to muster support for the Arghandab effort from Taliban groups located as far away as Helmand province and Pakistan.

Day 2: 31 October 2007

As dawn broke on Day 2, "B" Company's plan was to move onto the C-1 complex. The idea was to convince the enemy he was about to be outflanked, forcing him to disengage or, if he was not thinking, the move would drive him towards the wadi and into the 25mm guns of the Zulu LAV-IIIs. The 2nd kandak was up bright and early, moving at strength into Objective J which they cleared thoroughly all morning. ISTAR assets detected a section of insurgents heading north who subsequently split up, individually, and went in separate directions. Another Taliban section was detected heading north away from the river and was engaged with artillery fire before it could 'starburst'; an estimated seven enemy fighters were killed.

Once the companies were symmetrical on both axes of advance, "B"

Company prepared to move on C-1 around 1400. 2 Platoon and the company TAC struck out for the compounds where the enemy engaged at 100m range with harassing fire from the C-1 compounds. LCol Gauthier instructed "B" Company to get into the C-2 complex as quickly as possible and back off on C-1.

The Sperwer TUAV spotted enemy movement behind these objective areas and two AH-64 Apache attack helicopters arrived on station to support the effort. One of the machines loosed a Hellfire missile against a mud wall on C-2 to 'rattle the cage' of any occupants. There was no reaction and "B" Company started to methodically search the compound complexes. The search was slow-going as there was concern that the enemy may have laid anti-personnel mines, or left booby traps behind, so that by nightfall only 60 percent of C-2 had been examined.

On the northern axis, the Afghan force prepared to assault into Objective I. The Leopard 2 tanks and engineer LAV-IIIs manoeuvred to form a firebase to the north-west, while the 2nd kandak and the OMLT prepared to rush the compounds. This move was delayed because it was getting dark. Two bewildered enemy wandering around the area were detained. Another Taliban section was spotted moving among several compounds, but as the fleeting target could not be engaged with artillery, the AH-64 Apaches were asked to hunt them down. The attack helicopters had no luck finding them in that built-up area. As the force moved into the compounds south of Jelawur, a short, sharp firefight broke out, leaving two Taliban dead.

The Afghan kandak and "B" Company consolidated in three locations for the night and conducted re-supply. There were no engagements that night.

Day 3: 1 November 2007

"B" Company cleared the other 40 percent of the Objective C-2 compounds throughout the morning. A local national, who had stayed behind and hid, emerged and told the soldiers that the enemy was placing IEDs or mines on some of the routes. The combat engineers conducted a recce and discovered an IED between C-2 and the wadi. On careful examination, two other IED sites were located, again on routes leading to the wadi. It appeared as though the weapons were laid back on the first night in anticipation of an ANP/Police Mentoring Team (PMT) attack across the wadi. When that did not materialize, the IEDs were left in place. The clearance effort was conducted by combat engineers and took an hour. The enemy clearly anticipated a mounted attack and planned accordingly. Once again, a dismounted operation had caught the Taliban by surprise and dislocated them.

The "B" Company platoons moved on to Objective C-3 and cleared it as well. Maj Abboud then sent a platoon back to C-1 just in case the enemy surreptitiously re-occupied it during the night. Again, no contact. LCol Gauthier believed that the enemy had exfiltrated, so he sped up the advance. "B" Company moved on to the D series of objectives and were surprised to find local nationals returning. Almost all had been informed by cell phone that it was safe to return to their homes, that the enemy had left. On encountering the Canadians, the hospitality component of Pashtunwali[5] came into effect and the platoons were invited to move into the houses and bed down in the compounds by overjoyed Arghandabians.

The Afghan army and OMLT assault on Objective I went on, but there was no resistance. ISTAR surveillance picked up what amounted to an enemy evacuation of the Jelawur and Chalgoa communities. The enemy, apparently, was dispirited over the loss of leadership and the unwillingness of other Taliban commanders in the region to reinforce the Arghandab effort. They withdrew from the field, split up into small groups or individually, buried or concealed their weapons and left. LCol Gauthier decided to accelerate the advance so, once the ongoing clearances were completed in their present locations, "B" Company moved forward to Objective D and the ANA company to Objective K. By this time, the Canadians and Afghans were running out of district as they headed north and the terrain tapered between the hills and the river. The rest of the day was spent methodically searching the remaining objective compounds. There was no enemy contact.

Endgame: 2 November 2007

As the district population flowed back in, 2nd kandak and the ANP moved on to Jelawur in a massive show of force while "B" Company cleared the last objectives in D-2, E-1 and E-2. There was an atmosphere of jubilation, not only in the district, but in Kandahar City as well. When "B" Company was reunited with its LAV-IIIs, they drove out of the district and back to FOB Wilson with cheering crowds lining the roads, something not seen in Kandahar after any previous operation. The Taliban left behind a surprise in the form of a lone suicide bomber. Before he could detonate his vest, however, the locals in Tabi-e Sofia prevented him from doing so and turned him over to the ANP. On 4 November, a Taliban IED team that infiltrated the area succeeded in disabling a Leopard 2 tank that was supporting Recce Squadron in maintaining a presence in the district; but, without the forces to follow up, the Taliban action amounted to nothing. By January 2008, the district shura was more interested in electricity and irrigation issues than security matters.

After the action, there was some finger-pointing by local officials and 'Monday-morning quarterbacking' by other locally based commentators who were upset that the enemy had 'got away' or had somehow outwitted Task Force Kandahar during their exfiltration. The reality of the situation was that the terrain is porous and not all of the screening forces were in place throughout the course of the battle. If an insurgent divests himself of weapons and equipment, he can easily blend in with the returning population and escape. None of this should detract from the most important success of the operation; namely, that the enemy did not retain any control over Arghandab district or its population. They retreated to areas of the province that do not matter, areas that consist of rock and sand and which are difficult to re-supply from Pakistan in the face of other coalition forces' operations in Regional Command (South), with small population bases and, thus, fewer recruits.

In addition, the elimination of experienced leaders would have had a cumulative effect on those Taliban cells that were engaged in this operation; indeed, these effects have been felt throughout the Regional Command (South) area. The really telling aspect is that the other Taliban commanders in adjacent areas, and even in the provinces, declined to join the fight for Arghandab when it became evident the Taliban force was in trouble.

The ability of 150-200 enemy to generate panic in a city with a population of half-million inhabitants, whether deliberately or inadvertently, was astounding. Could this have been prevented? Yes, but only by a concentrated and concerted information operations campaign and only when the coalition forces recognized that such panic was spreading like wildfire.

The action in Arghandab district will prove to have been a critical one once the overall history of the campaign is assembled. The vital nature of the district, its proximity to Kandahar City and, most importantly, the fact that the enemy was unable to gain a foothold in the community – let alone control it – are stark indicators of success. The Canadian-led operation was mounted extremely quickly and used methods unanticipated by the Taliban. This thoroughly dislocated them psychologically, in contrast to the more deliberate set-piece actions conducted in Zharey district back in 2006. The geographical and psychological aspects of Operation INTIZAAR ZMAREY need to be understood, especially by counterinsurgency practitioners operating in Afghanistan.

A Note on Sources

This chapter is for the most part based on a series of interviews conducted by the author in-theatre in Kandahar two months after the operation with: the primary Canadian command and planning personnel; Maj Dave Abboud and his staff; members of the Kandahar Provincial Reconstruction Team; and Afghan personnel. Certain details relating to intelligence sources have been blurred and the code names of all route-control measures and geographical identifiers have been altered for operational security considerations.

NOTES

1 One Westerner with romantic and emotional attachments to the Alokozai tribe asserted to many Afghan officials and international aid workers in Kandahar City that "Canada" (not just TFK or ISAF) had been surprised by Taliban infiltration of Arghandab, thus the belief that Canada's response was needlessly slow gained credence in the media and within the population.

2 A shura is a governance meeting between the representatives of several adjacent communities at the village or district level.

3 The ANAP are essentially an auxiliary militia and are different from the Afghan National Police or ANP. The ANAP was an experiment and was supposed to be disbanded; but in 2007 it was still in place in Arghandab.

4 Zulu vehicles have had their infantry debussed but are still manned by their crews.

5 Pashtunwali is the tribal code of the Pashtuns that emphasizes hospitality to guests and blood debts among enemies.

The Viking over-snow vehicle was adapted for use in Afghanistan. Crewed by Royal Marines, this Viking troop acted as a mobile screen during cordon and search operations around Band-e Timor.

CHAPTER SEVEN
OPERATIONAL MANOEUVRE GROUP: OPERATION SOHIL LARAM II
KANDAHAR PROVINCE, FEBRUARY 2008

It is natural for military historians to focus on purely national issues and national history. Indeed, writing about coalition warfare is notoriously difficult, particularly when it comes to using sources from all of the key national players, sources subject to uneven availability. Then there is the Canadian proclivity to make up for lost time in military history affairs; this leads to an examination of Canadian combat arms units to the exclusion of the activities of higher headquarters and support units. Indeed, we expect our larger allies, with their more robust history-production apparatus, to take care of our coalition history as well as their own. As a result, a danger exists that we may overlook critical aspects of our military history, particularly when we have allied forces under Canadian command.

In addition to providing a Battlegroup, a provincial reconstruction team, special operations forces and mentoring teams to the war in Afghanistan, Canada has rotating command of the NATO-led International Security Assistance Force's Regional Command (South) Headquarters. RC (South) is responsible for four brigade-sized national commands, or task forces, that conform to the main provinces in southern Afghanistan: TF Helmand (British); TF Oruzgan (Dutch); TF Zabol (Romanian and American) and TF Kandahar (Canada). In addition, an Afghan corps headquarters, 205 Corps, is the counterpart to RC (South) and each province boasts an Afghan National Army brigade. For the most part, each ANA brigade is twinned with each ISAF brigade and they will control between one and four kandaks, or battalion-sized Afghan forces.

Scarce national resources, or 'enablers', like helicopters, (UAVs), various (ISTAR) capabilities, (CIMIC) and artillery operate everywhere in RC (South), depending on where they are needed; however, they usually come under the control of a provincial brigade headquarters for the duration of a given operation and then revert to national control. Consequently, few operations in Afghanistan are conducted by a single country on its own.

In January 2008, Canada took command of RC (South) Headquarters. Led by Major-General Marc Lessard, RC (South) HQ deployed resources in Kandahar province in order to supplement the operations already underway and commanded by BGen Guy Laroche, the commander of Task Force Kandahar. One of those resources was an entity called Regional Battlegroup (South) or RBG(S). The RBG(S) acted as a regional reserve force and could be employed by RC (South) HQ anywhere in the region it deemed necessary. The only self-imposed caveat was that the force had to be used to generate enduring operation-level effects, not only short-term tactical or province-level effects.

The United Kingdom assigned the 1st Battalion, The Royal Gurkha Rifles as RBG(S) in the fall of 2007 'without strings', meaning that the usual restrictive national caveats were lifted for the duration. This light infantry battalion, composed of Nepalese Gurkhas, led by British officers and supplemented with Canadian 'enablers', proved to be a formidable and agile asset that significantly contributed to achieving ISAF's aims in Kandahar province. This article will examine Operation SOHIL LARAM II, an operation conducted by the Regional Battlegroup (South) in Maywand district of Kandahar province in late February 2008.

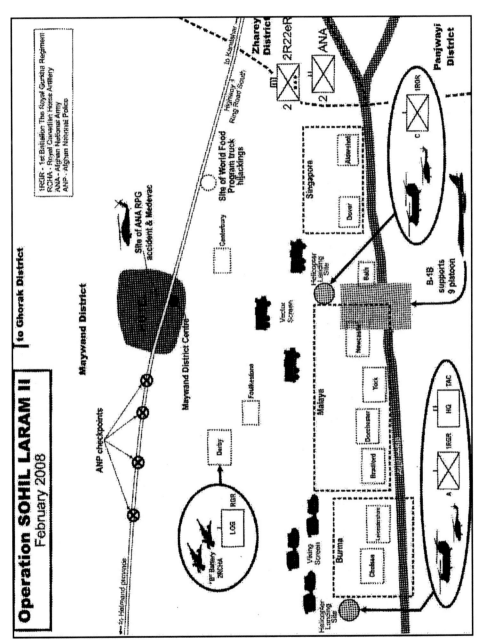

Operation SOHIL LARAM II, February, 2008.

The Operational Level Situation

The situation in RC (South) in early 2008 was calm relative to previous years. The United Kingdom had, since 2006, tripled the size of its forces in Helmand province from a Battlegroup to nearly a brigade. Headway was made in the Musa Qala area and even some senior Taliban commanders were starting to join the PTS amnesty program. In Oruzgan province, the Dutch task force controlled the main population centres, while an Australian special operations task force kept the Taliban off-balance elsewhere. Zabol, recently taken over by a Romanian Battlegroup, still boasted an American PRT and, for the most part, kept open the vital Ring Road South (RRS).

In Kandahar province, the Canadian Battlegroup and an Afghan National Army company kicked the Taliban out of Arghandab district, less than five kilometres from Kandahar City. This last move was the latest in a campaign to block Taliban attempts to take control of a district that abutted Ring Road South and the city. The enemy had, since 2006, tried to interdict the four main routes into Kandahar City. Zharey district was, in January 2008, garrisoned by ANA and Afghan National Police and there was a substantial

The 1st Battalion, The Royal Gurkha Rifles (RGR), acted as the Regional Battlegroup (South) reserve force in 2007-08. 1 RGR developed a close working relationship with the Canadian task force.

amount of development taking place. Over in Panjwayi district, Taliban that had been pushed out of Zharey mounted an IED campaign on the main roads there. Taliban still operated in Zharey but, unlike back in 2006-07, they were unable to seriously control the population. There was virtually no enemy activity around Kandahar Air Field, nor was the enemy operating along Highway 4, the main trade route between Afghanistan and Pakistan in the south.

Task Force Kandahar and the ANA's 205 Corps did not have the forces, nor the resources, to garrison the entire province, so they focused on districts that were vital ground. Northern districts like Khakriz, Ghorak and Sha Wali Kot had varying levels of Taliban influence but, for the most part, that influence remained local.

The Taliban maintained training sites, weapons dumps and command nodes inside Pakistan, notably in and around the city of Quetta where the Taliban command for the south, the Quetta Shura, was located. The *modus operandi* was to infiltrate fighters into Afghanistan, individually or in small numbers, smuggle in weapons and ammunition separately, mate the two and then fight. Suicide bombers had a separate but parallel system.

A pair of M-777 155mm guns from "A" Battery, 2 Royal Canadian Horse Artillery firing from the DERBY box in support of "A" Company, 1st Battalion, The Royal Gurkha Rifles.

To mount any sort of operation inside Kandahar City or in the adjacent districts took time. A command node (or nodes, depending on the size of the force) had to be established first, then followed by a G-4 (logistics) node to stockpile weapons and ammo. 'Rat lines', consisting of safe houses, sympathizers in the transportation community and facilitators of all types, had to be positioned and activated. Notably, the 'rat lines' sometimes worked in reverse for Taliban casualty evacuation. These shadowy networks were notoriously difficult to track down, partly because the police forces were not capable of the sophisticated approach needed to do so. The exception was the small, but fairly effective, National Directorate of Security. Checkpoints and police patrols could be bribed, others could be intimidated; still others adopted a 'live and let live' policy. ISAF and Operation Enduring Freedom (OEF) forces, however, maintained steady pressure on the enemy system to generate as much friction as possible within that system.

The Taliban also tried their hand at establishing a parallel government, but this generally took negative forms as opposed to competitive forms. Attacking schools and the healthcare system in order to deny effective government services was not the same as actually providing parallel services. However, there were small numbers of Taliban 'judges' and there were 'wandering mullahs' proselytizing in the rural areas, all backed up by a sophisticated intimidation campaign that made the Taliban look more powerful than they actually were, especially in the rural areas. In other districts, the Taliban co-opted corrupt local leaders or other men who played both sides against the middle for sheer survival, or profit, or both. These people tended to overlap with the narcotics producers in certain areas of RC (South).

The situation as it stood in late January 2008 was that the enemy was incapable of interdicting the main highways throughout RC (South) and failed to interfere with operations at Kandahar Air Field. The highways and the air field are absolutely critical to the ISAF, OEF and Afghan efforts in RC (South). Also, the Taliban had not taken Kandahar City. Control of Kandahar City is critical to the control of southern Afghanistan, both geographically and psychologically; not only is it a transportation hub, it is also the religious/political centre of the region. Weakened in all the adjacent districts, thwarted in their latest endeavour in Arghandab district, the Quetta Shura was at a crossroads.

The Quetta Shura hoped to move back to the heady days of 2006 when they seriously contested coalition control of Zharey and Panjwayi districts, mounted an incessant suicide bomb campaign in the city and showered Kandahar Air Field with rockets nearly every night. The networks, command nodes and G-4 nodes had to be rebuilt nearly everywhere. The cells already in place had to be revitalized, reinforced and re-supplied. Consequently, the networks in the districts in the next ring away from the city had to be revitalized first, as a precondition. As it stood in early 2008, if the Taliban were unable to achieve the salience they had in 2006, they would lose even more credibility with the population. That credibility was eroded daily with each new government reconstruction or governance initiative.

The generalities of this situation were known in RC (South) and in Task Force Kandahar in early 2008 and the pressure had to be kept up, in an overall sense, across the region. The issue in Kandahar province, however, was the upcoming relief in place (RIP) of the 3rd Battalion, R22eR Battlegroup with the 2nd Battalion, Princess Patricia's Canadian Light Infantry. In the past, the enemy exploited less than seamless RIPs to the detriment of the departing and arriving forces. The arriving force was usually inexperienced and took time to get up to speed with the deep nuances of operating in the districts and communities. Disruptive activity by coalition forces could shield the RIP and buy the incoming forces time to acclimatize.

At the same time, enemy forces in the peripheral districts tended to operate in 'seams'. They understood the problems of coordination between coalition partners on the artificial boundary lines established by staffs, and they understood that coalition control lessened the further away from the main population centres they operated. If the Taliban hoped to revitalize their networks, they would work out of those seams first, use them as staging areas and then infiltrate and support their forces in districts adjacent to the city. The combination of these factors pointed the planning staffs from RBG(S), TFK and RC (South) towards one particular district: Maywand.

Maywand district lay, from east to west, between Zharey district and Helmand province; Ring Road South ran straight through the middle of the district, through the prosperous agricultural community of Hutel. From north to south, Maywand was sandwiched between the mountainous Ghorak district and the Arghandab river, and then the inhospitable Reg Desert. The Dasht, as the wide-open plain was called, was a millennia-old trade and transit route between the Indian subcontinent and Persia.

Operationally, Maywand was a seam between Task Force Helmand and Task Force Kandahar, smack dab in the middle. The district had a reputation as a singularly large 'rat line' connecting the extensive infiltration routes from Pakistan in the Helmand river valley to the western edge of Zharey district and the western-most point of Panjwayi district. Intelligence analysts assumed over the years that the southern part of the district, an elongated series of communities called Band-e Timor, was a Taliban stronghold and out of reach due to the priorities to protect the city and to being far enough south from the main highway to be off the beaten path. Word had filtered out during the previous year that there was even a functional Taliban shadow government operating there, complete with judges.

The district leader and his police had a reputation for being brutally corrupt but, because he had been appointed by the current governor, he appeared untouchable. Rumours abounded that, back in the summer of 2007, his police hi-jacked World Food Program (WFP) aid trucks with impunity and even executed their drivers because the WFP refused to pay him off. There was no Afghan National Army presence. Tribally, Maywand was dominated by Noorzai and familial connections between the district and the border city of Spinboldak and which, reportedly, involved narcotics smuggling. In short, it was an ideal district to house a Taliban G-4 node and 'rat line'.

There had been two coalition forays into Maywand back in 2007. The 2 RCR Battlegroup conducted operations in May through the eastern portion of Band-e Timor with a company group, while the 1 RGR's predecessor RBG(S) The 1st Battalion, The Royal Welsh Fusiliers, essentially conducted a similar operation in the fall, but these were independent and temporary operations and generally not coupled with Afghan efforts conducted in the district.

The potential operation-level effects of inserting the Regional Battlegroup (South) into Maywand district were considerable. It would disrupt the 'rat line' into Zharey and Panjwayi districts, especially during the RIP. It would demonstrate to the Taliban that coalition forces did not fear operating in districts in which they did not traditionally operate and that coalition forces would operate with impunity. Such an operation would also enhance security along Ring Road South, the link between Kandahar Air Field and Task Force Helmand.

The main problem, as the planners knew, was that without an enduring coalition presence the enemy would eventually re-infiltrate the district and be back in business; however, 'emptying the garbage', as the Canadians called it or 'mowing the lawn', as the British named it, had its uses. Disruption without occupation was not optimal, but there was no apparent solution to that problem in the initial stages of the planning process; so, conceptually, SOHIL LARAM II started off as a large-scale RBG(S) raid.

Task Organization

RBG(S) or Task Force TIGER was based on 1st Battalion, The Royal Gurkha Rifles. Led by LCol Johnny Bourne, 1 RGR normally had three light infantry companies. In Afghanistan, however, 1 RGR detached one company to Helmand province, leaving two infantry companies available for RBG(S) operations: "A" Company led by Maj Paul "Pitch" Pitchfork, and "C" Company led by Maj Will Kefford.[1] There was a Support Company broken down into two Fire Support Groups (machine-guns, snipers) and a mortar platoon of six 82mm mortars. 1 RGR had its own doctor and medical team. In terms of mobility, one company was transported in Vector vehicles, essentially a six-wheeled, uparmoured Pinzgauer truck, and WMIK Land Rovers with .50 cal machine-guns and M-19 grenade-launchers mounted on them. The other company was carried by a squadron of Viking tracked over-snow vehicles armed with 7.62mm General Purpose Machine Guns and crewed by Royal Marines. Small portable bridges and fascines were carried to assist in moving across water obstacles that criss-crossed the areas near the river. 1 RGR had also just conducted two airmobile operations, one in northern Kandahar province and the other into the Chora Valley in Oruzgan with the Australian SAS Regiment.

1 RGR had also worked closely with the Canadian Battlegroup on at least two occasions in Zharey and Panjwayi districts. In each operation, a Gurkha

company operated under Canadian Battlegroup command. 1 RGR was short on long-range firepower, however. Though the Gurkhas were equipped with a variety of mortars, LCol Bourne requested and received a two-gun detachment of M-777 155mm guns, two 81mm mortars and a troop of TLAV APCs[2] led by Lt Candice Dunn from the newly arrived "B" Battery, 2 Royal Canadian Horse Artillery. Since 1 RGR was the regional mobile reserve, it normally did not have its own specialist 'enablers'. Canadian (CIMIC) and Tactical Psychological Operations (TPT or PSYOPS) teams were also attached. For intelligence collection and liaison purposes, the Afghan National Directorate of Security attached a number of officers. A Canadian Joint Terminal Air Controller (JTAC) from Air Command, and another from the RAF Regiment (a squadron of which was protecting Kandahar Air Field) with their specialist communications gear, also joined the force in order that 1 RGR could communicate with close air support and attack aviation resources.

The Plan

Planning SOHIL LARAM II was essentially a three-way dialogue between the 1 RGR, TFK and RBG(S) staffs. That dialogue established: the justification as to exactly why the Gurkha battalion would be employed in Maywand district; conceptually how the Battlegroup would be employed, with several options depending on transportation availability; and the coordination and de-confliction aspects. All of this had to be approved by MGen Marc Lessard after his multinational staff at Regional Command (South) gave the thumbs-up.

Operation SOHIL LARAM II were designed to achieve a number of effects. The most obvious was the disruption of enemy activity in Maywand district, the flushing out and destruction of leadership targets and, thus, the positive effects that both would have in both Helmand and Kandahar provinces. As for the district itself, the operation was designed to leave a positive impression with the population of the coalition forces, the ANA and the ANP in the hope that this would serve as a basis for future operations aimed at establishing a permanent Afghan government presence throughout the district. Finally, the operation was designed to improve the police presence along Highway 1 by reconstructing ANP checkpoints, many of which were rudimentary at best, partially manned and nearly indefensible.

There were a number of other reasons to conduct a Maywand operation at this time. One particular event on 13 February 2008 was significant. A Sperwer TUAV observed three World Food Program trucks being hijacked in broad daylight, just east of Hutel. The attackers bogged one truck down attempting to escape while an RG-31 Nayala raced to respond along with a section from the Canadian (OMLT) and two platoons from 2nd kandak in Howz-e Madad. With a B-1B in support and the TUAV tracking the movements of the hijackers, the OMLT and the Afghan National Army determined that police from Maywand district were responsible for this latest attack. This was the final straw and the Kandahar provincial Chief of Police, General Saquib, replaced all 160 police in Maywand district.

This unplanned, wholesale replacement of the Maywand police during the operational planning process provided a window of opportunity to renew the district. Rather than just raiding into the remoter parts of Maywand, the RBG(S) would be able to generate synergy by facilitating a combined coalition forces-police presence, in effect helping the new police establish themselves, a move which would ultimately prove critical in improving governance in the district. There was an operating theory that the district chief and the corrupt police were in cahoots in the shakedowns of aid convoy, but no action had been taken against him for a variety of reasons. The removal of 'his' police meant that he would lose 'muscle' and therefore be more compliant. As the planning process progressed, 2nd kandak was brought into the operation, initially at company strength, but then with a second company. Even though 2nd kandak would be committed for a limited period, the information operations and governance benefits that could be derived from highly visible joint ANA-ANP patrolling could be substantial, especially on the Maywand population.

The assessment of Taliban forces in Maywand suggested that the Band-e Timor strip north of the Arghandab river concealed a facilitation network with a line of arms dumps, and that there was also a C-2 node on the boundary with Zharey district. An enemy IED cell was known to operate in

Ghorak district, north of the Garmabak Pass, but it had previously sortied south and killed both British and Canadian troops passing through the district. The presence of static enemy fighting forces could not be confirmed; the Taliban generally moved through the area singly or in small groups, but sometimes they coalesced to shoot up the Maywand district centre for its info/ops effect. Enemy medium value individuals (MVIs), or leadership targets, were present from time to time, most likely using the Band-e Timor area as a 'rat line'. Significant movement of coalition forces into the district would set these pieces in motion – either to escape or to engage – and then 1 RGR Battlegroup would generate tactical responses accordingly. With a dispersed enemy hiding among the population, this was one of several ways to flush them out.

Much of the staff effort dealt with coordination and de-confliction as a way to avoid situations like the Tarnak Farms tragedy in 2002. For example, at least three types of special operations forces operated throughout the region, none of which belonged to RC (South). They possessed their own ISTAR resources and air support, but those had to be coordinated with ISTAR and air support assigned to RC (South). To make matters more complicated, some of these platforms were the same; i.e., they worked for NATO ISAF and the other entities. The priority was not always NATO ISAF, depending on what was going on elsewhere in the country, so availability had to be locked down.

There were legal aspects that men like LCol Marc Gendron, the LEGAD (Legal Advisor) at RC (South), had to sort out. What rules of engagement were going to be used – Canadian, British, NATO? Under what conditions would they change? Who would approve those changes? What could be blown up and what could not?

At Task Force Kandahar, control measures had to be established between the battle groups' forces operating in neighbouring Zharey district and the RBG(S). For example, the templated range of a 120mm gun on a Leopard 2 A6M was in excess of four kilometres. If the tanks were firing at something to the west of Zharey, could they accidentally hit the manoeuvring units? Or, if the Van Doos used artillery on a target in Panjwayi, nobody wanted lumbering CH-47s flying through the rounds as they arced through the airspace. These are not mundane matters when millions of dollars of helicopters and several hundred priceless human lives are at stake.

One of the main issues in planning SOHIL LARAM II revolved around the early warning problem. The expansion of the cell phone network in Kandahar province since 2003 meant that any person with a cell phone was a potential sensor. The Taliban had non-insurgent insurgents (locals paid to do a specific, one-time task), ideological sympathizers from the old days or people coerced into providing information. In effect, each district had an insurgent reporting network that was activated the moment coalition forces arrived on the scene. The network could communicate in a variety of ways and extended all the way from Maywand to the gates of Kandahar Air Field, and probably within those gates as well. Deception, therefore, was a critical component of the plan.

When 1 RGR war-gamed the operation, the presence of 100+ vehicles on Ring Road South, during the day or night, would be more than enough to activate the enemy warning system. The enemy would not know exactly where the force was going, however. It would take time to get from the high-way and into Band-e Timor as it was a distance of over 12 kilometres with no roads. It would be enough time for the enemy to hide or disperse before the force arrived.

The obvious answer to achieving surprise was to conduct an airmobile insertion at night. There were two problems with this course of action. The first was helicopter availability and the second was the perfidious weather situation. Night airmobile operations were complicated enough, but throw enough dust into the mix and the risk level rose dramatically, as the Americans found out during the Desert One disaster in 1980. There were only so many helicopters and they were heavily tasked. 1 RGR generated two courses of action: a ground move and insertion; and a combination ground move and airmobile insertion.

The second course of action was the best. The ground convoys would move along Ring Road South, the enemy would activate the early warning system and then watch it. As the ground force moved off the roads south towards Band-e Timor, the enemy would be fixated on its progress. Without warning, the airmobile force would emerge out of the desert from the south and surprise them. The first course of action was second best but the planners came up with a scheme to use various forms of airpower to take out any enemy forces trying to exfiltrate the area.

The elongated nature of Band-e Timor posed some challenges. There were clusters of compound complexes all along the river for some 15-20 kilometres. There were irrigations systems, including a canal with fast-running water moving through and between the complexes. Each compound cluster was separated by rolling, but open and arid terrain. The planners decided that the two companies would be inserted at either end of the Band-e Timor river zone and then work towards the centre. An Artillery Maintenance Area (AMA) for the Canadian guns and the 1 RGR logistics echelon would be established on the Dasht, in part to act as a block but also to give the artillery a reach to the south.

On the way through Hutel, one platoon would be dropped off and start working with the new police while the battalion command post would be set up in the district centre. Part of one of the companies would later be brought north to Hutel to join in operations there when the Afghan National Army arrived. If enemy forces appeared in the north near Ghorak, a contingency plan was formulated to respond to that move.

Ch-47 Chinooks like this one conducted the night airmobile insertion of 1 RGR into the Band-e Timor communities in Maywand district during the opening stages of Op SOHIL LARAM II.

Execution: Insertion and Pursuit

During the afternoon of 20 February, the weather situation was not good as the infantry companies rehearsed embarking and disembarking their helicopter chalks in an open field. A small dust event was moving into the Kandahar area and the hills that were normally visible from the air field were obscured with dust. On the evening of 20 February, elements of 2nd kandak moved to Camp Roberts, the 1 RGR camp on Kandahar Air Field, to link up with the Vikings and Vectors. The weather cleared enough by then so the air-mobile insertion was given the go-ahead. The convoys departed around midnight while the two infantry companies awoke from forced rest, prepared their equipment and were bused to the helicopter hanger area.

At 0235 hours, Identification Friend-Foe (IFF) control measures (glow sticks and mini-beacons) were activated and attached to helmets, and weapons were checked. RAF ground personnel mustered the chalks in the dark as the crews of the CH-47 and Lynx helicopters prepared their aircraft. The Auxiliary Power Units (APU) whined as they started the engines and soon the loud whop-whop-whop of the huge blades smacked the air. The Gurkhas filed in and, when everybody was loaded, Royal Air Force (RAF) Chinooks and Army Air Corps Lynxes taxied into a line and levitated off the runway into a sharp banking turn, taking the force into the Reg Desert. Army Air Corps AH-64 Apache attack helicopters, already in the air, joined up to escort the force. Helicopters are loud by nature so everything possible was done to mask the noise signature and achieve surprise. In this case, the desert is empty and the enemy early warning net does not extend to the south out of the built-up areas between Kandahar and Maywand. The circuitous route also gave time for the slower convoys moving along Ring Road South to get into position. Indeed, enemy 'eyes' were focused on the Vikings and Vectors as they drove by towards Helmand.

With the doors open and gunners with night vision leaning out checking the ground, the temperature inside the Chinooks was near freezing for the forty minutes it took to fly from KAF to a point south of Maywand district. The full moon bathed the desert sand making it look like an ocean as the helicopters surfed the ground at low level. At this point the force split into two and headed for their respective company helicopter landing sites (HLS).

The loadies held up two fingers indicating 'two minutes to the HLS' and the Gurkhas tapped each man ahead of them with two fingers. Everybody stood up and, seconds later, the machines' noses lurched up to flare into the HLS. "A" Company had a rough time. Its Chinooks hit the ground hard, probably because of the moon-dust-like powder that obscured the distance to the ground. There were several injuries, including broken noses and twisted knees.

The Gurkhas poured out into a defensive posture as the Chinooks and Lynxes lifted off, showering the soldiers with large rocks and dust for several seconds. Once the birds were gone the company commanders checked the surrounding area with night vision and, when satisfied, started to move off in the dark towards the objective compound complexes. At first, there was no contact.

"A" Company got into complex CHELSEA without incident and initiated several searches. "C" Company, on the other hand, immediately bumped into the Taliban after insertion near NEWCASTLE and BATH. 7 Platoon and 9 Platoon disembarked on the HLSs, with 7 Platoon to the north. A group of enemy in a compound complex south of 9 Platoon's HLS were spotted by an orbiting MQ-1 Predator. 7 Platoon swung into a blocking position to the west of the complex as 9 Platoon moved in, but the enemy pulled out to the south towards another group of compounds. 7 Platoon moved south in parallel and there were some shots fired. The company commander moved 9 Platoon in a leapfrog to the complex to the south of where the enemy was but, while this was in progress, the Taliban continued to move south. At this point, they could not be engaged from the air because of a Rules of Engagement (ROE) issue, so the pursuit continued.

The Taliban force, numbering some 17 personnel, crossed the river. 7 Platoon engaged with 7.62mm machine-gun fire when the Taliban silhouetted themselves on the skyline. Then the enemy split up. One group of six struck south-west into the desert while another group of eleven dodged 9 Platoon and swung north, trying to cross the river and flank them. At this point, they were engaged by a B-1B using three GBU-38 500-pound bombs. The strike, conducted around 0810 hours, killed an estimated four enemy and wounded three. The survivors turned east, heading towards Zharey. 7 Platoon moved east, south of the river, and 9 Platoon moved east while the Fire Support group manoeuvred into several blocking positions to the north. In time, the pursuit turned up nothing as the enemy hid their weapons and melted away in the compound complexes in the area.

The effects of the dance between "C" Company and the Taliban in Objectives NEWCASTLE and BATH were immediate. ISTAR resources reported that an enemy leadership target was in the area. The combination of the MQ-1 and the B-1B were kept on station as long as possible in case more enemy appeared.

Meanwhile, "A" Company's searches continued in CHELSEA. The NDS team working with the company discovered suspect materials of what might be IED production materials of a new type, but it turned out not to be the case. Of more interest was the discovery of a modified white Toyota Corolla, a type commonly associated with Suicide Vehicle Borne Improvised Explosive Device (SVBIED)s in RC (South). Numerous papers, identification cards and notebooks were uncovered and sent off for translation. ISTAR resources then reported that another enemy medium value target was located in a compound complex adjacent to CHELSEA. That made two significant enemy

In the field the 1 RGR Battalion TAC headquarters has the ability to link to imagery provided by a variety of unmanned aerial vehicles, including MQ-1 Predator and MQ-9 Reaper.

leaders present in Band-e Timor. "A" Company then detained an individual who was part of the Taliban early warning network. It was 0845 on the first day.

Execution: Influence Operations

An important aspect of operations like SOHIL LARAM II is how the manoeuvre force relates to the population, so the intended effects of this relationship were built into the plan. Indeed, the deployment of the battalion CO and his tactical headquarters early in the operation was meant, in part, to influence operations. These operations essentially combine information operations and CIMIC assessments with on-the-spot assessments of the religious/political, tribal and community dynamics while the operation is in progress, with the aim of positively influencing the population. There are fundamental local dynamics that cannot be captured by the broader examination of tribal dynamics or of provincial political processes in southern

"A" Company 1 RGR conducts a compound search on Objective CHELSEA.
This action will stimulate enemy movement and make their leaders more vulnerable to other coalition action.

178

Afghanistan. The only way to do so is through immediate and close contact with the population.

The primary tool in the case of SOHIL LARAM II was the Key Leader Engagement, or KLE, where 1 RGR sought out local leaders and met with them in shuras along with other local elders and powerbrokers. Using interpreters and the accompanying National Directorate of Security (NDS) personnel, the meetings yielded valuable information on the attitudes and needs of the community in addition to tactical information on enemy activities. The meetings also permitted PSYOPS to disseminate their messages in subtle ways or, simply put, to explain to the local leaders and people what coalition forces were doing in the area, and why. In theory, CIMIC activities and development assistance from the Provincial Reconstruction Team would follow later but, in the case of a foray like SOHIL LARAM II, only assessments could be made, and then only within the constraints of the tactical situation. Development could only take place with the long-term domination of the area by Afghan national security forces.

1 RGR conducted numerous KLEs and shuras in the Band-e Timor communities during the course of SOHIL LARAM II. The presence on the ground of the 1 RGR Commanding Officer (CO) and his tactical headquarters with "A" Company was also used to good effect. Having an older head man from the coalition meeting with the local elders facilitated dialogue in ways that were not as effective with younger men meeting with older men in similar circumstances. Respect goes a long way and respect is generation-based in the Pashtun culture.

The picture that emerged after several KLEs, though generalized, was at odds with the perception that the communities were pro-Taliban and had been for several years. The message transmitted to the coalition forces was that the bulk of the population would, in fact, welcome an Afghan National Army presence, even ANA strongpoints. They were generally not supportive of the Taliban, but they had no choice because there was little or no government presence. They did not, however, want an Afghan National Police presence. The population had extremely poor relations with the ANP in Hutel and even referred to them as "bastards". They informed coalition personnel that they had problems getting produce to the markets in Hutel. Whether this was the result of actions by corrupt police, insurgents dressed as police, or a combination of the two, was difficult to determine, but practically all elders called for the removal of the current district leader. The people were interested in improved healthcare and an education system, but the attitude of "we'll believe it when we see it" prevailed. Surprisingly, the CIMIC teams learned that many landowners lived in Kabul and rarely visited Band-e Timor.

Note that KLEs were not always a matter of just sitting down and drinking tea. On one occasion personnel accompanying the CO were menaced by a dishevelled, crazed young man wielding a pick. He was tied to a tree by two elders to prevent him from interfering with the shura.

The insertion and manoeuvre of the 1 RGR Battlegroup had a number of other effects on the enemy forces throughout Band-e Timor-Hutel triangle. ISTAR resources detected enemy activity consistent with a plan to screen the exfiltration of leaders, some of whom appeared to be in Objective YORK. One enemy group of observers had 'eyes on' the Canadian 155mm gun position and Gurkha echelon located at DERBY. The CO was concerned that the enemy, though psychologically off-balance, would stay put and wait out the operation, so he pressed for more manoeuvres with the intent to get the enemy moving, get him to make mistakes and make him vulnerable to strikes

Influence operations include the use of Key Leader Engagements. In this case, a local shura in Band-e Timor sits down with LCol Johnny Bourne for a chat about local expectations and conditions.

or capture. The low level of civilian activity was surprising and was a possible indicator that the population was not interested in providing cover for enemy movement out of fear of being targeted by coalition forces.

As the day progressed, ISTAR resources paid more attention to the compounds in Objective YORK. It was increasingly apparent that one or more enemy leaders were located somewhere in there. At least one was ordered by his high command in Pakistan to exfiltrate and avoid being captured at all costs. Other enemy groups in Operation Boxes BURMA and MALAYA were ordered by their higher headquarters to escape while they could. "A" Company was ordered to prepare for a future tasking in that area. As ISTAR assets scoured the district, the 155mm guns were readied; requests for more air power were put in, just in case anything moved. The ISTAR priority remained Objective YORK.

The enemy knew there were coalition forces in CHELSEA and he could see that the cordon and searches had been extended from the compounds in CHELSEA to those in LEICESTERSHIRE. To the enemy, it looked like "A" Company was plodding its way east through the various complexes. The 1 RGR plan was to finish with LEICESTERSHIRE and then 'tab' (route march)

"A" Company 1 RGR moves out from Objective CHELSEA. The terrain in this photo is typical for southern Maywand district.

to DONCASTER, make it look like the force was bedding down to deceive observers, and then conduct a rapid, night-approach march along the Arghandab river to arrive at YORK at first light and search the compounds. The Viking squadron would depart DORCHESTER just before first light to establish a screen north of YORK to catch any 'leakers'.

Meanwhile, the Fire Support Group snipers who were screening to the north of "C" Company were observing people moving about Objective DOVER, but they were unable to determine whether they were enemy forces. When "C" Company got into the compounds, they determined that the leadership target that had been there had slipped away, possibly heading north to Hutel. The presence of two Harrier GR-7 close-support aircraft flying up and down the river appeared to have deterred any enemy movement south.

While "A" Company was laying up in DONCASTER and preparing for the night tab, ISTAR resources identified one of the leadership targets as a logistics facilitator, but he was located west of DONCASTER about a kilometre away. This target appeared to be different from the one(s) in YORK. Should the plan be altered to take him out, or not? The decision was made to search for him but to carry on with YORK. Attempts were made to insert an American Pathfinder Platoon from TF EAGLE ASSAULT to get him or, if that were not possible, bring in a section of U.S. Army OH-58D Warrior recce helicopters; but the forces were not available. To the east, "C" Company reported the seizure of a small number of weapons in their areas. The locals claimed the Taliban "left yesterday"; this was most likely the group engaged by the B-1B. More importantly, "C" Company reported that the closer they were to Zharey district the more hostile locals were to coalition forces. Thus far, it looked like there were at least three leadership targets on the loose south of Hutel.

"A" Company's night tab and early morning entry in YORK was anti-climactic. A major KLE was held, however, late in the morning at YORK. The elders here told the coalition forces that they welcomed an ANA, but not an ANP, presence; and reported that the enemy moved through the area but that the locals would not let them stay out of fear of coalition air strikes. It appeared as though the Taliban acquiesced to the locals without a lot of intimidation because this was the only way to re-supply its forces in Zharey district and because they did not want a hostile population on such vital ground. Interestingly, the local leaders explained that Taliban forces moving through their complexes spoke Punjabi, not Pashtun, and that this was a common occurence.

There were no contacts and ISTAR resources detected no leadership target movement in that objective area, though it looked like the DONCASTER contact wanted to make his way to Helmand province to the west. "A" Company was ordered back to LEICESTERSHIRE with the Viking screen sent to try to hunt the DONCASTER contact.

ISTAR then reported that another leadership target was on the move and was no longer in YORK. How he got out was a mystery, but clumps of newly shaved hair were discovered near a compound he may have been hiding in, so he may have altered his appearance before departing. ISTAR resources reported yet another medium-value leader who evacuated Operation Box BURMA as the Gurkhas moved towards it. Unfortunately, the resources needed to identify and engage him were not available.

Moving along Highway 1 from the DERBY box to Hutel, the battalion tac Vector vehicles halt so the Gurkhas can conduct a defile drill to deter IED attack.

Execution: Consolidation

Concurrent activity in Hutel and the surrounding area on the second day of the operation produced immediate results. The Gurkha platoon and Canadian CIMIC and PSYOPS initiated a series of joint patrols with the newly arrived ANP and awaited engineering resources to start the reconstruction of the ANP checkpoints on Highway 4. The joint patrols discovered that there were hard feelings towards coalition forces dating back to at least 2002 when the poppy eradication program was initiated by the Afghan Interim Administration. At some point, around 20 farmers were killed during demonstrations. The presence of patrols immediately explained that the coalition and the Afghan security forces were not in Maywand to eradicate the poppy but, rather, to improve security and hunt Taliban. This impromptu information operation countered the prevailing Taliban information ops message that the coalition presence would disenfranchise and starve the farmers and their families.

Hutel bazaar was a thriving collection of establishments despite Taliban attempts to intimidate the populace; the latest attempt had been six weeks earlier when sixteen policemen were executed after their checkpoint was seized west of the town. ISTAR resources discovered that, in fact, the enemy was present in the western part of Hutel and had 1 RGR under observation. An enemy cell planned to place an IED on Highway 1 but the plan was thwarted by the presence of the joint patrols.

Two of the ubiquitious white Toyota Corollas seized by one of the joint patrols before they could be converted for use as suicide improvised explosive devices.

The joint patrols also turned up some significant finds on Day Three. Two white Toyota Corollas, concealed with a tarp, were discovered in a wadi, full of fuel and in good running order. No weapons were found, but it was likely that these vehicles were pre-positioned so they could either be quickly modified for suicide IED use or used as getaway cars for enemy leadership. Indeed, ISTAR reported that there were enemy nearby, but the details remained vague. The vehicles were confiscated and none of the locals complained.

"C" Company continued with its operations to the south-east. A sniper lay-back observation post spotted two pickup trucks behaving suspiciously in the evening near the locations of the B-1B strikes. They appeared to be cleaning up the remains of the strike or looking for wounded. The vehicles disappeared into the desert before they could be engaged by a pair of F-16s that were on station.

"C" Company remained interested in the area because there were indications from KLEs that the locals were annoyed with coalition operations (probably special operations forces operations) that bothered them at night. The NDS detachment confirmed from the locals that leadership targets had been moving through the area and that it was a waypoint for personnel, not for weapons storage. They also developed a theory that the Taliban groups who took off during the first night were a protection party for a significant Taliban leader and that their starburst actions were designed to distract the coalition forces from locating and engaging the enemy leader.

A joint Afghan National Army-Maywand District police patrol prepares to deploy into Hutel from the district centre. These patrols are crucial in establishing government presence in this volatile district.

185

Other information developed by the NDS and various ISTAR resources confirmed that there were still leadership targets in the area between the river and Hutel. They also learned that there was a safe house somewhere near Objectives SINGAPORE and CANTERBURY that catered to Taliban commanders. As there was a lack of 'fidelity' on the target, 1 RGR Battlegroup remained focused on securing the district centre in Hutel and working on the checkpoints before expanding the joint patrols outwards.

Then the enemy detonated an IED in the midst of an ANP convoy, wounding four. Incredibly, the ANP apprehended two insurgents who had other devices or components on them. They were brought to the district centre for interrogation by the ANP. Not to be outdone, "A" Company searches to the south-west uncovered IED components in a village west of DERBY. Two more prisoners were taken, both of whom had cell phones and they coughed up useful information on enemy movements in the district and on the types of vehicles they were employing.

At this point, the shift of emphasis was confirmed by the CO: "C" Company would focus solely on influence operations with the ANP in and around Hutel while awaiting the arrival of the ANA, while "A" Company would search and exploit any information it collected along BURMA, MALAYA and SINGAPORE.

The plan for SOHIL LARAM II took into account the possibility that Afghan National Army forces might participate, but the 2nd ANA kandak in Zharey district was itself preparing to rotate out and it was not clear what forces would be available, or for how long. LCol Shareen Shah, CO of 2nd kandak, determined that two companies would deploy from Howz-e Madad in Zharey to Hutel for two days. The idea was to conduct as many joint ANA-ANP patrols as possible in the area in order to demonstrate to the population that the ANA and the new Maywand ANP were going to cooperate effectively from now on, cement the linkages procedurally between the two forces and get them used to working together.

On day four, around 0830, a seemingly endless stream of ANA vehicles started to arrive in Hutel, including Ford Ranger pickup trucks, International 2.5-ton trucks, and even several mottled Hummers equipped with 12.7mm machine-guns. At the end of the column, several Canadian RG-31 vehicles discreetly entered the district headquarters compound.

This 12-man Operational Mentor and Liaison Team, led by Maj Corey Frederickson from 3rd Battalion Princess Patricia's Canadian Light Infantry, was the team who mentored elements of 2nd kandak. The stream of vehicles continued for some time and the entire population turned out to watch. These ANA soldiers, unlike their predecessors from two years ago, wore helmets, body armour and chest rigs and they carried themselves with some professionalism. The ANP were visibly envious. The PSYOPS team working the crowds detected a feeling approximate to 'the cavalry has arrived'. It was evident from conversations with the people that they were surprised, and even proud, that the ANA was in Hutel. This psychological effect was identified and exploited as soon as possible. LCol Shareen Shah immediately linked up with the Hutel ANP and launched a series of foot and vehicle patrols throughout the area with the police and with "C" Company.

While the ANSF saturation of Hutel and environs was underway, "A" Company continued its movements to the south-west near DERBY and around LEICESTERSHIRE and CHELSEA. Using the Viking squadron as a screen, "A" Company collected significant low-level intelligence related to Taliban activities in the area. Then the Royal Marines bagged a 'leaker' from one of the searches who was identified as Taliban. This individual gave up a relative and the NDS identified both as local Taliban leaders. They were passed on to Hutel for exploitation in the hope they would give up more elements of the facilitation network. The NDS exploited several document and laptop finds and they found lists of enemy personnel and a list of judges who had been paid off by the Taliban to release captured insurgents. Other documentation detailed links to support areas in Pakistan. There was so much material it had to be transported elsewhere for exploitation. The hunt continued.

Canadian CIMIC and PSYOPS teams accompanied the joint Gurkha-ANSF patrols throughout Hutel. The picture they developed was at odds with previous assessments. Only part of Hutel was seriously pro-Taliban. This was a series of communities approximating the north-west quadrant of the area. ISTAR reportage confirmed this. For the most part, 75 percent or more of the population supported the government. As before, they were intimidated by the Maywand police forces and tended to sit on the fence. Indeed, the local clinic sold medical supplies to the Taliban to keep them away.

7 Platoon deployed west along Highway 1 with engineers and ANP continuing to refurbish the checkpoint system. The Gurkhas conducted a series of clearance patrols and vehicle checkpoints to clear each site and facilitate construction. ISTAR reportage also identified possible enemy leaders in a compound complex south of the district centre, so LCol Shah deployed two of his platoons, accompanied by Gurkhas and Canadians, to conduct searches.

ISTAR reportage continued throughout the evening. First there was a threat warning of possible IED placement west of the district centre, on the highway. This IED attack was to be accompanied with an ambush. ANSF foot patrols flooded into the areas and successfully deterred this attack. The device was found and blown up, really annoying the local Taliban cell leader. Further reportage indicated that an enemy medium value leadership target was present somewhere in the compounds east of the district centre.

While night was falling, "C" Company developed an outline plan to go after him. The problem was the complexity of this particular built-up area: it amounted to a rabbit warren of compounds, alleys, walled cultivated areas and streams. It would be difficult to seal off the area and would require the whole battalion, but the close proximity to the district centre weighed in favour of an audacious move. A platoon from "C" Company went in trying

During a night raid in Hutel, private property was damaged. A Canadian PSYOPS/CIMIC team accompanied by a Gurkha patrol conducts compensation activities with the local population.

188

to get as close as possible to the enemy leader. A chase ensued, doors were kicked in and some rounds fired. Unfortunately, the target escaped.

The next morning, a Gurkha patrol with Canadian CIMIC and PSYOPS personnel went back into this community to conduct effects mitigation. The patrol offered compensation to house owners who had sustained property damage during the pursuit. Interestingly, nearly every citizen had doors kicked in and all demanded compensation. Despite some hard feelings, the patrol assessed that this community was still pro-government and was not knowingly hiding the enemy leader. It appeared that a non-governmental organization with an office in this community was assisting this individual to move around and hide.

The day the 2nd kandak was scheduled to re-deploy back to Zharey was wrought by tragedy. An ANA soldier negligently discharged an RPG launcher inside a concrete room, essentially shredding the lower extremities of eight Afghan soldiers. Gurkha medics, led by Dr. D.F. Reid, rushed to the site while the Canadian OMLT soldiers worked to stabilize the wounded. A U.S. Army UH-60 and a USAF HH-60 flew in to evacuate the wounded. Unfortunately, seven of the stricken Afghans eventually died of their wounds. ISTAR determined that the enemy had 'eyes on' the whole process and steps were taken to deter their planned actions against the MEDEVAC helicopters.

A US Army UH-60 prepares to lift off with some of the Afghan National Army casualties.

Gurkha medics, under the direction of Dr. D.F. Reid, and members of the Canadian Operational Mentor and Liaison Team work to save the lives of wounded Afghan soldiers.

The Taliban immediately exploited this event for information operations purposes and spread the word throughout Hutel that they had attacked the ANA and caused the casualties. The situation was complicated by the fact that 2nd kandak was leaving. This could become an information ops victory for the Taliban as they could portray the scheduled withdrawal as a response to the casualties they inflicted, thus reducing the positive effects generated by the joint ANSF patrolling. To counter the enemy message, the Canadian PSYOPS and CIMIC operators deployed with Gurkha and ANP patrols during the course of the next day. Surprisingly, the teams learned that local people, some of them four kilometres from Hutel, already knew that the blast was an accident and was not a Taliban action.

One of the other enemy medium value leadership targets was moving between NEWCASTLE and a position south of the district centre. There was some concern that he might collect fighters and, emboldened by the RPG tragedy, mount a night attack against the district centre to profit from the situation to enhance the Taliban's stature with the Taliban-supportive population and to intimidate the pro-government population. The attack did not materialize, for unknown reasons. Other cells to the west of the district centre, thwarted in their activities and frustrated, were trying to bring RPGs and another IED into the area to ambush any coalition travelling down Highway 1. Foot patrols sent into the area, coupled with the low-level pass of a pair of Mirage 2000 fighters, deterred this activity.

ISTAR reportage indicated that one of the enemy leaders had made his way to Helmand province while another was trying to get out of the area south-east of the district centre. Operation SOHIL LARAM II was winding down and the resources to conduct a detailed search for this individual were not available, but it was clear that the raid to the east of the district centre, looking for the third leader, had unsettled the enemy that remained in the Hutel area. In effect, they ordered their people to go to ground, stop communicating and cease operations.

Resolution

After seven days of operations in Maywand district, Task Force TIGER redeployed to Kandahar Air Field and made its preparations to depart Afghanistan and return to its home station in Brunei. The Canadian CIMIC and PSYOPS teams were sent back to Maywand almost immediately once RC (South) and TF Kandahar assessed the situation and realized that an opportunity presented itself. The forces did not exist for a complete occupation of the district, but creative ways to maintain the momentum generated by Operation SOHIL LARAM II were explored and implemented in March 2008.

As with any operation in Afghanistan, determining what the specific long- or short-term effects will be is no easy task. One of the most important effects, short of some IED activity, was the relative lack of enemy action directed at the relief replacing the Canadian Battlegroup in Zharey and

Panjwayi districts. When the enemy did attempt to engage Canadian forces in western Zharey/Panjwayi, he lacked the ammunition to do so effectively and even complained about it. Similarly, for some weeks there was almost no ambush or IED activity directed against forces travelling along Highway 1 between Helmand and Kandahar. Again, determining exactly why this was the case is open to some interpretation, but a tentative conclusion can be made with some confidence.

Substantial information on the Taliban's structure in Maywand district was collected during the course of the operation. The Afghan police and army also demonstrated increased confidence outwards towards the population and internally between the two organizations. Taken together, this provided a solid base for future action or security measures by any follow-on force. Demonstrating to the enemy that Maywand is no longer a safe haven or a seam, though ambiguous on the surface, also has the potential to contribute positively towards a pro-government orientation later on.

Finally, Operation SOHIL LARAM II forced several enemy commanders to scatter from what they viewed as a comfortable no-go zone. This in turn made them vulnerable to other coalition action and, at the same time, disrupted whatever plans they were working on at the time.

Operation SOHIL LARAM II confirmed that an operational manoeuvre capacity by Regional Command (South), when wielded properly, could generate positive operational and tactical effects in the complex environment of southern Afghanistan in the face of an insurgent enemy. To commemorate the new link forged between the Canadian army and the Gurkhas, 1 RGR was awarded the Canadian Forces Unit Commendation in May 2008;

FOR OUTSTANDING ELAN AND EXEMPLARY COMBAT SKILLS THAT DIRECTLY CONTRIBUTED TO THE OVERALL SUCCESS OF TASK FORCE KANDAHAR DURING OPERATION ATHENA, AFGHANISTAN, SEP 07 TO MAR 08.

A Note on Sources

The author observed the operational planning process for SOHIL LARAM II at Regional Command (South), Task Force Kandahar and 1 RGR Battlegroup and then accompanied the Gurkha battalion into the field for the duration of the operation. Certain control measures have been altered and intelligence sources blurred for operational security considerations.

NOTES

1   The Helmand-deployed 1 RGR company occupied a forward operating base near Garmsir. Not coincidentally, the Joint Terminal Air Controller (JTAC) assigned to that company was a certain "Capt Harry Wales", better known as Prince Harry. Or was the company in fact assigned to the JTAC?
2   The Tracked Light Armoured Vehicle (TLAV) is a dramatically re-engineered M-113A3 APC.

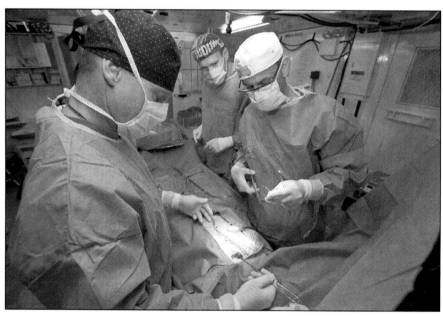

The Canadian-led Role 3 Multinational Medical Unit at Kandahar Air Field was responsible for saving hundreds of lives – coalition soldiers, Afghan security forces and civilians. (DND-Combat Camera)

CHAPTER EIGHT
INTERLUDE:
MASCAL AT KANDAHAR

It was a clear, warm day; the first after a cold, early February. I had just come back to Kandahar Air Field after observing operations at the remote Canadian outpost in Spin Boldak, an Afghan border town to the south. My enforced espresso fast had ended and I was sipping a nice strong roast at the British National Army, Air Force and Naval Institutes (NAAFI) canteen around 1230 when I saw the bottom-crawl on Sky News blandly announce in block letters: Suicide attack in Kandahar City kills dozens. Before I could down the dregs of my drink, the Big Voice public-address system warbled the up and down tones alerting the base to a Mass Casualty event. I have worked out of KAF since 2003 and this was the first time I had heard the Mass Casualty (MASCAL) go off, so I hurriedly left the NAAFI and thumbed a ride towards the Multinational Medical Unit, or what everybody calls the "Role 3".

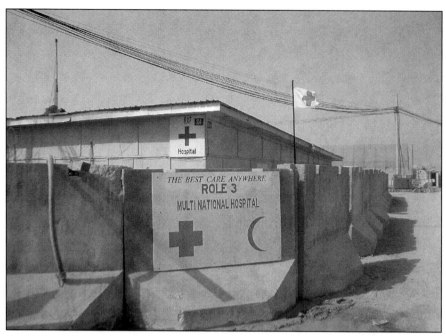

The Role 3 Multinational Medical Unit started off as "Charlie Med" under American command in 2004 before transitioning to Canadian command in 2006.

Coincidentally, I had received a briefing from the hospital staff just a week before in the green Weatherhaven that was the Multinational Medical Unit's (MMU) headquarters. I was greeted by LCol Pierre Charpentier, LCol Errol Villeneuve and Lieutenant-Commander (LCdr) Charles Gendron.

"Dr. Maloney? What specialty are you?" they asked, quizzically.

"Military history. But my dad's a gynecologist," I hastily added. We had a good laugh.

In NATO's world, medical facilities are designated Role 1 to Role 4, depending on capability. A Role 1 facility is essentially a Unit Medical Section, while a Role 2 can do everything short of surgery. A Role 3 has surgical capacity. In Afghanistan, a Role 2 (plus) type of hospital existed in some locations, which was a Role 2 with limited surgical capacity. The all-singing, all-dancing full-service Role 4 is located at Landstuhl, Germany. At Kandahar Air Field, the United States had been the lead nation at the Role 3 until

2005, with Canada taking over the following year. In its 2008 iteration, the MMU had Canadians, Americans, Dutch, British, Danish and New Zealand personnel, plus a small number of Afghan staff.

The Kandahar Air Field Role 3 Multinational Medical Unit (R3 MMU) is organized into four components: In-Patient Care, Clinical Support, Primary Care and an administration section. In-Patient Care is composed of the Operating Room, the Intensive Care Unit, the Trauma Bays (Resus) and the Acute Care Ward; the pharmacy (Forward Medical Equipment Depot, mental health services, X-Ray and the Lab) fell under Clinical Support. Primary Care was responsible for physio, dental services, preventive medicine and the unit medical services. There was also an entire Canadian Role 1 that had medics deployed with the Canadian units throughout Kandahar province.

Normally, the Role 3 took referrals from British, Dutch and American Role 2s in adjacent provinces, from the Mir Wais hospital run by the Red Cross in Kandahar City and from an Afghan National Army hospital located at Camp Hero, adjacent to the air field. Kandahar Air Field also had Role 1s from Bulgaria, the Netherlands, the U.S., the U.K. and Slovenia along with Kellogg, Brown and Root contractors.

While we were flipping through the Powerpoint slides during the briefing, the Regimental Sergeant Major (RSM), Chief Warrant Officer (CWO) David Horlick, stopped in the middle and pointedly said: "These Powerpoint slides don't really capture what we do. You have to see us in action." I secured an invitation from LCol Charpentier to do just that. Now, when I least expected it, it was time to see the moving parts in action.

The Sky News crawl quoted initial reports that there were fifty dead and fifty wounded in the attack. Mir Wais hospital in the city took the influx of wounded until it was full, then the Afghan army hospital near the air field filled up, too. I arrived at the R3 MMU at 1240 hours and headed to the entrance to the trauma bays. The R3 MMU is a plywood, one-story building, almost a western frontier town hospital in external appearance. Its rudimentary exterior, however, belies its sophisticated interior. I could see the staff through the trauma bay doors and I knew from previous visits in 2006 (when my convoy was attacked by a suicide bomber) that after you went through the bays there was an operating theatre to the right and an intensive care unit (ICU) to the left.

Some of the staff were gowning up, but the entrance was starting to get crowded. There were U.S. Air Force and Canadian medics, British doctors, Dutch nurses, a clutch of photographers and even a whole platoon of Gurkhas. I asked the soldier beside me what she did. "Oh, I'm a physiotherapist," she told me. "Almost all units have somebody assigned in the event of a MASCAL. Manpower is manpower, after all."

A Canadian medic was stacking up fold-out stretchers six-deep next to the door when LCol Pierre Charpentier, with his graying buzz-cut, emerged and held his hands up to quell the babble of voices.

"Attention please. We have a MASCAL event. There has been a suicide attack in Kandahar City. We will be taking the overflow from Camp Hero. The bulk will be coming by ground, not by air. There are numerous head and neck injuries."

The crowd continued to mill about the J-shaped road. It looked like there were too many people preparing to do too many different things. RSM Horlick sensed the emerging confusion and took control, his voice booming.

"Ok, we have the first ambulance coming in. Everybody not involved, back up." The assembled augmentees parted to either side of the road as a U.S. Army ambulance arrived.

"Litter and gurney!"

The civilian victim had a black beard and was about thirty years old. He had a serious neck wound and one of the medics was holding his head so it could not move. I could see bandages circling his chest as he had been hit there too. He did not make a sound. The orderlies carefully removed him from the vehicle and whisked him inside.

Without a pause, a white civilian ambulance with Pakistani markings wheeled around the drive and screeched to a halt, heading the wrong way. Two Canadian medics emerged from the back with another casualty. He had a head injury, his skull muffled with an Israeli-type combat bandage. And then a tan-coloured Afghan National Army truck pulled up in front of the

Pakistani ambulance. A U.S. Army medic and two Afghan Army medics kicked open the back to reveal two victims, one of whom had a gut wound and the other was missing his right arm; a tourniquet had been applied and the stump covered up. A third victim was assisted from the truck tailgate by a pair of Gurkhas. He was a man with a long, grey beard; he was an elder. He was mobile, but looked shocked.

As the RSM untangled the ambulance 'Mexican stand-off', a camouflaged Afghan Army Land Cruiser pulled up and the Afghan medics, assisted by Canadian medics, unloaded more shattered bodies. The blood dripped and pooled into the dust on the road as the staff unfolded and stacked more stretchers and deployed a number of gurneys. These were not the regular hospital gurneys; these came equipped with two large black wheels to facilitate movement in crowded spaces.

I noticed a bloated guy in shorts and a loud t-shirt avidly taking pictures with a professional camera. "Who are you with?" I asked, figuring he was media. He blushed red. "Oh, I, uh, take pictures."

"For who?"

"Um, myself. These'll be worth something on the Net."

When he saw that RSM Horlick was taking notice, he backed up to run away and was narrowly missed by two more incoming ambulances. Fortunately, the staff had stacked enough kit; there were six casualties jammed into them, along with the medics who were keeping them alive. More blood. People were walking through the blood – now mud – and I could see the imprint of a desert combat boot – except it was red. A young guy with head trauma, assisted by an Afghan civilian medic, walked around the corner, seemingly out of nowhere. Two medics rushed forward and gently laid him on a blanket and he was then transferred to a gurney.

A green Canadian ambulance rounded the bend with its call-sign 83H visible on the door. A Capt Michael leapt out.

"One lower body and hands, one lower body and upper extremities, plus a penetrating chest wound," he called out.

"We have only one bay left," a voice rose above the noise.

The next in the procession of carnage was a U.S. Army ambulance with its siren needlessly on.

"One head, severe neck, extremities, gut, possibly spleen. Number two: neck, head, jaw."

"Okay, start moving new patients to the headquarters building." Orders went out to clear away the briefing tables and projectors and use the Weatherhaven as overflow. Another Afghan ambulance, then another U.S. Army ambulance.

"Head, face, priority."

"Head, upper arms."

This went on for some time. At no time did any of the patients cry out or display any emotion. Was it Pashtun stoicism or was it really good drugs? I could not tell. Then four French soldiers with their full protective gear and armed with MAS assault rifles ran around the corner and reported to the RSM. They conversed off to the side. There was a force protection issue. It is easy to assume that the R3 MMU, being in the middle of Kandahar Air Field, was secure. With the influx of civilian and non-ISAF vehicles and personnel, coupled with the sense of urgency, there was a possibility that the enemy might infiltrate a suicide bomber disguised as a casualty, or even a vehicle-borne IED, into the Role 3 and blow it up. The results of such an attack would be catastrophic. All civilian vehicles, already searched once on entry to the base, were searched again by the troops and the patients were all re-checked by the medical staff, just in case. There is no 'rear area' in Afghanistan.

Two men walked up to me wearing beards, Oakley sun glasses, tan civilian clothes, non-standard side-arms, unmarked ball caps and carrying nondescript pouches.

"Are you here from [insert super-secret organization code name here]?"

"Uh, no. I'm a military historian. I think you want to talk to him." I gestured towards the RSM. They nodded slowly and went inside to join the fray.

LCol Charpentier emerged and addressed the crowd again. He stepped around the blood drying in the dust.

"All ambulance crews are back. No more patients are coming. We are standing down the MASCAL status. You can return to your parent units." The crowd started to disperse.

"Come with me," he said. "You get to see how we do business. This one is going to be a challenge. It's the biggest so far."

The activity in the trauma bay nearly blew my mind. I counted a large number of trauma bays, each marked by a red Roman numeral. Each bay was a pod, a microcosm of frantic, purposeful activity; yet, all were connected as if it was one large organism. It was not as mechanical as I thought it would be. It was organic.

I counted no less than four different nationalities at work in each bay. There were Canadian doctors and nurses, Dutch nurses, U.S. Air Force pararescue jumper medics, U.S. Special Forces, British and Australian surgeons and nurses, French orderlies and a bearded Dane. Then a Slovak doctor arrived, asking if he could assist. What struck me was how there was no arguing, no debate, no national histrionics; it was all inter-operable, so to speak. If only NATO politicians could perform as well together. Maj Sandra West handled 'traffic control' with a specially marked white board that listed the severity of wounds, bay location and a potential priority for triage purposes. There was a red line on the floor to keep people back, so the board was unobstructed.

"We have 14 confirmed so far, with two more possibles," she indicated. "One of our problems is interpretation. We put the word out to Task Force

Kandahar for more 'terps', but we've had to press some of our cleaning staff into service." One of the Afghans was getting gowned and masked by an orderly who sported elaborate Maori arm ink.

Imagine the situation if it were reversed. You, an English- or French-speaking Canadian, have been wounded in Afghanistan and been taken in the dark back of a vehicle to an Afghan hospital where nobody speaks English or French. How would you communicate how or where you were wounded? What would your mental state be if you did not understand what was being done to you, let alone having to deal with the pain of wounds? It was imperative that the patients' anxiety level be lowered as quickly as possible.

It was now 1330 hours. Only one hour had passed since I had left the NAAFI.

I saw a sign over the operating room (OR) door: "Kandahar Institute of Surgical Science".

"Valium! IV!"

"Are there more casualties?" A man with a red ball cap and a clip board pushed by and headed to a groaning man lying on his side on a gurney. Another man was wheeled to the X-ray, suspected of having head trauma. A cluster of imagery techs were crowded around the computer screen looking at the interior of a casualty. One of the techs shook his head. "The C-6 and C-7 are severed. There's nothing we can do. He's 19 years old…."

Three staff members were working on the guy with the jaw wound.

"Terp!"

"What does he need?"

"He needs to pee."

"Catheter!"

I conferred with the Task Force surgeon, LCol Heather Coombs and made a list of the casualties and wound types to get a sense of the nature of the attack. Of the fourteen, there were three chest injuries, ten head injuries and one patient who had an emergency tracheotomy. It looked to me at the time like all of the casualties had been looking down at something or sitting in a stadium or amphitheatre when the device was detonated.

A nurse in greens, wearing a shoulder holster, reported to LCol Heather Coombs that Camp Hero had delivered another casualty; he had a penetrating skull wound that the Afghan hospital could not handle. The man's skin was dark with dried blood and he was unconscious. Without space in the bays, he was taken to the headquarters lecture room and a team went to work on him there. Two F-16s thundered down the KAF runway, temporarily blotting out any form of verbal communication. At around 1405 Camp Hero sent over another casualty. This person had a severed femoral artery and they did not have the resources to repair it.

The staff in the R3 MMU Tactical Operations Centre collected as much info as they could and relayed it to the Provincial Operations Centre. Unlike a civilian hospital, R3 MMU is a tactical unit and, like any military unit, it relays tactical data to decision-makers who will use that information for subsequent operations. This is important for a number of reasons. First, the type of device and its effects could help lead us to the perpetrators who conducted the attack. Secondly, the location of the attack and the tribal affiliation of the casualties could be indicators of future enemy action; or, it might give warning of a larger attack that was underway in the city or elsewhere. Thirdly, the willingness of the victims to publicly condemn the enemy could be used for information operations purposes, but that was time-sensitive. Information operations are critical to counter enemy attempts to influence the population, especially in a environment where the will of the people is the critical element for success in the conflict.

Some information about the attack came from the patients who were lucid. The bomb was detonated around 1130 outside Kandahar City, but it was not clear whether it was in Zharey, Daman or Arghandab district. Later on, it turned out that the Taliban had bombed a sporting event in Arghandab district. Abdul Hakim Jan, a senior police figure in that district, was killed pro-

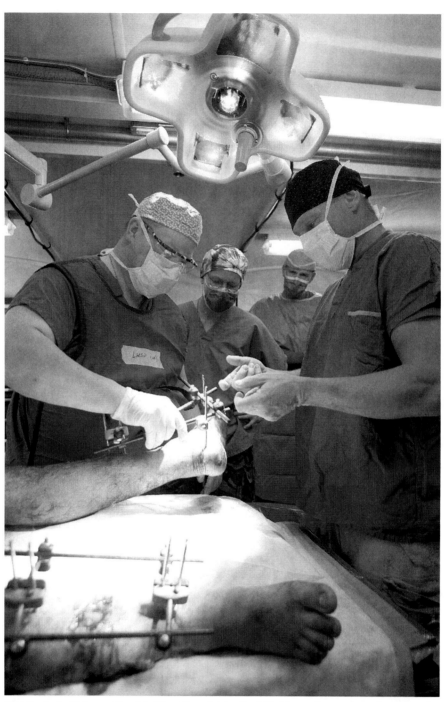

Medical staff from the Multinational Medical Unit work to save the leg of a wounded Afghan. (DND-Combat Camera)

ducing a level of instability in that district that the enemy could exploit. By deploying more police and replacement leadership in a timely fashion, it was possible that the Taliban were deterred from making another move on Arghandab (the enemy had tried to take over that district in November 2007 but failed in the face of combined Afghan-Canadian action).

A counter-IED team arrived and asked that the shrapnel be collected from the wounds so they could assess what type of device was used. The bits and pieces did not appear to have a pattern, no nuts and bolts or washers, just jagged metal. At this time, it was not clear how the bomb had been infiltrated into the event, but later on it was determined that a suicide bomber conducted the attack using a vest device. The casualty numbers were adjusted upwards as the afternoon progressed: 80 killed and 100 wounded. Mir Wais hospital was dealing with 48 wounded and estimated the dead at 55.

Back at R3 MMU, two of the more severely wounded died by 1455 hours. I saw a masked surgeon and four staff in the Kandahar Institute of Surgical Science working quickly and deliberately on a man with a severe head wound. Unlike the trauma bay's white and wood look, the OR had a bluish-green hue to it, most likely from the lights reflecting from the bevy of surgical greens bent over or moving around the table. It was different in there through those doors, quiet and comparatively serene, but no less purposeful.

LCol Charpentier moved throughout the facility keeping a quiet watch in the background. R3 MMU staff was now confronted with a number of dilemmas. The possibility existed that they would have to take more casualties from Mir Wais or Camp Hero, but it was getting crowded. Could some patients be moved to the Role 2 in Camp Bastion the British base in Helmand province? Or to Bagram Air Field north of Kabul? How would they get there? Who would provide the aircraft? Helicopters to Bastion, C-130 Hercules to Bagram? What about triage; who would go where? The crowd around the white board brainstormed solutions. The issue revolved around sending people with the patients. Were they qualified for aero-medical evacuation care? And then how would these people, both medics and civilians, get back to Kandahar?

The interpreters moved back and forth between the bays as the nurses and medics bantered about, hooking up a 'bloody mary and vodka' to the IV stand. The information operations team then arrived. They secured permission

U.S. Army UH 60 extracts wounded from the blast site.

from the CO to interview patients about the attack, as long as the patients consented to the interviews and understood how the information would be used. Working through one of the 'terps', the team asked one man, whom I will call Zia, if he would allow himself to be interviewed for Kandahar radio. Zia was propped up; he had an injury to his skull and to one of his shoulders, and he had a few tubes in him. He periodically spat blood into a bowl from an injury inside his mouth. Zia explained that he was watching a dog-fighting match, a common sports event in the region. He was engrossed in the event (he had some Afghanis down on the prime contender) when the bomb detonated. He blacked out and did not remember a thing until he woke up in the Role 3.

"Does this attack contravene Islam?"

Zia agreed vehemently and spat out more blood. "Yes. Those who did this are un-Islamic bastards."

"Mr. Zia, we pray for the return of your health, God willing. Thank you very much."

206

The sun was starting to get low and the mountains were casting indigo shadows. I stepped outside for some air and to get a coffee just as two CH-47 Chinook helicopters thundered by. The R3 MMU smoking area was full to capacity with people in OR greens and Crocs. I had forgotten how many medical people actually smoke. I took out a Romeo y Julietta, circumcised it, lit it and puffed away with the rest of them. Things were winding down and plateauing as the patients stabilized, the tension and drama ebbed, replaced with fatigue. The CO and I walked in the direction of the dining facility. "That is what we do," he simply said and quietly regarded the route as we walked on.

It was the end of one bloody day and another was about to begin. The next morning, Taliban terrorists mounted a suicide attack down in Spin Boldak, the latest in a series of futile attacks designed to kill Colonel Rezziq, the local militia commander. It wounded three Canadians and 27 Afghans. Thirty more Afghans were killed by the bomb. The Role 3 MMU once again prepared to receive the carnage.

Operation ROOM SERVICE was the periodic Mushan re-supply task executed by the Strathcona's tank squadron and other mechanized forces.

Chapter Nine
Panjwayi Alamo:
The Defence of Strongpoint Mushan

Throughout 2008, a small band of Canadians living and working along-side soldiers of the Afghan National Army occupied an isolated outpost in Panjwayi district designated Strongpoint Mushan. Once the pivotal leg of an ambitious security and development plan, Strongpoint Mushan quickly became an orphan as priorities changed, the plan shifted, and the number of available friendly forces contracted to the eastern part of the district. At the same time, abandoning Strongpoint Mushan after such a lengthy occupation would not only result in a Taliban propaganda victory, but would also remove the only coalition presence in that part of Panjwayi, a presence that was aggravating the Taliban leadership in its attempts to challenge Canada and Afghanistan for control of the vital districts west of Kandahar City. There was no good solution to this operations-level dilemma, so the position was kept manned and re-supplied in an increasingly dangerous environment, even when it was cut off on the ground. This is the story of the Canadian soldiers of the Operational Mentor and Liaison Teams and the Afghan soldiers they worked with in the defence of Strongpoint Mushan.[1]

Why Mushan?

Mushan is geographically important to coalition efforts west of Kandahar City. Looking at a map, the embattled triangular Zharey District lies south of Ring Road South, the main ISAF service route to the forces fighting in Helmand province and the primary commerce artery in and through Afghanistan. Panjwayi District, also triangular in shape, complements Zharey District, with the Arghandab River separating the two. The forbidding Registan Desert is directly south of Panjwayi district, with the Dowry river separating the two. The tapered point of Panjwayi district denotes the confluence of the Arghandab and Dowry rivers and it is also the meeting place of Zharey, Panjwayi and Band-e Timor communities over in Maywand district. Maywand leads to the Helmand river valley, and routes from that region branch out to Baram Cha in Pakistan (see map).

The enemy needed to facilitate the movement of personnel, supplies and weapons from the Baram Cha-Helmand valley-Maywand 'rat line' into Panjwayi. Once in Panjwayi, there are other 'rat lines' that lead both into the south-west suburbs of Kandahar City and into the 'rocket box' north-west of Kandahar Air Field where 107mm rockets are fired at this vital ISAF logistics and support facility. This route is also one of several used by those engaged in the transport of narcotics product into Pakistan. Mushan, when occupied by coalition forces, is an extremely inconvenient 'burr under the saddle' for the Taliban, HiG and other anti-government and criminal elements.

Back in 2006, Mushan was a 'sleepy hollow' as the Operation MEDUSA battles raged in Pashmul and Sperwan Ghar. It had a limited security presence that was enhanced sometime in late 2006. The reasons for this remain controversial as the definition of what constituted 'police' was very loose during that time. In the main, it was widely believed that the 'police' presence in Mushan at that time was really a militia belonging to elements in the provincial power structure who had some relationship with the narcotics trade. Mushan was important to them because product could not move along Ring Road South or through Zharey district due to the fighting that raged there throughout the year.

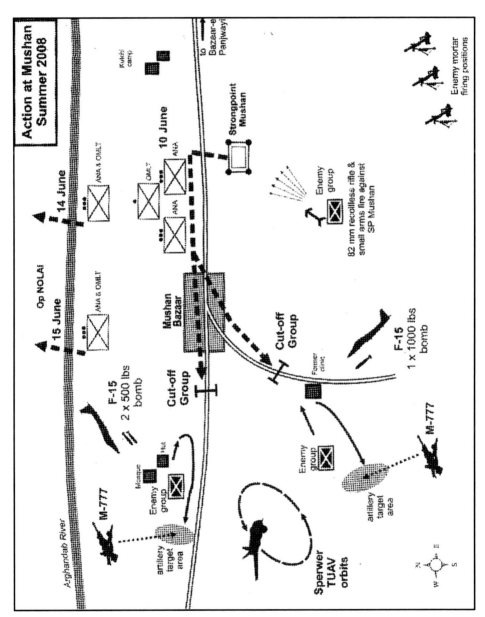

Action at Mushan, Summer 2008

This picture, taken from a Canadian CH-47 and facing west, show the confluence of the Arghandab and Dowry Rivers where the Reg Desert, Maywand district, Zharey District, and Western Panjway District all meet. Mushan is approximatly at the 11 o'clock position from the gun-mount.

In mid-2007, Task Force Kandahar formulated a plan to construct one road from Panjwayi town to Mushan and then another from Mushan to Ring Road South. There were a number of reasons for this but, in general, the idea was to facilitate commerce and security in this extremely fertile district. Mushan was the pivot for this project and its enhanced stature in the plan resulted in the construction of better defensive facilities there. In time, Afghan National Police replaced the 'police', the defensive works were designated a 'police sub-station' and a detachment of the National Directorate of Security moved in. This, in turn, increased the enemy's interest in Mushan as demonstrated by a significant increase in insurgent violence in the western part of Panjwayi district. Subsequently, the decision was made to designate the police sub-station as a Strongpoint and then deploy Afghan National Army troops to Mushan.

At this point in early 2008, Strongpoint Mushan was one of a line of police sub-stations and strongpoints along the Panjwayi-Mushan road. Enemy forces mounted a campaign against this chain of facilities, escalating throughout the spring of 2008. Mechanized forces had to be used to re-supply and replace personnel along this chain and this, in turn, attracted enemy IED cells. The battle along the Panjwayi-Mushan road itself nearly became a sub-campaign, aggravated by the absence of Canadian helicopters, which forced TFK to mount costly ground re-supply operations. There were no less than 14 IED attacks against Canadian vehicles during this period. Eventually, the decision was made to cease ground re-supply and a variety of aerial solutions were explored, leading in part to the contracting of civilian Mi-8 helicopters for the task.

The situation also resulted in contraction from some of the police sub-stations along the Mushan-Panjwayi road, adding to the physical, and even psychological, isolation of Strongpoint Mushan. There were higher-level aspects to these measures, however. The Canadian Forces were under pressure by the Canadian Government to present a 'no-casualty' situation, partly because of opposition criticism over the conduct of the Afghan war which, in turn, was linked to the fact that the Canadian Government was a minority government anticipating an election campaign sometime in 2008. Any enemy analysis of Canadian media would have concluded that Canadian casualties in Afghanistan would have a strategic effect on Canada's will to fight. At the same time, Canadian and Afghan forces could not retreat from Mushan for operational and psychological reasons. These factors collided in the fight over Mushan, with the Canadian soldiers from the OMLT and the Afghan soldiers from the kandaks caught in the middle. Mushan had to hold.

The OMLT and the Kandaks

Using coalition soldiers to train the emergent Afghan National Army was a tortuous process dating back to 2002. When Operation ENDURING FREEDOM was the primary coalition in Afghanistan, Embedded Training Teams, or ETTs, were the primary connection point, at the tactical level, between the Afghan National Army and the coalition forces. As NATO ISAF gradually supplanted OEF and more non-North American countries joined the effort, new terminology emerged: the Operational Mentor and Liaison Team.

Initially, the ETTs were akin to Vietnam-era Special Forces "A" teams working with non-professional indigenous forces. Indeed, the burden of ETT work initially fell on the 19th and 20th Special Forces Groups in the early days of the war. As the ANA emerged as an institution, the ETTs shifted to a more conventional posture as the intent was to create a professional army to replace the Special Forces-backed militias. A U.S. National Guard brigade took over this mission from the special forces by 2004. The NATO-led OMLTs were originally supposed to supplement the OEF ETTs and provide higher-level mentoring at brigade and higher levels, but as NATO took more and more control of the coalition effort, the NATO OMLTs increasingly handled tasks previously done by the ETTs. ETTs and OMLTs confusingly shared the same battlespace throughout Afghanistan.

Canada's involvement with mentoring at the tactical level went back to 2003-04 when a Canadian ETT worked with Afghan National Army units in Kabul. At that time, the singular Canadian ETT consisted of 15 personnel led by a major who worked closely with a 'kandak', the ANA equivalent of a battalion. That commitment evolved into significant Canadian involvement with the Kabul Military Training Centre from 2003 to 2006. Canadians worked alongside Americans, French, British and American soldiers and their Afghan counterparts to raise, train and equip the kandaks that would form the manoeuvre forces for the ANA.

For a variety of reasons related to the deterioration of the situation in Kandahar province, Canada committed more and more resources to the ex-pansion of OMLTs in fall 2006. By this time, 205 ANA Corps was stood up and the kandaks assigned to operations in Regional Command South came under its control. By 2007, 1st Brigade of 205 Corps, or 1/205 Brigade, was established to handle ANA operations in the province. 1/205 Brigade's kan-daks varied in number, however, and it would be a mistake to assume that 1/205 Brigade had the same level of stability as a Canadian brigade. In 2006, it wavered between one and three kandaks at a time when the Canadian OMLT was capable of mentoring only a single kandak.

The OMLT requirements increased dramatically in 2007 to the point where nearly an entire Canadian infantry battalion was required to reorganize into OMLTs assigned to mentor the various components of 1/205 Brigade. 3rd Battalion, Princess Patricia's Canadian Light Infantry, was selected. This was an organization filled with soldiers and officers who had, on average, two tours in Afghanistan. Afghan experience played a critical role in the approach taken by this particular OMLT rotation. 3 PPCLI was the first Canadian infantry battalion to have any contact with Afghans, back in 2002. Subsequently, "B" Company was the force-protection company for the Provincial Reconstruction Team when it was first established in 2005. In other words, these soldiers had experience working with Afghans – and specifically Afghans from Kandahar province – in non-traditional situations.

In 2008, 1/205 Brigade consisted of five kandaks totalling, on a good day, around 2900 personnel. There were three infantry kandaks (1/1, 1/2 and 1/3), a Combat Support (CS) kandak (4/1) and a Combat Service Support (CSS) kandak (5/1). For transport, each kandak had a varying number of Ford Ranger pick-up trucks, Hummers armed with 12.7mm machine-guns and International 7-ton trucks. Paper organizational charts are deceiving, however, when dealing with Afghan units. In general, not all three infantry kandaks are deployed at once. Some are undergoing refit, others have personnel on leave. There is always a percentage of personnel who are absent without leave. The reasons for this vary greatly and cannot always be attributed to a shirking of duty or to laziness; indeed, the situation in the country means that it can take days for soldiers on leave just to get home. The CS and CSS kandaks were not fully manned at this point and the more specialized trades such as engineers and logisticians, were not fully trained.

Introducing 1/1 Kandak and the Kandak 1/1/205 OMLT Team[2]

The kandak assigned to Zharey district in the spring and summer of 2008 was 1/1 kandak, commanded by Colonel Anwar. 1/1 had: three infantry companies, with about 70 men each; a Weapons Company of 188 personnel divided into four platoons; a Headquarters and Headquarters Company; and a Combat Service Support Company of around 70 men.

1/1 and its support companies were based out of Forward Operating Base Masum Ghar, with two companies deployed to FOB Sperwan Ghar and another to Strongpoint Mushan. Three of the Weapons Company platoons occupied strongpoints along the Panjwayi-Mushan road. 1/1 kandak's leadership included a tactically and politically proficient executive officer who kept things together. 1/1 kandak's strength lay in its Non-Commissioned Officers (NCOs) and their RSM. The operations sergeant and company sergeant majors were rated as strong. Their officers, however, were generally weak. They suffered from poor French training in Kabul and some were appointed because of political or tribal relationships. The OMLT constantly strove to present a national outlook to the Afghans. That said, an estimated 60 percent of 1/1 were Pashtun and Uzbeks dominated the other 40 percent. Dari was the language of choice, with Pashtun used informally. Notably, the NCOs publicly declared that "We are one Army" and generally did not engage in divisive ethnicity issues.

1/1 kandak was fairly experienced, as kandaks went. It was formed in Kabul back in 2002 where it initially acted as part of President Hamid Karzai's protection force. 1/1 spent a lot of time projecting from Kabul to provinces in Regional Command (East) when a surge was required. In 2005, it was sent to Oruzgan province where it worked with a Dutch OMLT and an American ETT. While in Oruzgan, 1/1 focused on becoming proficient at platoon-level operations. Two companies of 1/1 were deployed to retake the Chora District Centre in an action that took place in 2007. This required what was euphemistically called 'heavy mentoring' by the ETT and the Dutch OMLT. 1/1 was not proficient at independent kandak-level operations when it re-deployed to Kandahar in November 2007. In late February 2008, 1/1 entered the line in Panjwayi district.

The Canadian OMLT paralleled the kandak structure. kandak 1/1/205 OMLT Team, as it was formally known, was initially commanded by Maj Mark Campbell (until he was critically wounded in June and replaced by Maj David Proctor) and consisted of 26 Canadian soldiers. Sixteen of these were the company mentors with each team consisting of four men and an RG-31 armoured vehicle; their call-signs were 71 A through 71 D. The Team also had a five-man command post with an RG-31 armoured patrol vehicle and an eight-wheeled Bison, call-sign 71. There were three specialized mentors (logistics, medical and operations) and a Sergeant Major mentor. Each company team consisted of a Captain, a Warrant Officer (WO) and two Corporals (Cpl) or Privates (Pvt). However, the leave plan and field injuries meant that, on many occasions, the four-man teams could be reduced to one or two men. Similarly, not all of the vehicles were operational because the OMLT had no integral Electrical and Mechanical Engineering support and could not always draw on other Canadian resources, especially if 1/1 and the kandak were operating in areas that differed from, say, the Canadian Battlegroup. In effect, a skeletal Canadian light infantry company mentored a motorized Afghan kandak that was operating in a static role.

Working with Afghan soldiers was an eye-opening experience to Canadian soldiers trained in the context of Western culture and a European-based military system. The ANA had uniforms, most of which were various versions of the American woodland pattern Battle Dress Uniform (BDU) and wore different coloured berets. For the most part, all had helmets and 95 percent had body armour in the infantry companies and, even if they had access to it, a sense of bravado deterred them from wearing the protective gear. Chest rigs predominated instead of traditional webbing.

Culturally, the Afghan troops were uneducated, which was not surprising given what had happened to the country over the past twenty years. The mentors noted problems with learning, problem solving and abstract thinking. The Afghan soldiers had problems conceptualizing second- and third-order effects but, more importantly, many had problems associating ground with its depiction on a map. Even math skills were limited. "The planning cycle," as one mentor explained, "was moment to moment." Again, this was not surprising since the young men emerged from a survivalist culture where life expectancy was short and the Taliban discouraged studying anything other than the Koran.

The Afghan soldiers were extremely polite and respectful of elders. They understood 'place' and rank, and they tended to be non-confrontational. They would go out of their way not to humiliate guests in any way, as hospitality was a cornerstone of the Pashtunwali code and of Afghan society generally. Their faith was an integral aspect of their daily lives, to the point where it could interfere with operations. Soldiers would pray collectively before, after and even during patrols; a sentry would be deployed as the prayer mats were pulled out.

217

For the most part, the Afghan soldiers understood the basics and they could work as a team. The main problems lay in planning and in combat service support and in their tendency to be reactive. The danger in any OMLT was that the mentors would take over the problem-solving tasks, so the teams had to be vigilant in passing on this responsibility to the Afghan leaders. Clearly, there was no impetus to improve if the Canadians did everything for them. The Afghan NCOs did lead by example and that was considered to be a major positive factor.

The war around Mushan in early 2008 revolved around efforts to affect a relief-in-place, or 'RIP', of the forces stationed in Mushan. The outgoing OMLT and ANA company from another kandak was replaced with a new rotation in early March. This was a complex operation involving a strong mechanized force which encountered significant enemy resistance. By the end of March, for the most part, 1/1 kandak had a company in Mushan, another in and around Panjwayi town and bazaar, and another deployed up at a district centre in Ghorak. The kandak and its mentors initiated a patrolling program along the Panjwayi-Mushan road, but with the lack of police in these locations, the best the teams could provide was a temporary presence, and then only during the daytime. Another task involved providing over-watch security to the Panjwayi-Mushan road-paving project that had just started near Panjwayi town. On occasion, coalition operations damaged property in the battle area. As the kandak and the OMLT had no integral CIMIC capability, they also sent out assessment patrols to note any damage and pass the information back to the Civil-Military Cooperation teams at the Provincial Reconstruction Team.

Mushan: Environs, Occupants and Initial Operations

The Strongpoint itself is located two kilometres east of Mushan village, next to the unpaved road. The Mushan Bazaar is approximately 300m northwest of the position. On market days, the bazaar, which is the economic centre for the area, swells to 400 people. Just south of the bazaar is a building that had been used as a clinic. A small Kutchi[3] camp is situated to the northeast. For the most part, the terrain is flat and consists of traditional Afghan compound complexes with high mud walls, grape-growing trenches, grape-drying huts and walled growing areas for the crops.

Strongpoint Mushan is 100m by 150m square. The main wall is made from Hescobastion and has two observation towers, one to the north, the other to the south. There are three run-up positions which were used by Ford Ranger vehicles with DsHkA and PKM machine-guns mounted on them. A mortar pit with a 60mm mortar occupies the centre. It has no air-conditioning and is infested with sand fleas and rather ugly camel spiders. The ANA and the OMLT lived in modular tentage, but there were several bunkers consisting of a layer of sandbags, one-man high. Concertina wire surrounded the perimeter backed up by Claymore area-defence weapons. ANA strength wavered between 62 and 68, amounting to two platoons. The ANA company at Mushan had a mix of PKM, DshKa, KpV 14.7mm and .50 cal machine-guns augmented with RPG-7 rocket launchers. The first OMLT team into Mushan[4] was 71B; it was led by Capt Craig Robertson and included WO Rob Crane, Cpl 'Rusty' Myroniuk and Cpl Shaun Copeland. Generally, the Canadian OMLT team had three to four personnel stationed at Mushan. The OMLT personnel had their personal weapons plus a Carl Gustav rocket-launcher and 203mm grenade-launcher attachments for their weapons.

For the most part, the platoons at Mushan ranged out three to four kilometres from the Strongpoint. These 'framework' patrols in and around Mushan and the bazaar produced significant information on the insurgent activities through KLEs and casual contact with the population. More conversant with local culture than the Canadians, the Afghan soldiers had insight into the situation that an array of technical collection means could not match. For example, around 7 March an ANA company commander held an impromptu shura at the bazaar. The local merchants told him that the enemy would mount significant operations against the Strongpoint in a month's time. The merchants were upset by this development and asked the Taliban to stay away from Mushan. This information was confirmed by a follow-up patrol. The remains of two failed 107mm rocket launches, discovered on separate patrols, pointed towards a higher probability of future enemy action.

On the whole, though, the locals within the three- to four-kilometre security 'bubble' around the Strongpoint tended to be apathetic but, at the same time, openly positive about the ANA's presence. They would back whomever was in charge, or appeared to be in charge. They were caught between the insurgents and the Afghan government and determined that, in effect, it was too risky to take up position in Mushan. It was easier to do nothing and just carry on with day-to-day life.

Further patrolling and KLEs started to flesh out the enemy situation. There was a spotter or facilitator close to the Strongpoint and an estimated 12-15 insurgents within Mushan itself. Information suggested that the regular patrolling had a deterrent effect on this cell's operations and that they were somewhat frustrated and wanted help. They were particularly concerned about the coalition presence at the bazaar, for reasons that remain speculative. A week later, two men monitoring the movements of a patrol were detained. Around mid-March, higher-level ISTAR reportage on enemy interest in Strongpoint Mushan's activities started to pick up in the area.

71B and the 3rd Company soldiers then had a contact on 25 March three kilometres south of the Strongpoint. Five insurgents armed with a PKM machine-gun engaged the patrol from a compound. When the ANA deployed and fired back, the enemy withdrew. The Afghans then caught a man who had enemy logistics documents in his possession. The following day, another ANA patrol and 71B were engaged by what was believed to be ten insurgents firing RPGs and PKMs at them from behind walls and a grape-drying hut. During the 40-minute firefight, 71B fired M-203 grenade-launchers at the hut as a pair of OH-58Ds from Company "B" 2-17 Cavalry ("The Banshees") arrived on the scene. Using the splash of the grenades as a marker, the helicopters made six runs on the target, firing .50 cal machine-guns and rocket pods at it as the ANA kept the enemy pinned down. Enemy firing ceased and, because the ANA patrol was critically short of ammunition, it withdrew while covered by an MQ-1 Predator. One detainee was apprehended by a hasty vehicle checkpoint and three enemy were seen to flee from the engagement in the direction of a Kutchi camp near the Reg desert. Follow-up KLEs suggested that the locals were concerned about increased insurgent activity around Mushan, and that it was unusual.

Notably, the ANA started to bring Afghan National Police along with them during search operations. There was, however, a notable difference in the professionalism of the two forces. On one joint patrol, the ANA were appalled by the police's behaviour towards women and by their lack of respect for property. The discussion between the two forces became quite vocal on one occasion.

At the beginning of April, the coalition mounted Operation TOOR AZADI along Route FOSTERS. TOOR AZADI was designed to re-supply all of the police sub-stations and strongpoints and to conduct relief in place for individuals and sub-units, as required. 3rd Company was supposed to be part of this RIP. 71B and the ANA extended patrols to the east of Mushan as a part of this effort. Unfortunately, as vehicle casualties from IED attacks mounted, the force halted to the east, less then half-way to Mushan. On 3 April, the link-up between the forces occurred and 71A, consisting of Capt Matt Aggus, WO John McNabb and Master Corporal (MCpl) Trevor Saina, replaced 71B while 3rd Company RIP'd with 1st Company. The team and its Afghan counterparts mounted daily framework patrols and compound searches throughout April. ISTAR reportage revealed that the enemy was annoyed at the continued presence of the force and planned to bring a mortar into the area, but their logistics system was having problems deploying the weapon and its ammunition.

Re-supply was a significant problem for the men occupying Strongpoint Mushan. The American and British transport helicopters supporting operations in Regional Command (South) would not fly into Mushan unless they had AH-64 Apache support. The operational tempo in RC (South) in the spring and summer of 2008 meant that there were few AH-64s available for a mundane re-supply task. The Helicopter Landing Site at Mushan was exposed and subject to dust clouds which were hard on helicopter engines. Emergency re-supply became the order of the day with food, water and ammo kicked out of the doors of helicopters when they were available. Consideration was given to using C-130 Hercules from the multinational pool to conduct parachute re-supply drops using GPS-guided pallets, but the decision was made to use 'Jingle Air', civilian contractor-flown Mi-8 HIP helicopters, to re-supply the combat outposts and strongpoints. One 'Jingle Air' HIP dropped its load in a panic when confronted with a volley of RPGs on approach to another combat outpost. The enemy set an ambush that deterred recovery of the supplies. They then raided the pallet and exploited the contents of the mailbag for PSYOPS purposes against the Canadians manning the outpost.

After this debacle, aerial re-supply of the strongpoints along FOSTERS was limited to the 'emergency Administration Request (AMR). A U.S. Army UH-60 from Task Force EAGLE ASSAULT, escorted by a pair of OH-58D Kiowa Warriors from The Banshees (if AH-64 Apaches were not available – and they usually were not), would land at the Mushan helicopter landing-site, the crew chief would kick out boxes of ammo and the Blackhawk would immediately lift off, covered by the orbiting OH-58Ds.

When OMLT personnel had their mid-tour leave, they had to be escorted by a foot-patrol east to the police sub-station at Talukan; this became a staple of life at Mushan. The 71B team then instituted night-patrolling in the area in order to increase the ANA's proficiency at that art. This produced results in the ISTAR system, so more and more patrols were mounted as part of a 'manoeuvre to collect' program designed to flesh out the size and intentions of the enemy apparatus in and around Mushan. As patrolling became more regular around the bazaar, enemy forces from across the river in Zharey started to engage at a distance. The mentors recommended that the patrol plan include those areas, but the ANA company commander was reluctant to do so without air support so, for the rest of April, patrols focused on the bazaar and areas west of the town.

In May, the 71A team, consisting of Aggus, McNabb, Saina and Cpl Dan Meeking, a medic who was attached from the Police OMLT, replaced 71B at Mushan during Operation TOOR AZADI II (Corporal Tyler Latta arrived back from leave later on and Meeking rotated out). There was an immediate spike in reports of unarmed enemy personnel observing this RIP operation but, again, there was little enemy activity with the exception of an IED attack against a patrol from "B" Company, 2 PPCLI, an ANA section and mentors from 71A. This was a particularly gruesome attack in which the enemy used a ten-year-old boy as an improvised explosive device. This child was pushed ahead by an older man in the direction of the patrol, and was then remotely detonated. The attack killed an ANA soldier and wounded two Canadians and one Afghan.[5]

By this time, battle procedure for Operation NOLAI was in progress. This was a 2 PPCLI Battlegroup operation over in Zharey district designed to move south from Ring Road South towards Mushan. The Mushan force was to play a supporting role by providing a feint to the south. On 26 May, however, a number of insurgents shot at an ANA patrol (accompanied by Warrant Officer John McNabb) from a compound. The Afghans mounted a clearance operation with 'minimal prompting' and their leadership retained a 'cool demeanor' during the engagement. The enemy fled north into Zharey with "B" Company, supported by an MQ-1 Predator hot on their heels. Within two days the insurgents attacked the Strongpoint with small-arms fire from the direction of the old clinic.

The situation around Mushan deteriorated again on 31 May. Between 15 and 20 insurgents, split between four compounds, ambushed a 20-man Afghan patrol and three Canadian mentors in a three-sided ambush while the Strongpoint simultaneously received harassing sniper-fire. The ANA patrol endured ten minutes of small-arms and RPG fire before the patrol sergeant organized his PKM machine-guns to respond in kind during a lull in the fire. The mentors joined in with an M-72 LAW and a M-203 grenade-launcher. An enemy sniper then started to pick away at the Afghans who had gone to ground in a nearby wadi. The two M-777 guns from "C" Troop, "B" Battery, 1 RCHA, under the command of Lt Candice Dunn (who later became known as 'The Angel of Death' by some of the soldiers her troop was supporting), fired smoke to screen the ANA as they broke contact, leapfrogging back in two groups and in good order. ISTAR reportage indicated that a Taliban cell leader and five other insurgents were killed during the course of these engagements. They were attempting their own version of a Key Leader Engagement at the time the patrol appeared.

The next day, several mortar rounds landed near the Strongpoint. The Sperwan Ghar M-777s fired several smoke missions to screen the compound from any potential observers or from mortar fire controllers. Subsequently, an insurgent commander told the shopkeepers at the Mushan bazaar to close up and go home because "the war has started".

The Defence of Strongpoint Mushan

The number of engagements from the north bank of the river continued to mount in early June. In almost every case a patrol that was involved in a Troops in Contact (TIC) event was mortared once it returned to the Strongpoint. None of these rounds initially hit the compound, but incoming rounds were seen to bracket it at about 100m in each direction. This was an indicator that a trained, enemy mortar fire controller was in the area.

Between 8 and 10 June, ISTAR reportage indicated that the enemy forces were annoyed at a perceived pro-government tilt of the population in Mushan, so they intended to enter the bazaar to intimidate the merchants. One theory was that they wanted to stop merchants selling fresh food to the ANA in the Strongpoint in order to aggravate the supply situation. A local source complained to the Joint District Coordination Centre in Panjwayi about the intimidation.

As a result of this information, the company in the Strongpoint surged two platoons into Mushan bazaar as a show of force to demonstrate to the local people that the government would not be intimidated. As the two cut-off groups deployed, they came under enemy fire. One platoon, moving in behind the bazaar, took rounds from a grape-hut to the west, while the second platoon received small-arms and RPG fire from positions west of the old clinic. A Canadian Tactical Unmanned Aerial Vehicle was orbiting the battle and a pair of U.S. Air Force F-15s were available, but there were problems in employing the firepower because of how close the engaged forces were. The firefights stalemated after about 30 minutes and the Strongpoint started taking fire. The Afghans in the run-up position were able to identify and engage one of the compounds from where the enemy was shooting, and so did the platoon near the bazaar. The enemy then started to exfiltrate from the position opposite the bazaar. Warrant Officer John McNabb, who was not trained as a forward air controller, got on the radio to the F-15s. The orbiting fighter-bombers dropped two 500-pound bombs on the hut and a 1000-pound bomb on the old clinic. These strikes reduced both structures to six-foot piles of rubble. The M-777s from Sperwan Ghar then fired an additional five 155mm rounds to catch the enemy as they withdrew.

The first platoon from the bazaar swept south to link up with the second platoon at the old clinic where they found a lot of casings and some salvage, but no bodies. Low on ammo, they made the decision to head back to the Strongpoint and call in a CASEVAC flight. Two Ford Rangers loaded with ammo and led by SMaj Bashir sortied out to the bazaar to act as a reserve as the withdrawal took place. The F-15s remained overhead as long as they could.

ISTAR then reported that the enemy was attempting to hide his dead bodies and assorted body parts in culverts so they could then deny the coalition forces an accurate battle-damage estimate, though these remains were later retrieved. The enemy's estimate was 15 killed.

As the situation heated up throughout June, a ground re-supply operation named ROOM SERVICE was spun up by an armoured combat team from "B" Squadron of The Lord Strathcona's Horse (Royal Canadians) led by Maj Chris Adams. This particular 'river run' brought in an additional mentor and five more ANA soldiers just in time for Operation NOLAI. The Mushan force's role in NOLAI was to cross the river with a platoon and two mentors and then distract enemy forces further north right before they were pummelled by an infantry company from 2 PPCLI and an infantry company from another kandak, all supported by the Strathcona's Leopard 2A6M tanks. The Mushan force was ordered not to get decisively engaged.

As the Afghans and Canadians crossed the riverbed into Zharey district on the morning of 14 June, an Afghan soldier spotted an insurgent with an RPG in a compound. As the platoon took up firing positions, the enemy unleashed a high volume of small-arms fire against the coalition forces from a grape-field to the west. An OH-58D from The Banshees, already on station, swept up from the riverbed, but communications between the ground forces and the helicopters were not working. Corporal Tyler Latta jumped up onto a wall and pointed in the direction of the enemy so the Banshees could go to work raking the grape-field with .50 cal machine-gun fire.

Then, between eight and 10 insurgents opened up from covered positions in a tree-line to the north. The Afghans returned fire that was inaccurate but voluminous. Pumped on adrenalin, the RPG gunners fired too high, arcing their rockets to no effect.

One of the other mentors, Corporal Tyler Latta, fired a 203mm grenade round into the northern tree-line to mark the target while ISTAR reportage confirmed that a force of between 10 to 15 Taliban was in the area. The OH-58D made gun-run after gun-run on the tree-line until its .50 cal was 'Winchester' (out of ammunition). The snub-nosed rocket-pod was employed until it, too, was out of rockets. This engagement lasted 15 minutes. A Canadian Tactical Unmanned Aerial Vehicle then spotted an insurgent lugging an 82mm recoilless rifle heading north. An orbiting MQ-9 Reaper subsequently dropped a 500-pound GBU on him.

The fire from the tree-line dropped off and the Afghans and their mentors moved in and found seven dead enemy. Then two elders approached, but some of the Afghans believed that they were being used to plant false information or, worse, trying to suck the platoon into an ambush in the compound complex to the north-west. Since the OH-58D was low on fuel, it headed home. Once the helicopter departed, five insurgents opened up with small arms. The decision was made to move back to the river-bed and hold, so a request was put in for fire from the 1 RCHA M-777s at Sperwan Ghar. There was a lot of smoke, however, so the mission could not be executed. With the Afghans running low on ammo, McNabb and Latta decided to use their smoke grenades to cover a withdrawal across the river-bed as an Afghan section sortied out from Mushan to the south bank to assist them. However, once the platoon was back at Strongpoint Mushan, three mortar rounds landed right on the south-west edge of the wire. Shrapnel hit an Afghan commander in the shoulder and Capt Hyatt was slightly wounded. The .50 cal and C-6 machine-guns in the towers immediately opened up on the point of origin, using the 'uneducated guess' method. ISTAR reportage later estimated that 12 enemy were killed during the course of the day's operations, all on the north bank.

On 15 June, a similar cross-river operation was mounted from Mushan, but this time the entry point was shifted 800m west. Starting out at 0300 hours, the probe immediately ran into trouble due to a navigation error that put them 200m further west in an area that had virtually no cover when the sun came up around 0430. ISTAR reportage indicated that the enemy "just went nuts" and ordered local forces to observe and engage as rapidly as possible. When this information was relayed to the platoon, the interpreter started to panic and started to urinate every five minutes. Some of the ANA soldiers started to panic too, which put McNabb and Latta in a bind. Knowing that panic is contagious and must be countered immediately, McNabb and Latta decided to have the "C" Troop M-777s drop some smoke to the north of their location. ISTAR reportage came back and told the platoon that the enemy was worried about how close the smoke was to their position, so McNabb called in a fire mission of proximity-fused high-explosive rounds in the same area after he saw three enemy moving in that area.

An Afghan soldier then spotted a single insurgent and dispatched him with an RPG round. The fight was on as a five-man insurgent group then opened up on the platoon. Lt Dawa Jan, who had been trying to calm the panicked 'terp', ordered the platoon to move back to the south bank. As they moved across, they saw the Kutchi camp on the south bank, but the Kutchi were packing up and moving west with a trail of people. Not a good sign. An ISTAR asset reported that there were several non-Kutchi present, some wearing black turbans, but they appeared to be unarmed. As the enemy fire resumed from the north bank, Lt Jan prepared to move the platoon east along the river when an Afghan soldier spotted men with weapons on a wall parallel to the river on the south bank. The Sperwan Ghar M-777s fired a linear smoke mission followed by a high-explosive mission onto the wall. The platoon dashed across the river-bed to secure the position. The wall, however, was 25 feet high forcing the platoon to continue east once more; this produced a repeat of the same situation. The artillery fired smoke, but the enemy then opened up with 12.7, RPG and 82mm fire from the north bank. McNabb's helmet was knocked off by an RPG blast, while Latta sought out an extraction route. The guns fired a linear HE mission down the river bank in a bid to stop the fire. The rounds 'walked' down the north side of the river causing an attenuating effect on the enemy's aim.

As the platoon finally made its way back to the Strongpoint, it came under ineffective speculative fire from the bazaar. The guns from Sperwan Ghar now had to shift fire since combat outposts elsewhere along FOSTERS were under attack. An orbiting MQ-1 Predator spotted four insurgents 500m away from Mushan who were preparing to fire RPGs. They were successfully engaged with an AGM-114 Hellfire.

Operation NOLAI disrupted enemy harassing fire that was being directed at patrols near the bazaar, in addition to the distraction being generated to support the 2 PPCLI company operation. The heavy contacts during Operation NOLAI, however, left the company in Mushan low on almost every consumable. While awaiting re-supply, the Strongpoint and its occupants were engaged in a gunfight almost daily throughout June. The insurgents then mounted a bold attack on 22 June. 14.5 and 12.7mm machine-gun fire raked the position while enemy RPG rockets were fired from the west. To ward off the attackers, the Canadian mentors and the ANA responded with a high volume of direct and indirect fire. During the course of the firefight, ISTAR reportage indicated that the enemy wanted to generate casualties so that the coalition would respond with a MEDEVAC helicopter which, in turn, could be targeted for destruction. After this engagement, the enemy force in the Mushan area was short on ammunition, attenuating their operations for a time.

The next day, an ANA patrol noted that women and children were evacuating the area west of the bazaar. This was an ominous sign. Twenty-four hours later, on 28 June, RPG volleys, small arms and now an 82mm recoilless rifle poured fire onto the Strongpoint. This time, the mentors dragged out the Carl Gustav and blasted back with 84mm rocket-assisted projectiles. They bombarded the attackers with the 60mm mortar and emptied box after box of .50 cal ammunition as the Afghans moved the Ford Rangers into the run-ups and engaged with 12.7mm DshKa's.

On 29 June, a smaller volume of small-arms fire was directed at the Mushan force from a pair of grape-drying huts to the north-west. The ANA returned fire. The next day, what appeared to be a coordinated small-arms fire attack from the north-west and south-west was repelled. The situation quieted down until 4 July when an ANA patrol in the bazaar was shot at and the Strongpoint was mortared. The insurgents said 'goodbye' to 1st Company and the 71A team with a devastating mortar attack which wounded five ANA soldiers and disabled the 60mm mortar. One of the wounded suffered an extruded brain which was attended to by the Canadian medic MCpl Ian Mothas. Almost all of the medical supplies were used up. The severely wounded Afghan soldier later succumbed to his wounds.

Mortar Games

The Strathcona's Leopards deployed again on 5 July during Operation ROOM SERVICE 2 and had multiple engagements along the Arghandab River as they fought their way to Mushan. 2nd Company and the 71B team took over from 1st Company and 71A who had deployed into a 'bubble' around the Strongpoint in order to receive the column. 71B and 2nd Company were greeted with a mortar attack on 9 July that killed two more Afghans and took out the communications equipment to the Strongpoint. In this attack, five mortar rounds were fired from the vicinity of the clinic and two hit inside the compound. A subsequent fire destroyed the accommodation tents and most of the Strongpoint's stores. The 71B commander, Capt Slade Lerch, requested that a Joint Terminal Air Controller (JTAC) and other assets be deployed to Strongpoint Mushan to deal with the mortars.

On the return trip, the 71A team and the ANA company were tucked into the 'bubble of steel' provided by the tanks of the Operation ROOM SERVICE column snaking its way back along the Arghandab River towards Mas'um Ghar forward operating base. 71A's ordeal was not over yet. The column was hit by enemy fire and Capt Matt Aggus dismounted with the Afghans to engage the ambushers as the Strathcona's Leopard 2s returned fire with their 120mm guns. The enemy fled. 600m further on the column was hit again, but this time the enemy focused on the ANA's soft-skinned Rangers with inaccurate RPG and small-arms fire from both the north and south banks. The ANA stood and fought back as artillery was called in. Sergeant (Sgt) Abdul Haq, seeing an Afghan soldier fire his machine-gun in a jerky and ineffective fashion, grabbed the PKM, ran up and fired the weapon, stunning and scattering part of the ambush force. Then, in what has to be the dumbest move in Taliban military history, an insurgent, armed with an RPG, ran onto the river-bed right in front of a Leopard 2 and tried to engage the tank. Two tank commanders apparently argued over who was going to take him out, so both fired simultaneously and vapourized the insurgent with 120mm HEAT rounds before he could fire his rocket launcher.

Meanwhile, back at Strongpoint Mushan, Afghan National Army patrols were engaged from Zharey district any time they went near the bazaar and the indirect fire attacks continued.

From 7 to 26 July, Strongpoint Mushan and its occupants, now augmented to include seven Canadian mentors, were engaged on 14 separate occasions by various combinations of small-arms fire, RPG attacks and mortar fire. In one of these engagements, the Strongpoint took several mortar rounds, one of which landed two metres from the mortar pit and its ammo stash. Capt Lerch, using his binoculars from one of the towers and covered by Corporal Duarte with a .50 cal machine-gun, called down corrections to MWO Rod Dearing and Corporal MacDonald who were manning the 60mm mortar. Corporal John Prior fired the 25mm from a LAV-III with MCpl Todd Woods in the other tower spotting. The next day, the insurgents held a funeral for their mortar expert and credited the "government mortar team" with the kill. Several Afghan soldiers received wounds and were medevac'd by UH-60s covered by Banshee OH-58Ds. The Afghans and the mentors maintained their rigorous patrol schedule in the surrounding area.

Operation LEWE, a sweep by "B" Company 2 PPCLI, was put together to disrupt enemy activity and give the Strongpoint force some breathing room. Fighting patrols from 1st Company and 71A Weapons Company, 71D and "B" Company fanned out west of Mushan resulting in several TICs, but no mortars.

At the end of July, 2nd Company and the 71B team returned to Mushan on Operation ROOM SERVICE 3, and Capt Aggus, MCpl Saina and Cpl Latta returned. While the RIP and re-supply were in progress, the enemy was bold enough to engage the tank leaguer with seven rounds of ineffective mortar fire the first night. When they tried it again the following night, the mortar was engaged by two GBU-38 500-pound bombs from a pair of U.S. Marine Corps F-18s, while insurgents manoeuvring to engage on the ground were discouraged from doing so by 120mm gun-fire from the Leopard 2 tanks. An estimated five insurgents were killed.

Once ensconced in the Strongpoint and the tanks had gone home with the 71A team, the new occupants were subjected to coordinated small-arms direct fire and a mortar attack, resulting in two mortar hits inside the compound and three casualties. On 26 July, 71B and an ANA patrol were engaged by a section of insurgents. Patience had worn thin and "C"

Troop's M-777s from Sperwan Ghar were called into action to deal with the ambush. As if in retaliation, five mortar rounds were fired at the Strongpoint the next day, but this grouping was not as accurate as previous attacks and none of the rounds landed anywhere near the compound. This attack was replicated the following day, leading some to speculate that a new mortar team was now in play. Patrols found numerous duds in the ground around the Strongpoint and the ammunition was determined to be of Iranian origin.

The enemy now resorted to something new and different. A delegation of people arrived at the Joint District Coordination Centre in Panjwayi town and asked for a shura, which was granted. They petitioned the government to have the Strongpoint and its forces removed. They asserted that crops and compounds were damaged by the various re-supply operations and they demanded restitution for the damage. The problem was that this delegation did not, in fact, represent the people of Mushan at all and the Afghans identified one man as a relative of a known Taliban fighter.

When this approach did not work, small-arms attacks on the Strongpoint resumed on 14 August, followed by two more mortar attacks on 20 August. This time, an ISTAR system was able to identify the point of origin of the mortar attacks and the M-777s from Sperwan Ghar blanketed those positions with 155mm rounds in an effort to kill the mortar teams. What emerged later was that an enemy mortar specialist was brought in to replace the one killed in a previous engagement. This individual's *modus operandi* was different. He would establish the mortar base-plate and sight in the weapon. Other insurgents, obviously more expendable than 'the specialist', were used to actually fire and reload the weapon while the specialist buggered off long before the counter-battery fire could arrive. As the counter-battery fire improved and the patrol program expanded the security 'bubble', the enemy mortar specialist and his apprentices were forced to move north of the Arghandab River.

Relief in Place

After successful participation in another incursion into Zharey district, 1/1-205 kandak and its mentors extracted from Mushan and, by September 2008, rotated back to Camp Hero for refitting, training and rest. Canadian engineers deployed to the FOB Mushan and laid 'Rhino Snot' and Moby Matting to improve the helipad. Canadian CH-47 Chinook helicopters, escorted by CH-146 Griffons, took over the re-supply and RIP missions. A company from 2/2-205 'Strike' kandak moved into the FOB. Families started to move back into the area at this time. During a shura with the local elders, Capt Sahim Ravatullah personally guaranteed that he and his men would provide security to the area. Constant framework patrols demonstrated his resolve over a two-week 'honeymoon' period.

By the end of October 2008, relations between the local population and the new ANA company were improving. The Taliban noted that the bazaar was the nexus of this improved relationship, so they established a rival market three kilometres west of Mushan town along with checkpoints to protect it. They also used intimidation patrols to demand that the locals close the existing bazaar near the FOB. Attendance at the regular bazaar dropped to 25 percent over the course of one week. The ANA and the OMLT responded by pushing out west of the town. The Taliban's response was to resume harassing mortar-fire against FOB Mushan in late November and they even brought in one of their scarce 82mm recoilless rifles. On 17 November, three first-round hits eventually landed inside the FOB, killing two and wounding four Afghan soldiers, while other mortars were fired towards Zangabad and IEDs laid on the road to the east in order to discourage reinforcement. Unlike the previous locations, the new mortars were emplaced by their teams inside houses and fired through holes cut in the roofs. Clearly, any aerial retaliation that resulted in destroyed buildings and dead civilian 'human shields' would be exploited by the enemy and condemned by the Western media. ISTAR reportage confirmed that this was another professional team that had infiltrated in from Pakistan. As U.S. Army UH-60s conducted the MEDEVAC, Canadian M-777s and a British 81mm mortar team from 42 Commando worked with the OMLT and the ANA to suppress the new enemy teams as best they could, given the new circumstances.

"M" Company, 3 RCR eventually surged into the area and captured three mortar tubes; one was still warm after having been fired. After these operations, the bazaar near the FOB re-opened. In January 2009, the local merchants told the ANA that they were not getting the same amount of business in the 'Taliban bazaar' and preferred the previous arrangements where they could make some real money.

End Game

Strongpoint Mushan was clearly a disruptive element to the enemy program for Panjwayi and Zharey districts as evidenced by the significant resources, varied and escalatory methods, and scarce expertise that the insurgents employed in their attempts to remove the coalition presence. The willingness of the Afghan soldiers to continuously exert a presence in the area, even if limited at times to a three-kilometre security 'bubble', demonstrated to the local people that the government was there to stay, even while under heavy contact over several days. Given the security situation, the question of how to expand that bubble so that governance and development activities could expand could not be addressed during that time. In the Afghan cultural context of the war, the sort of obstinacy projected by the defenders of Strongpoint Mushan can have a positive effect on the population if the message is conveyed properly by the defenders themselves with a PSYOPS team, by CIMIC quick-impact projects and by the methods employed by provincial and national governments. Sadly, this level of coordination does not yet exist within the Afghan National Army structure so the ANA remains dependent on the coalition forces for such support. As of February 2009, Strongpoint Mushan continues to hold and provide a security presence to the people at the western end of Panjwayi district.

Postscript: In May 2009, the decision was made by the Afghan National Army authorities in Kandahar province to dismantle Strongpoint Mushan and withdraw Canadian and Afghan forces from the area. A combined Canadian-Afghan operation, was mounted in June to dismantle the Strongpoint.

Notes

1   A note on sources: The author was present in the spring and summer of 2008 for the Route Fosters 'duel' and observed it from several levels. During a research trip to the forward-deployed elements of the OMLT in the summer of 2008, I interviewed the personnel involved in the Mushan operations as they rotated out of the position. I would especially like to thank LCol Dan Drew, Maj Dave Proctor, MWO Rod Dearing and WO Chuck Côté for their insights into OMLT operations at this time. I would especially like to thank Cpl Tyler Latta, WO John McNabb and Capt Matt Aggus for sharing their experiences with me. I also was briefed by the army aviators from Company "B", 2-17 Cavalry on their role supporting Canadian and Afghan forces in Panjwayi district. I would also like to thank Lt Candice Dunn and "C" Troop, "B" Battery 1 RCHA. Maj Steve Nolan, Capt Sean French and WO Joe Doucette, from the follow-on OMLT rotation, assisted me with the events of late 2008. Note that certain control measures and intelligence collection assets have been blurred in this narrative for operational security considerations. Some names had to be altered to avoid personal embarrassment.

2   The Canadian soldiers from 71A asked me to note that they do not view their actions at Mushan as extraordinary in the context of what other elements of the OMLT were engaged in at the time in Zharey and Panjwayi districts throughout 2008 and they wanted to convey that this is but one action in the course of their tour in Afghanistan. They took pains to express to me their concerns about being labelled 'self-aggrandizing' by others because their actions appeared in print and other actions did not. The full story of the OMLT and its other operations during that time will be told in a future narrative so that all OMLT elements receive equal historical recognition for their efforts.

3   The Kutchi are nomadic and can be found throughout Afghanistan. They tend to live in domed tents and maintain camel, sheep and donkey herds in addition to various agrarian pursuits.
4   At least from this particular rotation.
5   Those who observed this attack remain psychologically scarred by it.

A dozer-equipped Leopard 1 moves up to plow run-ups for the LAV-IIIs. The lack of air conditioning in the older vehicles resulted in the manufacture of heat reflective umbrellas which significantly reduced temperatures for the crews.

CHAPTER TEN
THE MECHS:
OPERATION TIMUS PREEM
AUGUST 2008

Tanks were first used by the Canadian Army in Afghanistan in the fall of 2006 during the MEDUSA operations. Simplistic public criticism was directed towards this deployment and focused on the argument that tanks were unsuited to counterinsurgency operations because of the amount of damage they caused to the infrastructure while moving around or discharging the vehicles' weapons. Others viewed the deployment of tanks as a sign that the coalition was 'losing' the war because the insurgents had 'escalated' to conventional operations and, in the Maoist schema, victory for the insurgents had to be near because they had supposedly transitioned from guerilla to conventional operations. Deployment of 'conventional' forces like tanks to counter this 'transition' was therefore problematic. Indeed, simplistic arguments made the rounds, such as "The Soviets used tanks and failed, Canada is now using tanks, therefore Canada will fail". Consequently, the presence of Canadian tanks in Afghanistan assumed political, as well as practical, dimensions.

By 2008, these arguments had all but died away in the 'mediasphere' and the 'punditocracy'. Tanks were no longer a novelty in the Canadian area of operations. The Leopard C-2s of 2006 were replaced by Leopard 2A6Ms by the summer of 2007, though many Leo 1s stayed on to push anti-mine and anti-IED implements that could not be mounted on the new vehicles because of the modular construction of their armour. What became evident to Canadian Battlegroup commanders very quickly, once they got on the ground, was how diverse the terrain was in Kandahar province. That diversity allowed that a variety of types of forces could be employed to meet coalition objectives. In this case, tanks would be unsuited for operations in Kandahar City or, say, the mountainous Maruf or upper Shah Wali Kot districts. In the open terrain in Maywand, however, there were advantages to using armour. Tanks could be used even in the built-up green belts around the city. The Howz-e Madad incursion described in Chapter Five was one example but, in October-November 2007, Arghandab 1 had a troop of Leopard C-1s covering open high-ground to screen a battalion-sized assault into a built-up area; this came right out of a Canadian FIBUA[1] doctrine from the Cold War. Armoured columns were used to re-supply isolated strongpoints like Mushan.

Operation TIMUS PREEM, led by LCol David Corbould and conducted by the 2 PPCLI Battlegroup in August was a mechanized assault involving nearly two battalion-sized units of Canadian and Afghan forces, with armour leading the main effort. By comparison, Operation TIMUS PREEM resembled Operation TOTALIZE on a smaller scale: the terrain is extremely restricted and similar to bocage in Normandy, and the operation involved the use of armoured breaching columns.[2]

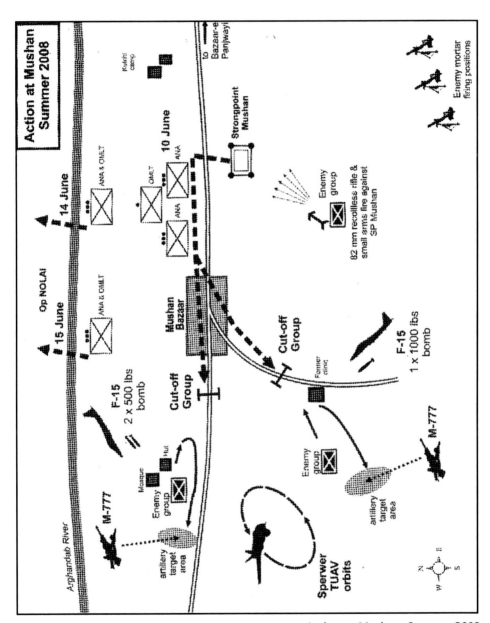

Action at Mushan, Summer 2008

The Origins of the Operation

The 2008 iteration of Joint Task Force Afghanistan, led by Brigadier General Denis Thompson, planned to create a 'stability box' in eastern Zharey District in Kandahar province. The idea was to select a key area and apply serious resources to it. Operations in the box would, in theory, dislocate insurgents, convince the 'fence sitters' to support the government, deny the enemy the ability to influence the population in the box and prepare the area for high-profile development projects.

Stability Box JUNO was established in June-July 2008. It encompassed Route SUMMIT from Highway 1 down to Bazaar-e Panjwayi in Panjwayi district. Stability Box JUNO was also supposed to give focus to Canadian development efforts. CIDA, DFAIT and other government departments now had a specific area in which to establish a joint inter-agency team and force it to work together on a dedicated series of projects. In theory, a second Stability Box would be established in Panjwayi District once JUNO was up and running. JUNO was limited to part of Zharey district because there were not enough resources to project Afghan governance and security throughout the whole district.

Several factors militated against the effective operation of JUNO, however. The primary one was the Sarposa prison break and the subsequent diversion of forces to conduct the Arghandab 2 operation in June 2008. The secondary factor was the ongoing demand for the 2 PPCLI Battlegroup's infantry companies to occupy legacy tactical infrastructure positions along Route FOSTERS. As usual, the dearth of Afghan police and the ongoing build-up of the Afghan National Army and its occasional diversion to Helmand province were impediments to establishing security in the stability box, as were the ongoing problems between the Afghans as to who constituted legitimate governance in the two districts. The Canadian inter-agency piece was still evolving. If JUNO was supposed to be a showcase, there was not much under the glass by the height of the summer of 2008. However, that did not prevent the continuing efforts to jump-start the process nor the consequent disruptive activities by the enemy.

Indeed, a series of operations along Highway 1 near Sanjeray assumed priority status. The enemy had conducted a series of high-profile IED attacks on the highway which threatened to cut off this vital east-west commercial and logistic route. Operation ASP-E-JANOUBI, (a.k.a. 'Ass Pain Janoubi' to the staff) was a complex operation involving the transport of a huge turbine from Kandahar Air Field all the way to the Kajaki Dam in Helmand province. The Kajaki Dam was the key hydroelectric producer in the region and, after years of neglect, it was failing. The logistics of moving such a piece of equipment over such a distance, and then protecting it from enemy action, was immense. Keep in mind that the effects of a failure of the information operations were potentially catastrophic for ASP-E-JANOUBI and this possibility overshadowed Canadian operations in Kandahar province.

Over the course of the summer, the Battlegroup planning staff, led by Maj Jay Adair, developed a series of plans designed to protect and enable Stability Box JUNO. ISTAR resources were focused on the area west of JUNO, specifically on a suspected enemy command node in a large compound complex dubbed Objective WEASEL. This node had some relationship to the IED cells operating along Highway 1, but it was also connected to the rocket attacks on FOB Mas'um Ghar. Another cell and a command and control node from Nahlgam to the south-west operated against Afghan National Police in western Zharey, while another cell harassed Strongpoint Mushan over in western Panjwayi district.

Objective WEASEL was a physical location, but the pattern of activity in that area varied. Enemy leaders came and went, including the notorious Jabber Agha,[2] and there were an estimated 40-50 enemy fighters in the vicinity. Zangabad boasted another 40 or 50 fighters, as did Nahlgam. A number of enemy IED specialists, based in Sia Choy and Nahlgam, used WEASEL as a transit point when they moved to and from Sanjeray. Adair and his staff discussed the possibility that Objective WEASEL also served as part of the enemy's early warning system. If coalition forces started to move west from JUNO, the forces around WEASEL would conduct some form of covering force fight until the 'deep' forces in western Zharey could be mobilized and deployed.

The planners struggled to identify objectives. There were not enough Afghan security forces to establish an enduring presence in the area cleared by coalition forces, so extending Stability Box JUNO was out. However, a major operation against these enemy forward positions could accomplish multiple objectives. First, it would probably interfere with enemy operations in Sanjeray and enemy IED operations on Highway 1. That would draw off heat from the turbine move. Secondly, in September 3 RCR Battlegroup was flowing in to affect a relief in place with 2 PPCLI Battlegroup. One lesson from 2006 was that the enemy would use every means available to exploit the lack of acclimatization of the incoming forces. A major operation that put the enemy back on his heels right before the RIP would positively contribute to the process and protect the incoming forces. Finally, an operation like this would force the enemy away from JUNO and give the inter-agency and governance processes some breathing room.

This was only a contingency operation as of 8 August and there was no inevitability about its execution. Were there enough forces available to mount it if Task Force Kandahar said 'go'? This was a serious problem. A combination of the leave plan, the protection of tactical infrastructure, a quick reaction force task and the siphoning off of infantry platoons to guard bridges in northeastern Kandahar province near Zabol meant that 2 PPCLI Battlegroup had less than 50 percent of its forces available for planning purposes. The planners had four available infantry platoons in LAV-IIIs, two tank troops, a recce troop with Coyote, two engineer platoons and the M-777 artillery battery. For command and control there were two infantry company HQs, a tank squadron HQ and the recce squadron HQ. Yet, this was not going to be enough. The planners looked at Afghan National Security Force availability. After consultation with the Canadian Operational Mentor and Liaison Team, there was a possibility that an ANA company and an ANA platoon, with their Canadian mentors, could be cut loose for the operation. Perhaps more. Perhaps not.

Between 8 August and 16 August the Contingency Operation (CONOP) continued to evolve. In a general sense, there would be a main effort in the centre against the western area of Pashmul along with two supporting attacks: one to the north-west down from Highway 1 and the other moving east-to-west south of Pashmul. In the CONOP plan, planners used phase-lines named after characters from the movie Transformers, a DVD that was popular with the armoured soldiers. The CONOP was thus formally designated Operation TIMUS PREEM. Regional Command (South), which consisted of older staff officers not familiar with popular culture, asked what TIMUS PREEM was. LCol Corbould told everybody it meant 'lawn mower' in Pashto.

On 16 August, Operation TIMUS PREEM was formalized by Task Force Kandahar. Coincidentally, there was more and more ISTAR reportage of enemy leadership in and around Objective WEASEL, including Jabber Agha and two other senior commanders. Structurally, the plan remained the same: a main effort directed against three successive objective areas with two disrupt operations in the flanks and aerial screens provided by OH-58D helicopters from the Banshees and UAVs. The only real debate at this point was how to hit Objective WEASEL, with what, and when. One planner wanted to use a particular missile system, but it was not available, so the idea emerged of unloading a B-1B onto WEASEL at the start of the operation. WEASEL's elimination at the start of the operation would, in theory, have a significant disruptive effect.

FOB Mas'um Ghar: "B" Squadron, The Lord Strathcona's Horse (Royal Canadians)

Canadian operations in eastern Zharey district had evolved significantly over the course of three years. During the summer operations in 2006, Task Force ORION relied on deception, night operations and stealth to infiltrate the Pashmul area with LAV-III-mounted infantry. The mass deployment of improvised explosive devices altered that approach and, in 2007, 2 RCR Battlegroup conducted daytime, tank-led, mechanized incursions into the district coupled with early morning, dismounted infantry insertions. In 2008, 2 PPCLI mounted several company-sized dismounted incursions supported by tanks. Operation TIMUS PREEM would be the first Battlegroup-sized operation of the 2008 rotation where the tanks led.

The three designated objective areas in Operation TIMUS PREEM require some explanation. Each objective area was a collection of compound complexes, almost like islands. Each cluster of complexes was surrounded by grape-growing trenches, drying huts, tree-covered irrigation systems and, because it was August, lush and dense vegetation (corn and marijuana, mostly). The only roads into and out of these areas were one-lane, unpaved routes with multiple irregular twists and turns and innumerable culverts. That is, these routes were perfect for IED emplacement.

The only way to avoid IED attack and subsequent canalization and delay was, in effect, to unpredictably create new roads as the operation progressed. This is where the armoured vehicles came in. The Badger Armoured Engineer Vehicle, or AEV, employed at this time was a Leopard 1 hull with engineering modifications, including a durable dozer-blade. The armoured engineers were also experimenting with fascines carried not only on the AEV, but by armoured trucks and the Mercedes AHSVS, as the Beaver AVLB vehicle was too unwieldy to use in the Zharey environment. The AEV boom, or any vehicle crane, could lift fascines from the truck's cargo area and emplace them. Then there were the older Leopard C-1s equipped with dozer blades.

"B" Squadron, led by Maj Chris Adams and Squadron Sergeant Major Tony Batty, experimented with these and other measures throughout their tour. They built on tactical ideas that their predecessors used in previous rotations, particularly the employment (and recovery) of tanks in mobility-restricted environments. The vehicles themselves were fine-tuned as much as possible by Tango Maintenance at FOB Mas'um Ghar. "B" Squadron's proficiency level was at its peak in August 2008 and it would contribute to the success of Operation TIMUS PREEM.

In terms of structure, "B" Squadron had three troops, each consisting of a mix of vehicles. As a rule, there were four Leopard 2 A6Ms, plus one or two Leopard C-2s equipped either with anti-mine ploughs, rollers or dozer-blades. The make-up of each troop depended on the type of mission: River Run, incursion or Quick Reaction Force. There were also a mechanized infantry platoon on rotation from one of the 2 PPCLI companies, an artillery FOO and his LAV-III, a troop of armoured combat engineers with AEVs, an Explosive Ordinance Disposal team, armoured recovery vehicle assets and armoured ambulances. The Leopard 2 A6Ms with their 120mm smooth-bore guns were capable of firing canister, or HEAT, rounds. The "M" on the designation stood for 'mine resistant' as the Canadian vehicles had a variety of modifications designed to mitigate the effects of IED and mine strikes.

At the same time, "B" Squadron was responsible for supporting development efforts in the Panjwayi and Zharey districts. This took many forms, but usually involved attempts to coordinate efforts between the Canadian government departments, the PRT, the Operational Mentor and Liaison team, the Police OMLT and the Afghan security and governance people. "B" Squadron staff referred to themselves as the "Panjwayi East Combined Operations Centre" or the home of the "Whole of Panjwayi Program for Enhanced Reconstruction". "B" Squadron also handled FOB MSG security which included counter-rocket operations. Leopard 2s emplaced in over-watch positions regularly engaged Taliban rocket teams at night in Operation Box ELTON as they prepared to fire at the FOB.[4]

FOB MSG was also home to the Operational Mentor and Liaison Team supporting 1st kandak, 1/205 Brigade, of the Afghan National Army. Led by Maj Dave Proctor, the OMLT headquarters and support facilities were co-located but not under the command of "B" Squadron. There was also a Combat Service Support (CSS) detachment led by Lt Alison Lucas. The CSS detachment forward, consisting of vehicle techs, electro-optical equipment techs, weapons techs and supply techs, were responsible for non-tank maintenance and supply distribution at the FOB. The detachment had TLAV APC, an armoured AHSVS wrecker, a HLVW with a crane and a HET vehicle transporter. Importantly in this environment, the detachment had the ability to deploy a fire-control system- repair team, under armour, into the field. Tango Maintenance was a separate organization and included the Leopard 1 and 2 Armoured Recovery Vehicles.

RG-31s, LAV-IIIs, a Bison, and a fascine carrier establish themselves in the centre of a night leaguer.

The Enemy Draws First Blood

At 0730 on 19 August, the shock wave from an explosion rocked FOB MSG. The FOB's occupants initially thought a rocket had hit the camp but, in time, the crews from the Quick Reaction Force, consisting of Leopard 1 and Leopard 2s plus an ARV and Bison ambulance, moved quickly to their vehicles and started up. The Tactical Operations Centre staff was trying to ascertain what happened. The enemy, it turned out, attacked a Canadian-mentored Afghan national police patrol on the Bazaar-e Panjwayi-Kandahar City road when they were attacked by a suicide IED bomber. One interpreter was killed and a Canadian Police OMLT mentor was wounded. A local child was also wounded and a MEDIVAC chopper was called in.

This did not stop planning for Operation TIMUS PREEM. Capt Edgetar Manoucheri, the Battle Capt and the "B" Squadron staff fine-tuned their part of the plan. A confirmatory drill held later that day revealed that "C" Company, 2 PPCLI plus "B" Squadron would handle the main effort. The northwestern supporting effort would be done by the OMLT with two ANA companies, while "B" Company and an ANA company would handle the southern supporting effort. Knowing full well that the enemy kept close watch on FOB MSG, Maj Adams pre-positioned his vehicles inside the FOB as he normally would for a River Run down to Strongpoint Mushan to make the enemy think the upcoming operations were directed west, not north. Hopefully, the enemy would also re-position his forces which, in turn, would be detected by ISTAR resources; then other coalition resources could be directed from higher headquarters to interfere with the enemy's activities.

Enemy forces in and around the objective areas were estimated at around 325 fighters, of which 100 were assessed to be skilled. They knew how to exploit cover to protect themselves from ISTAR assets and they were well versed in how to exploit the limitations on the Canadian forces imposed by NATO rules of engagement. Enemy morale, however, was not high and there was some internal debate between the Zahrey-based commanders as to the future direction of operations. In terms of leadership, Jabber Agha was estimated to be around Pashmul planning more SIED and IED attacks, while Khaliq and Razaq, two of the Zharey district commanders, had been seen near Objective WEASEL.

Once Operation TIMUS PREEM was detected, the staff anticipated that the enemy would use his early-warning system to determine what axis of advance the coalition forces were using, and then lay multiple IEDs to delay the Canadians and Afghans while reinforcements were brought in from the west, married up with their weapons caches and deployed to fighting positions. The dissenting opinion was that the enemy would drop their weapons, walk away to the west and not engage. LCol Corbould believed that, in either case, there would be a significant disruptive effect on enemy operations in eastern Zharey and that this would meet the operation's objectives.

The main effort, consisting of "B" Squadron and "C" Company, was to conduct a rapid breach and isolate each objective area with a 'ring of steel'. The tanks and infantry were divided up into Breach Teams BT-1 and BT-2.

BT-1:

"B" Squadron HQ (2 X Leo 2)
"C" Company HQ (1 X LAV-III)
SLAYER (2 X LAV-III with FOO/FAC/JTAC)
1 Troop (4 X Leo 2, 2 X Leo 1)
Badger Armoured Engineer Vehicle
Leopard 2 Armoured Recovery Vehicle
Fuel truck (AHVSS)
Ammo truck (AHVSS)
Fascine truck (AHVSS)
1 X infantry platoon in LAV-III

BT-2:

3 Troop (4 X Leo 2, 2 X Leo 1)
Badger Armoured Engineer Vehicle
Leopard 2 Armoured Recovery Vehicle
1 X Leo 2 detached from "B" Squadron HQ for command and control
1 X infantry platoon in LAV-III
Four M-777 155mm guns and eight 81mm mortars on call.

The ANA, its OMLT mentors and the ANP with Canadian Engineer Exploitation Teams would then sweep the compounds and exploit any material or personnel found. The force would then move to the next objective and do the same thing. Any defensive works would be destroyed through demolition. Aerial over-watch would observe any 'squirters' and track them. There were three objective areas for the operation, which was estimated to take three days. Of note was that Operation TIMUS PREEM would also have PSYOPS and CIMIC detachments to support its effort.

While preparations for Operation TIMUS PREEM continued, the Red Phone in the "B" Squadron TOC rang to the theme from the movie "In Like Flint". A massive explosion occurred on Highway 1 around 1040 hours on 20 August. A Canadian engineer recce party supporting Operation ASP E JANOUBY consisting of an engineer section and a recce platoon from 2 PPCLI Battlegroup was subjected to IED attack. As the Quick Reaction Force (QRF) rolled out the gate, ISTAR reportage warned that an enemy commander in western Zahrey was preparing to send forces to attack those responding to the attack.

The drama continued all morning. The stricken vehicle had flipped over, the turret was wrenched off and the surviving crew was trapped inside. Then the vehicle started to burn. An Armoured Recovery Vehicle and a Bison ambulance approached the site to right the wreck and extract the crew, but there was no protected fire-fighting capability to stop the fire. Then ISTAR reportage noted that six to ten insurgents, with a significant enemy leader, were nearing the blast site. MEDEVAC helicopters were called in, but there were now concerns that the enemy may have laid IEDs on the nearest open space, so the American task force wanted engineers to clear an HLS before they would go in.

There were an estimated four casualties, but their status was in some doubt. One Canadian was outside of the vehicle but three were still inside. Then, ammunition in the stricken LAV started to cook off, slowing the recovery team's efforts. Back in the Battlegroup Tactical Operations Centre, the JTAC and intelligence staff were trying to track the in-bound enemy commander with the intent of using an MQ-1 Predator or an MQ-9 Reaper to kill him. Artillery could not be used because of an ROE issue. Fortunately for him, when the UAVs became available he could not be engaged because of another ROE issue.

The staff discovered that there was, in fact, an HLVW firefighter vehicle available, but they had not been told it existed. It was meant to suppress aircraft fires at the landing-zone and 'belonged' to another organization at Kandahar Air Field. Maj Steve Davies from the OMLT volunteered to lead this virtually unarmoured recovery 'package' through Zharey district to the strike site. This included the firefighting HLVW, a dump truck (to fill in the crater) and a HETT low-bed, escorted by OMLT RG-31 patrol vehicles. Another threat warning from ISTAR reportage came in: the enemy was deploying a mortar team to attack the IED strike-site. Resources were deployed to look for it. The flat-screen TV in the Tactical Operation Centre (TOC), set to a news channel, surreally announced that Christina Applegate was diagnosed with breast cancer. It was quickly shut off. The mortar team, it turned out, directed its efforts at Strongpoint Mushan, not at the strike-site. After two mortar rounds landed near the Strongpoint, M-777 guns were called in to suppress the mortar team.

Tragically, the QRF reported in that there were three Canadian dead and one wounded.[5] The belief at FOB Mas'um Ghar was that Commander Canadian Expeditionary Force Command (CEFCOM), who was in-theatre at this time, might put a hold on Operation TIMUS PREEM, anticipating domestic political sensitivities. This proved to be unfounded, however, and the enraged Canadians made their final preparations late into the night of 20 August. The crew of T-23, a Leopard C-2, spray-painted the visage of a Grim Reaper and his scythe onto the dozer-blade of their vehicle.

RG-31s, LAV-IIIs, a Bison, and a fascine carrier establish themselves in the centre of a night leaguer.

Day 1: 21 August

At 0415 the Battlegroup's TAC forward at FOB MSG was fully manned and at 0426 hours, a pair of U.S. Army AH-64 Apaches arrived on station and checked in. Inside FOB MSG, long lines of armoured vehicles from the breach teams sat in the dark with their engines off, their crews cupping their cigarettes. Foot patrols swept suspected rocket-launch sites outside the camp. Operation TIMUS PREEM was cocked and ready, awaiting clearance to engage Objective WEASEL. ISTAR assets were now closely watching the site, checking the pattern of life. When a control link failed between an allied ground station and an allied UAV that was operating on the flanks, a Canadian Sperwer was brought on station to check a 'deep' target in western Zharey district. Nothing. No movement. ISTAR reports "enemy quiet".

0445 hours: The breach team columns roared into life and headed out the gate, down the road and into the Arghandab River wadi. Instead of turning left and heading down the river to Mushan, the Badgers, Leopards and LAVs proceeded north on Route SUMMIT. No contact. 0515: The sun was just starting to come up, revealing dusty mountains in the distance. ISTAR resources still observed Objective WEASEL waiting for the enemy commanders to arrive. Breach Team 1 reported in: "The first breach is in". Unfortunately, a traffic jam developed on Route SUMMIT, slowing down the second breach team's movements. The ANA and the OMLT moved on to their objectives south of the breaches.

At this point, the enemy's early-warning network was not reporting anything, nor was the enemy activating reinforcements. LCol Corbould believed that the presence of the AH-64s was deterring enemy movement, so he ordered them to orbit elsewhere for the time being, hoping the enemy would 'come out and play'. By 0605, still no enemy movement was detected.

The Badgers, with their blades down, turned west off Route SUMMIT, ploughing tracks across the grape-trenches and smashing through high mud walls. Then a Leo 1 with a dozer-blade followed behind, ploughing four or five small paths off the main track. The Leo 1 dozer then backed up and the paths were occupied by the Leopard 2s. This 'herring-bone' formation was repeated as necessary, with the infantry following in a LAV-III. The tracks allowed the columns to completely bypass the roads which were assumed to have pre-positioned IEDs on them.

At 0634, the enemy finally reacted and their whole communications system erupted in an aural blur. LCol Corbould could not wait any longer and decided to engage Objective WEASEL. The Battlegroup TAC headquarters chatted with a B-1B that was orbiting high overhead. The staff filed out of the bunker with their binoculars to watch. It was now a dusty, hot dawn. Objective WEASEL was barely perceptible from FOB MSG. A loud "CRUU-UMMMMPPPP!", the shockwave of nine guided bomb units hitting WEASEL; it then hit the FOB and a plume of black smoke could be seen several kilometres away.

"B" Squadron got the first contact at 0637 hours. A volley of RPG and small-arms fire was directed at the lead vehicles. Leopards from 2 Troop returned fire. Then a U.S. Police Mentoring Team triggered some form of anti-personnel device as the vehicle manoeuvred, wounding one of its crew. By 0654 there were several contacts underway: the OMLT and their Afghan troops were engaged in two locations on the two supporting efforts; "B" Squadron was shooting it out with insurgents on their axis of advance; and "C" Company, moving in behind "B" Squadron, was engaging enemy in a compound. ISTAR detected four enemy, maybe more, moving to a compound to engage "C" Company, but the FOO called in a fire mission and 155mm rounds crashed onto the compound they had moved into. A second fire mission was called in to take out a similar attempt by the enemy to move up and engage.

Operation TIMUS PREEM was initiated by nine bombs dropped by a B-1B on Objective WEASEL, an enemy command and control compound.

A Leopard 2A6M advances through a field on Day One of Op TIMUS PREEM. The decision to avoid existing roads by the advancing forces resulted in no IED strikes during the operation. (Author) LEO2advance.jpg

The first objective was designated MIKE. It consisted of numerous compound complexes and was separated into MIKE 1 through MIKE 3. Breach Team 1 ploughed its way to MIKE and then ploughed a 'ring road' around MIKE. The dozer tanks then ploughed run-ups and paths from off the 'ring road'. Leopard 2s and LAV-IIIs then moved in. The idea was to isolate MIKE by having 360-degree observation and fire around the whole area. Anything trying to get into MIKE would be engaged, as would anything trying to get out. Once the 360-degree cut-off was established, the Afghans, their OMLT mentors and the Engineer Exploitation Team moved in to sweep the MIKE 1, 2 and 3 compound complexes. PSYOPS and CIMIC teams assisted, as required, when there were civilians in the area.

Searching one compound complex, let alone three, was arduous, Wearing body armour and carrying ammo and water in the nearly 45-degree heat was taxing for all involved. Indeed, it took all day to sweep and clear MIKE.

ISTAR detected enemy movement near KILO as the second wave of ANA deployed. Over in Panjwayi, two IEDs exploded on Route FOSTERS, but apparently not against coalition targets. As they had in the past, the enemy was trying to distract attention from the main effort over in Zharey.

Around 0800, an OMLT vehicle observed and engaged enemy moving around Objective ECHO. The two AH-64s were called in and unleashed their rocket pods on them. Another call-sign, 3 Platoon, identified enemy movement south of MIKE and started to engage. The JTAC accompanying Breach Team 1 cleared in a Harrier which dropped a Guided Bomb Unit (GBU), obliterating the enemy in the open. The ANA and the OMLT worked quickly in the Objective KILO complexes, declaring the first three clear by 0950.

In an effort to speed up re-supply and casualty extraction routes, combat engineers using counter-IED equipment cleared the roads parallel to the breaches. They found numerous pre-positioned IED components, including a massive culvert bomb. They also discovered multiple fighting positions with interlocking fire. These were destroyed with explosives. In a disturbing development, an OH-58D from the Banshees saw a suspected IED from the air on Route SUMMIT, so engineers were diverted to examine the site and remove the device. Then a vehicle from the American Police Mentoring Team accompanying the Afghan police in Objective KILO struck an IED. It was a mobility kill with no casualties.

The Afghans and the OMLT continued to get contact, particularly in and around Objective KILO to the west. An ANA platoon had a short but sharp engagement with a small group of insurgents who appeared to be trying to infiltrate Objective MIKE. Another small group was driven off by the cut-off force surrounding MIKE. Even the Battlegroup TAC got involved. At 1115 hours, a 9'r TAC LAV-III observed and engaged six enemy fighters with RPGs who were trying to skirt MIKE to the south and get in behind the cut-off force from the east. Heavy-calibre weapons were fired from the RG-31s and LAV-IIIs, and an AH-64 came in with 25mm to finish off what was left. The backpacks these insurgents were carrying went up in a series of secondary explosions. The AH-64s were then diverted to drop a Hellfire on a grape-hut where several insurgents had been seen to flee. An estimated four other in-surgents were taken out in that strike. By 1155 hours, Breach Team 1 re-mained in position around Objective MIKE, while Breach Team 2 passed through MIKE, heading south.

Normally, the enemy commanders in Zharey would be assembling and deploying reinforcements from communities in the west. This was not hap-pening to the extent that some hoped. Was the enemy discombobulated by the novelty of the operation? Or was the enemy choosing not to react to it and then flow back in later? Were there other reasons? Was this slow re-sponse an effect of the strike on WEASEL? It was not clear. What was clear was that ISTAR reportage indicated they were having problems activating a single suicide bomber to infiltrate MIKE, let alone mount a coordinated as-sault on the TIMUS PREEM forces.

By 1215 hours, the ANA and OMLT were consolidating Objective KILO when they found two IEDs. Objective MIKE was being swept, but was not yet clear. The initial battle-damage assessment of Objective WEASEL was that 90 percent of the target was damaged. ISTAR reportage suggested, but did not confirm, that forty enemy were killed in the strike, including some who had been medium-value leadership targets.

Breach Team 2 moved south of MIKE and, in the fields, started clearing leaguer areas for the assault force. The Badgers and dozers cleared three parallel lanes for each assault force. While this was happening, 4 Platoon got a contact inside MIKE and three insurgents were positively identified and engaged in the late afternoon.

LCol Corbould's assessment of the situation in the waning hours of 21 August was that the breaching operations were much slower than anticipated, that the operations on Objective KILO were a successful block with positive effects, and that the deep strikes were successful at engaging reinforcing fighters. He now had a decision to make: should the force go after Objective GOLF or Objective WHISKY? It was unfortunate that the coalition did not have the resources to permanently garrison Objectives MIKE, GOLF and WHISKY. The Battlegroup had temporarily expanded the 'security bubble' west of Stability Box JUNO, yet it was too bad that it could not be exploited.

The CIMIC teams were now reporting that there were some annoyed farmers. It could take years, even decades in some cases, to grow the huge grapevines in these trenches. Chunks of these fields were being obliterated by the dozer-blades. The message from the Battlegroup was not conciliatory: "If you told us where the IEDs were on the roads, we wouldn't have to make our own," they were told. That is, you locals are 'fence-sitting'. You want us to stop, come off the fence.

At 1830 hours, 120mm and 25mm fire erupted west of Objective MIKE and artillery started to land on targets. There were contacts all over the place and it seemed as though small groups were trying to infiltrate at dusk. They were unsuccessful. By 1845 hours, both breach teams were lined up in their lanes south of Objective MIKE when cries of "Stand To!" were called out. The lead tanks on the lanes then engaged targets 300-400m to the south, in the direction of Objective GOLF. As it turned out, three groups of fighting-age males pretended to be labourers during the day but recovered cached weapons at night and advanced on the leaguer. They were all taken out.

ISTAR resources reported that the enemy was bringing in an "82" in a vehicle. Was it a mortar or a recoilless rifle? Nobody was sure. "Crash harbour" was not an option, given the restrictive terrain. Four civilian vehicles and some 20 personnel were spotted moving in from the south-west, but weapons were not evident. Various systems continued to track them. Then coalition forces over in Objective KILO started tracking night movements, noting up to 50 personnel. ISTAR picked up that a significant enemy commander from Zharey was present, but the conditions were not right to engage. It might have been a funeral.

It was a cool night as the crews bedded down behind their vehicles. Capt Tom Neil and his PSYOPS crews in their RG-31s turned on their loudspeakers. Interpreters read out messages and letters to the Taliban in Pashto, trying to convince them to quit the fighting: "Taliban, if you want to use the children for suicide attacks, that is not good. They are innocents. If you are ready to fight grown-ups, we are here." "Taliban, if you drank your mother's milk, then come out to the fighting place and fight us. If you don't, then you are a bastard." A Scan Eagle MUAV buzzed the leaguer and orbited the perimeter.

A Leopard 2 advances through a breach and moves to a cut-off position near an objective compound complex.

Soldiers from the Afghan National Army and their Canadian Army operational mentors advance to search a compound complex. The ANA were responsible for all compound searches, while the Canadians handled cut-off security.

Day 2: 22 August

The troops put away their sleeping gear after they awoke in the morning cool. LCol Corbould decided to move on objectives WHISKY and GOLF, simultaneously. His decision was based, in part, on overnight ISTAR reportage. The enemy apparently believed that this incursion was payback for the three Canadians killed on Highway 1. They also were surprised that the force did not pull out at noon, but remained in the field. They were confused as to what the next move was going to be. They knew the force was aligned south in its leaguers, but that could mean it was headed to the compound complexes in GOLF or WHISKY. Therefore, LCol Corbould concluded, hit both objectives. Breach Team 1 would move on GOLF while Breach Team 2 would move on WHISKY and then, depending on how things went, onto BRAVO.

Again it took the enemy several hours to make any moves. ISTAR reportage had an 82mm mortar preparing to fire at coalition forces while over in Objective BRAVO fourteen insurgents, with what looked like a heavy weapon, were seen moving around, but could not be engaged. There was no movement around KILO.

There was now talk that JTF-A or CEFCOM might order Operation TIMUS PREEM terminated so that the engineers from 1 Combat Engineer Regiment who were in the field on the operation could go to KAF to participate in the ramp ceremony for their three dead comrades. There was additional talk that there was increased political pressure to avoid more casualties and that that was the reason for finishing the operation early. The idea that the combat engineers could extract separately from the operation was also floated and rejected. Ultimately, the operation continued at the behest of BGen Dennis Thompson who rejected the arguments that Operation TIMUS PREEM should be prematurely ended.

Breach Team 2 had 'eyes on' Objective WHISKY-2, where Objective WEASEL was located. There was no pattern of life. The breach was launched. To get at WEASEL, the breach team had to traverse complex terrain. The Badger AEV with its blade went first, ploughed through a marijuana field, took down a hardened five-foot-high mud wall, cut a path through a square cornfield, then took down the next wall, which was nearly eight-feet high. This put the AEV into a second square-walled field where the process was repeated. When the last wall was down, the AEV was in sight of Objective WHISKY. This route was selected because the ground was relatively flat, the walled fields to the east were full of grape-growing trenches and, to the west, there was a wooded stream with a wall parallel to it.

The Leopard 2 troop followed the AEV, burst out of the last breach and moved in open ground to isolate Objective WHISKY. The Leopard C-2 with the dozer followed and ploughed out the 'herring-bone' run-ups in the first field, which was occupied by the battalion TAC; it then moved to the second field and did the same for the infantry LAV-IIIs.

By 0837, Objective WHISKY was isolated with the cut-off forces and the exploitation started. With Warrant Officer Chuck Côté accompanying the lead Afghan infantry company, Maj Dave Proctor's OMLT dismounted, marched through the breaches, deployed and prepared to move on WHISKY. A pair of AH-64s orbited the proceedings looking for targets. In its initial search, Afghans and the OMLT found a large mortar cache and a pile of artillery rounds which were probably destined to become IEDs. A small bunker was found adjacent to the strike-site and the exploitation continued. A report came in that the stench of rotting flesh was noticeable around the Objective WEASEL strike-site. Further explorations uncovered large amounts of IED-making material. Another interesting discovery made by the engineers was that the enemy was re-using Canadian construction materials to shore up their bunkers and fighting positions; the materials had been used to build Afghan National Police Sub-Stations in Zharey district.

Objective KILO then started to take mortar fire; four rounds landed near the OMLT and ANA leaguer. These rounds bracketed the force and indicated that an experienced, or at least trained, enemy mortar-man was in play. The ANA and the OMLT engaged enemy spotters, while a quick analysis determined the firing-point for the mortar base plate. A distant explosion signalled the abrupt end of the enemy mortar team; a GBU from a Harrier had killed the whole team. ISTAR reportage indicated that the enemy commanders kept trying to contact the team throughout the afternoon, to no avail.

Breach Team 1, on the other hand, followed Breach Team 2 through its breach and then turned west at a point south of Objective GOLF. The Badgers and Leopard 2s swung north to isolate GOLF from the west while keeping an eye on BRAVO to the south. The shortage of Afghans meant that the Canadian infantry platoon with Breach Team 1 and the Engineer Exploitation Team had their hands full with GOLF.

Echelon elements carrying fuel, ammo, water and food followed the Breach Team 2 Badger, which had scraped out leaguer rows in a large, open field south of Objective WEASEL. The battalion TAC and the echelon moved into these positions. Around 1625, the enemy was able to get off a round or two of either mortar or RPG airburst exploding near the battalion TAC just as the Leopard 2 Armoured Recovery Vehicle, nick-named 'Calgary', hooked up a Leopard 2 that was having power-pack problems. The turret crews could see spotting pop-ups along walls, but they could not tell if they were enemy spotters or curious children – or both. Then an orbiting MQ-1 spotted a pair of men with binoculars observing the leaguers, so they started to track them.

Maj Chris Adams observed six insurgents in a nearby compound and the JTAC spotted two more carrying what looked like a heavy weapon – possibly an 82mm recoilless rifle. The orbiting Predator was cleared to engage. At the same time, the Afghans engaged a target with small-arms fire and a Leopard 2 then let fly with a 120mm canister round at a group of insurgents who were probing the leaguer positions.

Almost all Canadian groups in all of the objective areas reported people equipped with binoculars observing the new positions. Orders were given to engage anyone involved in this activity. An unknown vehicle crew commander whispered "I seeeee you!" onto the Net right before his gunner fired. Three enemy spotter teams were taken out using 25mm and 120mm fire.

Objective WHISKY was now 100 percent clear. Additional searches uncovered mortar, RPG and IED material caches. (The mortar rounds, incidentally, had Chinese markings on them.) A number of radios were found together with some cell phones and a significant amount of medical supplies. A detainee was taken and whisked away to KAF via UH-60 helicopter. Objective GOLF, however, was not cleared yet, so there was no update on material found. At 1645, the enemy ineffectively engaged the leaguer with RPG and small-arms fire from the west.

Information from Afghan sources indicated that the enemy had moved back in on the initial breach routes from SUMMIT to Objective MIKE and laid eight IEDs along them. They also determined that 15 wounded enemy fighters had been evacuated to one field hospital, and eight to another. For the most part, the bulk of the insurgents in the objectives areas retreated west, south-west and south to get out of the way of the armoured onslaught. The results of the airstrike on Objective WEASEL were in some dispute. The numbers of enemy killed were revised down so that the best estimate at this point was 25 killed and 15 wounded, including a small number of Arabs, Pakistanis and possibly Chechins. Further information came in that 15 enemy fighters were placing mines on routes south of the leaguer, trying to anticipate the force's movement. Again, reports of more inbound mortar teams came in so the Badger AEVs were tasked to dig shell-scrapes throughout the leaguer. The engineers used plastic explosives to take down large iron-wood trees that blocked the tanks' arcs of fire.

LCol Corbould assessed the situation. The enemy was reacting in a more coordinated fashion than yesterday, but still not strongly. The options were to move onto BRAVO, continue to 'muck out' GOLF, do both, or withdraw. LCol Corbould was also prepared to use the leaguer as a 'hedgehog' and rack up the kills, if the enemy chose to take it on. The enemy, on the other hand, seemed to be slowly reinforcing the area near Objective BRAVO with small groups. Small groups of young men on motorcycles were also seen entering the now-abandoned Objective MIKE and there was word that the two enemy commanders for western Zharey were on the scene.

LCol Corbould decided to clear Objective BRAVO. The night leaguer was oriented south, while Objective BRAVO was to the west. It was probable that the enemy would think the axis of advance would be south and not west, so some surprise might be achieved. The move on BRAVO would also avoid the mines the enemy had placed to the south. Both breach teams would isolate the rather elongated BRAVO objective area, then the ANA and

A Leopard 2 in a cut-off position.

OMLT would clear south to north to throw off anybody still in his position. The only issue was a pair of small wadis, but the fascines would be put to good use there. The Canadian and Afghan forces pulled into their night leaguers, dismounted and made supper. As the night closed in, the PSYOPS teams played Blue Oyster Cult's "Don't Fear the Reaper", followed by a succession of distorted tunes from Blink-182, Limp Bizkit and Linkin Park. There was no contact that night.

Day 3: 23 August

At 0630, observers saw a group of women and children leaving Objective BRAVO and heading north. An enemy observer with a cell phone was seen in the midst of the women and children, so the Leopard 2 tank crew that was tracking him refrained from firing its 120mm gun. Another group of insurgents, however, were seen to be signalling their compatriots and they had no human shield, so a 120mm HEAT round took them out over some distance.

Pre-positioned chambers for improvised explosive devices were discovered along the roads. Combat engineers cleared the roads behind the advance forces to permit re-supply.

Then, at 0655 The Badger AEVs with their fascines moved out of the leaguer, heading west-south-west. The two wadis were filled in with the fascines and crossing-points were established for the follow-on forces. A motorcycle was seen to leave BRAVO heading west at high speed. This was seen to probably be a 'Paul Revere', a backup early-warning fighter heading off to alert his commanders that the coalition forces were not moving as anticipated. Indeed, crew commanders and gunners started to see signalling mirrors blinking in the morning light. When he queried, LCol Corbould was informed through ISTAR reportage that the enemy was having serious problems communicating with their early-warning networks, particularly after they had been targeted.

Breach Teams 1 and 2 ploughed on through the rich soil of the tall cornfields. The Badgers put in the 'ring road' and, by 0725, the Leopard 2s and LAV-IIIs had isolated Objective BRAVO. The Afghans and the OMLT commenced their sweep in the south. Many fighting-age males were seen, but it was difficult to determine whether they were 'moving with intent' or were conducting 'agriculture-related activities'. A CIMIC team working with the Afghan soldiers conducted a Key Leadership Engagement in one of the BRAVO compounds as engineers found a locked trapdoor elsewhere. The local nationals told the Afghan soldiers that the insurgents had rounded up everybody in the area, put them under guard in a grape-hut, and told them not to leave or look out. The enemy did not want them telling coalition forces in what direction they went. The engineers then found IED equipment, while an orbiting UAV saw a man on a motorcycle headed west, stopping and talking

An example of the complex terrain encountered in Zharey District during Op TIMUS PREEM. This is a collection of grape-drying huts surrounded by vineyard trenches that are four to five feet deep and choked with vegetation.

to small groups of fighting-age males who were conducting 'agriculture re-lated activities'. Nobody seemed to be in a hurry to go anywhere near BRAVO. The local people in BRAVO, it turned out, were extremely friendly.

Almost 60 people remained in their compounds when the sweep forces came through and they were quite helpful in describing enemy activity in their area. The people were adamant that most of the enemy they saw were Pakistanis from Balochistan, with some Arabs and, apparently, Chechins. They forced local people to store vehicles, but did not force them to store weapons. For the most part, the insurgents stayed overnight in the fields, not in the compounds. They operated in groups no larger than eight and usually carried a mix of small arms and RPGs. 82mm recoilless rifles were carried by special teams of two to four. Local nationals with military back-ground told the ANA soldiers that the Taliban was low on ammo this season and were probably incapable of sustained actions, as they had been in 2006.

The CIMIC team decided to hold a formal shura. In that meeting they learned that the people in BRAVO were mostly pro-government; so much so, it seems, that the Taliban hanged a kidnapped police officer from a tree earlier in the year just to intimidate the people. More importantly, a local national with military experience confirmed that Objective WEASEL was, in fact, some form of forward headquarters and depot. The enemy commanders apparently had two command 'nodes' and rotated them through WEASEL so both would not be killed at once; BRAVO was a transit area for the backup command node. The enemy kept a small command team active in WEASEL at all times, augmenting it from BRAVO when necessary. If an operation was undertaken east in Sanjeray, the teams generally passed through WEASEL on the way.

The insurgents interfered with education in the BRAVO area. There was a school and a principal and the ANP had a checkpoint to protect it. The Tal-iban kidnapped and killed the police and threatened the principal. He was forced to hide the small school library to prevent it from being burned. The PSYOPS team was concerned that the enemy would portray the withdrawal as a victory. Discussions with local people confirmed that they understood that the coalition forces could not stay indefinitely and that they would resist the Taliban's claims of victory. They had seen the Taliban driven away by the coalition forces and knew the insurgents would be back by nightfall.

Continued sweeps in BRAVO turned up very little, though there was confirmatory information from other local nationals. By 1100 hours, LCol Corbould decided to extract the force and head back to FOB Mas'um Ghar. The extraction plan was tricky. The enemy was alerted and no doubt they would mine and IED the existing east-west routes between BRAVO and Route SUMMIT if they could. The enemy could not be sure, however, that the Operation TIMUS PREEM force might not continue to move south or west, and they had a limited number of devices. LCol Corbould decided to take the most direct option. The two breach teams would plough two parallel routes along the single east-west road, and set the forces in Objective ECHO to clearing the junction of that road and SUMMIT, and also from SUMMIT to FOB Mas'um Ghar, so there were no surprises on the way home. Alertness was a priority; it was a long and hot operation and thoughts of a shower and hot food could not be allowed to override vigilance.

Breach Team 1 headed south, while a Badger from Breach Team 2 ploughed a track and a 'parking lot' pointing west. The forces assembled in lanes pointing west. ISTAR reportage indicated there was enemy observation and they were trying to figure out where to set up an ambush. Once Breach Team 1 was well on its way, Breach Team 2 peeled back and headed south too.

By 1350, the lead Badger Armoured Engineer Vehicle (AEV) in Breach Team 1 started to overheat as it tried to traverse a muddied wadi system and the mechanics were brought up to repair it. Another Badger was pushed forward to maintain the momentum. A Scan Eagle MUAV flew ahead along the planned routes to check the tree-lines for possible enemy ambushes. Nothing so far.

At 1407, however, a Leopard 2 crew spotted several insurgents in tall grass south of the breaches. There was some debate as to who was going to engage: the artillery, Predator or the tanks. The enemy dispersed and withdrew as the tanks readied their coaxial machine-guns. Then Maj Adams spotted three more insurgents manoeuvring to the south and let fly with a 120mm canister round, killing all three. The orbiting Predator re-acquired the first group which was in the process of splitting into two teams; it was not clear whether they were running away or manoeuvring.

Breach Team 2, however, hit a wet wadi system and then ploughed into a wet cornfield. The Badgers and Leopards had to back up and find a route around this impasse. Could the vehicles now start using the road to speed things up? There were only 200m of it left before it hit the paved Route SUMMIT. The answer was no, continue to avoid the road in case it was IED'd. Maj Adams, quoting Back to the Future, said over the radio: "Roads? Where we're going we don't NEED roads!" It was just as well. When Breach Team 2 was forced closer to the road because of wet terrain, a sweep discovered an IED. It was blown in place by the engineers and the breach team swung north again into navigable terrain, continuing east.

By this time, Canadian and Afghan forces cleared and secured the junction as the Badgers and Leopards bashed through the rich earth of the fields. As soon as the vehicles hit the junction, they headed south to FOB Mas'um Ghar. There were no incidents during the extraction. Operation TIMUS PREEM was over, with no Canadian casualties.

Conclusions

Operation TIMUS PREEM had a number of effects on the enemy in Zharey district. First, it forced them to re-organize their command structure and re-place leadership personalities. Second, it wiped out their 'forward' IED-production capacity and the transit base to the Sangeray area. The cumulative effects contributed to the lack of IED activity directed at the Operation ASP-E-JANOUBI turbine-transit operation that took place days afterwards.[6] The operation most likely took out some of the people involved in the killing of the three Canadian engineers on the eve of the operation. The operation also bought time for Stability Box JUNO to consolidate. There may have been longer-term effects, but they were not measurable in August 2008. By spring 2009, Construction Management Team-2 was working with local Afghans to address volatile water diversion and irrigation issues in the 'box', all without significant, or even noticeable, enemy interference.

Operation TIMUS PREEM, however, continued to highlight the problem of not being able to install an enduring Afghan government security and governance presence in an area subjected to a clearance operation. The enemy forces were swept from the area and many were killed and wounded; but, without adequate security in place, they returned the night after the 'mechs' left for home. It was noted by all involved in the operation, and understood beforehand, that the populations of some of the objective areas were either pro-government or potentially pro-government and it is a tragedy for the Afghans and their Canadian allies that adequate forces were not available to expand the security 'bubble' west from Stability Box JUNO.

Notes

1   FIBUA: Fighting in Built-Up Areas. Facetiously called FART or Fighting Around Town or FISH, Fighting in Somebody's House by U.K. forces.

2   The author observed the planning process for Operation TIMUS PREEM and accompanied the Battlegroup for the duration of the operation in the field.

3   a.k.a. 'Jabba the Hut.'

4   As in, "The Rocket Man".

5   These were Sgt Shawn Eades, Cpl Dustin Wasden and Sapper (Spr) Stephan Stock, all from 1 Combat Engineer Regiment.

6   The enemy's 'rear' or depth IED production facilities were taken out the night after Operation TIMUS PREEM by special operations forces. I was told that it was the most successful SOF strike against Zharey IED cells in two years. This also contributed to the success of Op ASP-E-JANOUBI.

Preparing to move west: elements of 2nd (Strike) kandak at FOB HUTEL.

CHAPTER ELEVEN
STRIKE KANDAK:
THE CANADIAN OMLT AND THE
AFGHAN NATIONAL ARMY
IN HELMAND PROVINCE, OCTOBER 2008

Canada provided Operational Mentoring and Liaison Teams as part of its commitment to assist the Afghan government shield its reconstruction effort from the vagaries of the Pakistan-supported insurgency in southern Afghanistan. After nearly three years of working side-by-side with the Afghan National Army, a Canadian-mentored kandak, or Afghan battalion, deployed on two occasions from its home base in Kandahar province to the Lashkar Gah area when enemy forces overran ISAF and ANA positions protecting these vital central districts in neighbouring Helmand province. These were successful operations in that Lashkar Gah and its environs remained under coalition control.[1]

Of equal importance, however, were the operations in October 2008 and January 2009. These were indicators of significant progress in the Canadian-Afghan military partnership. In mid-2006, during that year's climactic battles, the Afghan National Army was nearly incapable of operating at the company level in Kandahar province. By 2009, however, the Afghan National Army's 2nd (Strike) kandak from 1st Brigade, 205 Corps was capable of battalion-level operations within a brigade context, albeit with coalition enablers and mentorship.

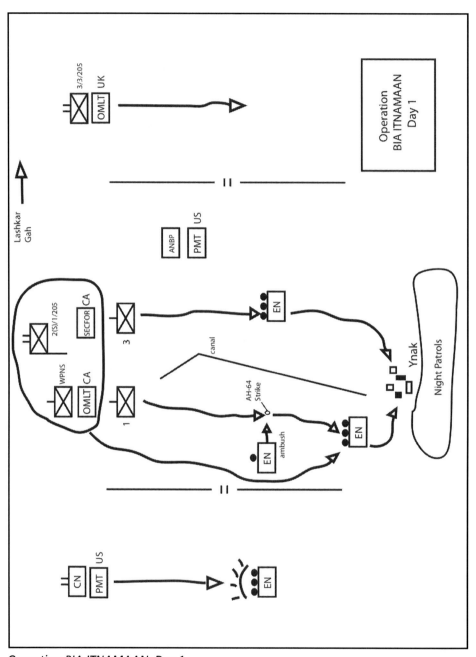

Operation BIA ITNAMAAN, Day 1.

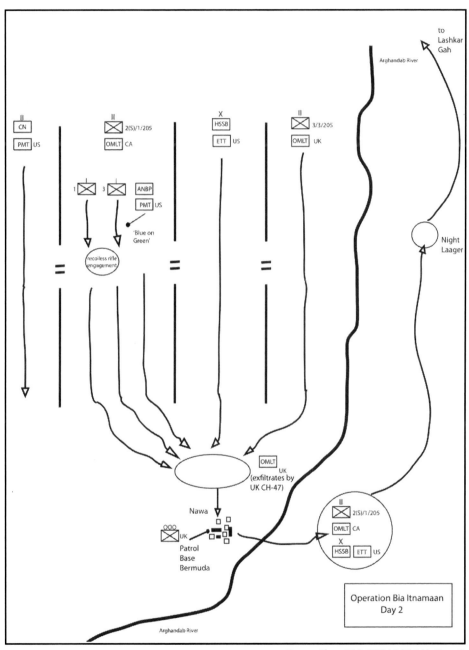

Operation BIA ITNAMAAN, Day 2.

271

The employment of Canadian mentors and the Strike kandak in Helmand province was also part of a complex inter-coalition competition for scarce resources. Consequently, the Helmand province operations highlight several key issues in how Canada understood coalition politics and their relationship with the employment of forces in the pursuit of larger national objectives in coalition warfare.

The Background: Kandak Politics

The scramble by coalition partners to gain influence over ANA kandaks in southern Afghanistan dates back to 2005-06. At this time, there were few kandaks and many of them had been mentored by U.S. Special Forces who were essentially focused on unconventional warfare operations whereby indigenous forces are trained and partnered with special forces to conduct guerilla and counter-guerilla missions. The Special Forces eventually handed over their responsibilities to Task Force PHOENIX, an American National Guard brigade, who had a more conventional outlook when it came to training. In the first instance, the indigenous forces were an adjunct to U.S. special forces operations; in the second instance, they were an independent, national, conventional army. In southern Afghanistan in 2005, U.S. Special Forces and 'their' Afghan National Army units operated in Joint Special Operations Areas, while conventional American forces generally operated in separate areas of operations alongside, but not necessarily partnered with, a small number of mentored Afghan National Army sub-units.

By 2006, however, more Afghan National Army forces were becoming available from the TF PHOENIX pipeline. These units and subunits were generally mentored by American Embedded Training Teams or ETTs, though other nations were involved, including Canada. The ETTs varied in their composition; in one instance, Canadians ran into an Afghan infantry company mentored by U.S. Navy submariner ETTs.

The distribution of the ANA units, however, was not even and had significant demands placed on it. Essentially, countries who contributed forces to Operation ENDURING FREEDOM, and later to the International Security

Members of 2nd (Strike) Kandak Weapons Company check comms before departure. Note that they carry Canadian C-7 rifles.

Assistance Force, competed with one another to get the Afghan Ministry of Defence to commit as many kandaks (battalion-sized units) as possible to their areas of interest. Within the American sphere, there was even competition between the special forces community and the conventional forces. There were only so many kandaks to go around and their quality varied. Obviously, a nation wanted both quality and quantity in its selection of kandaks so that a good 'Afghan face' could be placed on operations. The kandak would reduce the burden placed on that country's own forces in a given province, but it would also demonstrate to the population that OEF and ISAF were not occupation forces and that they were supporting a legitimate Afghan government.

Canada initially did not play this game well and did not understand that there was, in fact, a competition for the kandaks. The brigade-level combined task force deploying to Kandahar in 2006, CTF AEGIS, believed that it would be able to partner each of the four committed battle groups (U.S., Canadian, British and Dutch) with four ANA kandaks and that those kandaks would somehow magically appear from the loins of the training system in Kabul.

The U.S. Special Forces community, however, was more adept at getting what it wanted because it understood the rules of the game, so this contributed to the dearth of kandaks available for southern operations. During the climactic battles in the summer of 2006, there was only one Afghan infantry company available for operations in Zharey and Panjwayi districts. It was split into platoons, with one ANA platoon attached to each Canadian company in the Battlegroup.

By 2007, however, things had improved. The 16-man Canadian contingent at the Kabul Military Training Centre (KMTC) was used to do an active 'talent scout' for 'rock-star' kandaks while they were training and then pass that information to the Canadian task force headquarters in Kandahar so they, in turn, could bid for them. In time, Canadian commanders came to realize the importance of maintaining situational awareness on how the ANA was developing and how it could play a role in the defence of the Canadian area of operations. By 2008, Canadian commanders were getting better at using various levers in Kabul to bolster the number and quality of kandaks in Kandahar province.

Another strand in the kandak problem related to British issues over in Helmand province. The United Kingdom severely underestimated the nature and extent of the insurgent problem in their area of operations. On numerous occasions in 2006, Canadian and American forces were stripped away from Kandahar and Zabol provinces, and even from Regional Command (East), in order to stave off a complete collapse of the coalition position in Helmand.

In 2007, the British tripled the size of their task force from one Battlegroup to three. Then the enemy stepped up operations against forces that were already stretched thin in both provinces. One solution was the commitment of a light infantry battalion to act as the Regional Battlegroup (South) in late 2007.[2] This unit, usually a British one, was placed at the disposal of the Regional Command (South) headquarters and was to be used specifically to generate operations-level effects. This appeared to solve a British and a Canadian problem; namely, the low troop density in Kandahar and the need to counter the shifting enemy activity back and forth between Helmand and Kandahar provinces. It was not enough. The need to occupy areas that had been cleared assumed greater importance in 2008 and the competition for more Afghan kandaks increased steadily to meet that need.

The Afghan National Army in Kandahar province

There was an Afghan corps headquarters based in Kandahar that corresponded to ISAF's Regional Command (South). 205 Corps maintained brigade-sized headquarters in Helmand, Oruzgan, Kandahar and Zabol provinces. The number of kandaks assigned to these brigades varied. In Kandahar, there were three infantry kandaks, a combat support kandak (artillery, engineers and a recce company) and a combat service-support kandak (logistics) assigned to 1st Brigade, 205 Corps (1-205). Assigning a permanent, or even stable, troop-strength number to these units is impossible. Leave and rotation policies, absenteeism and special forces poaching all ensured that at no time was any kandak at anywhere near 100 percent of its strength. Infantry companies tended to have around 65 personnel, for example.

The disposition of 1-205 Brigade's kandaks was in flux by 2008. At some point in 2007, Canadian planners determined that a kandak, with its associated OMLT mentors, would become responsible for handling Zharey disrict and the vital Highway 1 as an area of operations, while a second kandak and its mentors would do the same in Panjwayi district. A third kandak would be at Camp Hero (1-205 Brigade's main base) refitting and training. kandaks would rotate between the assignments. The kandaks, therefore, were supposed to become the 'land-holders' occupying 'tactical infrastructure' (strongpoints, combat outposts, forward operating bases) and pushing out presence patrols while the Canadian Battlegroup would act as the mobile force and reserve. In theory, Afghan National Police would then establish police substations and expand the 'security bubbles' from those areas where there was tactical infrastructure.

This plan came under severe enemy assault in 2008 and the 'tactical infrastructure' became, in some cases, traps to pin down the Afghan and Canadian forces. More and more resources were allocated to defend the positions to the detriment of more mobile operations. At the same time, there were never enough police to work the security 'bubbles'. The Canadian Battlegroup became more and more involved with defending tactical infrastructure and the initiative was nearly lost by mid-2008. The ANA, particularly 205 Corps headquarters, also champing at the bit for more mobile operations, were loath to occupy 'tactical infrastructure', so they sought out operations where they

275

could improve their formation-level skills, not just patrol tactically and locally.[3]

2nd kandak from 1-205 Brigade 'ripped' into Panjwayi district at the end of August 2008 after linking up with its Canadian mentors. Mounted in 7-ton International trucks, Ford Ranger pickups and some unarmoured Hummers, 2nd kandak consisted of a headquarters company, three infantry companies of three platoons each, and a weapons company with four platoons (mortar, recce, machine-guns [12.7 DshKa]) and an SPG-9 recoilless rifle platoon. At that time it had between 75 and 88 percent of its personnel available for operations.

The Canadian mentors for 2nd kandak came primarily from 1st Battalion, The Royal Canadian Regiment. Led by Maj Steve Nolan, call-sign 72 normally had four 4-man teams, with one team assigned to each company and one interpreter for each team. There was also a small headquarters element. In many cases, the team strength was in flux because of leave, battle injuries and cross-attachments. For the most part, 72 was mounted in RG-31 armoured patrol vehicles equipped with remote weapons systems in either a 7.62mm or .50 cal variant.

Logistics support, always a serious challenge for the kandaks, came in the form of a barter economy between the kandak commanding officers and the brigade commander. Everything was a negotiation with the Afghans, even when operations were pending. An American Logistics Support Team, or LST, mentored the ANA in logistics but also provided monies to the ANA for humanitarian and CIMIC-type projects from American sources.[4] The kandaks identified projects on their own while in the field and the U.S. LST paid out the funds as required.[5]

2nd kandak deployed a company to FOB Mushan in western Panjwayi; another company to FOB Sperwan Ghar; and the remainder of the kandak was based out of FOB Mas'um Ghar. An ANA engineer detachment was also based there and a troop of Mongolian-mentored Afghan D-30 guns was based at FOB Sperwan Ghar. For the most part, 2nd kandak was involved in a series of 'pulse' operations into enemy-dominated parts of Panjwayi district, working alongside "M" Company 3 RCR and 42 Commando. 2nd kandak also surged into Kandahar City to support the ANP and NDS in a series of operations designed to round up terrorist cells. The Mushan-based company continued to act as a thorn in the Taliban's side, as had its predecessors.[6]

In mid-2008, there was an effort at the Canadian Task Force Kandahar headquarters to reduce the amount of tactical infrastructure in Zharey and Panjwayi districts. The objective was to get out of the outposts and strongpoints and re-introduce mobility. The idea of a 'strike' kandak emerged from these ruminations. A 'strike' kandak would not, theoretically, be wedded to tactical infrastructure and could be employed throughout the province as required, much like the Regional Battlegroup (South). 205 Corps looked at the idea, liked it, and wanted to use a kandak as a mobile reserve during voter registration and security surge operations; but they wanted to surge into Zabol province with the planned 'strike' kandak, not just to operate in Kandahar province. When there were low-key protests from the Canadians, the question was asked: did the kandaks belong to Task Force Kandahar, or to 205 Corps? Clearly, the Afghans wanted some say in how they used their own forces, but many suspected there were other players pushing that agenda behind the scenes.

Eventually, 2nd kandak was re-designated 2nd (Strike) kandak and this led the unit and its Canadian mentors down the path to becoming 205 Corps' RBG(S) equivalent, with obvious implications for Panjwayi district. Who would man the ramparts at Mushan, Sperwan Ghar and Mas'um Ghar when 2nd (Strike) kandak was deployed elsewhere? The answer was the mechanized 3 RCR Battlegroup. Even the 1-205 Brigade leadership was wary of the possibility that one of its three kandaks could be ripped away at any time. Various Afghan schemes were concocted to keep 2nd (Strike) kandak in Kandahar province, but the operations-level situation militated against them.

Helmand Province Heats Up (Again)

Those creative schemes failed in the fall of 2008 when the insurgents ramped up near-conventional operations in Helmand province after a discrete, two-month build-up had started sometime in August 2008. This enemy campaign was planned by the insurgents' primary commanders based in Pakistan and involved practically the whole insurgent command structure in the province. The first area to succumb was Nad-e-Ali district. The Afghan National Police were driven out almost to a man. More and more enemy fighters infiltrated in from Pakistan throughout September and were situated in three lodgements: Marjeh, Nad-e-Ali and Bolan.

On 8 October, the insurgent leadership initiated attacks on the provincial capital of Lashkar Gah, including suicide attacks, indirect fire with mortars and rockets, and small-arms fire. The three lodgements built up to the point where they could start moving fighters to the edges of the city and conduct operations by 10 October.

These attacks occurred within three days of the transfer of authority between 16 Air Assault Brigade and 3 Commando Brigade for command of the Helmand Task Force. The insurgents understand that new and un-acclimatized forces, and particularly headquarters, were more vulnerable than seasoned, acclimatized ones and they clearly waited for this opportunity.

On 11 and 12 October, British forces used indirect fire and attack helicopters to engage and disrupt enemy forces moving around the outskirts of the city, who themselves mortared the Governor's palace. Public estimates placed the number of enemy killed to be between 25 and 60. Insurgents were reported east of the city as well as to the west, and this was cause for some concern. Other coalition engagements eliminated a number of key enemy commanders in some of the lodgement areas, significantly disrupting their command and control. What became clear over the course of several days was that elements of the ANSF in Helmand had been co-opted by insurgent and other anti-government elements, so they were deemed to be unreliable. Consequently, there was a need for outside forces to help re-establish the government's position in Helmand province.

The Afghan government declared a national emergency and 2nd (Strike) kandak and its mentors were pulled out of Panjwayi district and sent east. On 14 October, Maj Steve Nolan received a phone call at around 1800 hours from the CO of the OMLT, Colonel Joe Shipley. He was told to be in Helmand province by 0600 the next morning. This had never happened with such rapidity before and it was clear that something was going very wrong in Helmand province. Maj Nolan did an estimate and determined that he needed another medic, more signallers, a liaison officer, an additional Armoured

Heavy Support Vehicle System (AHSVS) truck and a Bison APC command variant for communicating on the move from Helmand which was 110 km away from Mas'um Ghar and 139 km from Kandahar Air Field. He was told that he did not need any of these additions and that three RG-31 armoured patrol vehicles with trailers would be made available from the OMLT SECFOR (Security Force) that handled personnel and logistics movements. Consequently, Maj Nolan had to squeeze thirty Canadian OMLT personnel, four interpreters and their equipment into six RG-31s and deploy to another province without operations-level communications. Because a number of OMLT members were on leave, the OMLT company sergeant majors and captains became drivers for the RG-31s.

2nd (Strike) kandak mounted up two infantry companies, the weapons company and the headquarters company. Weapons company, based to the east in FOB HUTEL in Maywand district, was used to backfill the other two companies so that company-level mentors were only required for three companies (the third infantry company in the kandak was left down in Mushan).

RPGs figure prominently in Afghan National Army units. They provide a psychological boost for friendly forces and play into Afghan cultural norms regarding warfare.

This was all completed, more or less, by 0800 when the forces left Mas'um Ghar. Maj Nolan, along with Master Corporal Steve Pink, Private Eric Frandzen and 'Froggy' the interpreter proceeded down the road to collect Corporal Conrad Kippenhuck from FOB HUTEL while Weapons Company sorted itself out.

The situation was so dire and the operation mounted so rapidly, that the Canadian OMLT teams for 2nd (Strike) kandak were not even given a grid reference for a link-up with the British forces; they were simply given a cell-phone number and told to drive west to Helmand. Once the kandak and the mentors were on the road, Maj Nolan called the number reaching a British duty officer who then provided the headquarters with a grid. That grid turned out to be in the middle of nowhere, and nowhere near Lashkar Gah. Another grid was provided and that one was on a road east of the city. Without the Bison and its communications suite, the OMLT was effectively cut off from its higher headquarters back in Kandahar province and had only tenuous communication via a cell phone number.

When the cell phone rang again, the mentors were told to take 2nd (Strike) kandak to Lashkar Gah, and not Camp Bastion, the large British base that supported operations in Helmand province. When the force hit a Y-junction, the Afghans went south and the mentors went west, winding up in Camp Bastion. The staff at Bastion was taken aback. Then a U.S.-mentored force led by an American full colonel drove into the camp. This Afghan unit was the Home Special Security Brigade (HSSB), a three-kandak-sized cere-monial parade-ground unit from Kabul. They were not sure what they were supposed to be doing either.

Maj Nolan was concerned about three things at this point: re-establishing communications; re-establishing contact with 2nd (Strike) kandak; and get-ting situational awareness on what was going on operationally. He asked for two British radio operators carrying British radios, as Canadian, Afghan, British and American systems were incompatible. Instead he was given a British captain liaison officer with a Bowman radio, together with all sorts of caveats as to how the officer could or could not be employed.

As for the situation, the Canadian mentors were subjected to a 'nine-liner' MEDEVAC procedural briefing and an RSOI (receive, stage, onward move and integrate) briefing; but nothing about what the enemy was doing.

It was evident to the Canadians that Camp Bastion was not plugged into what was going on and was receiving its visitors as if they were inbound personnel from outside Afghanistan.

Communications collapsed immediately after the force left Bastion's gate. The British captain did not know how to use the radio other than operating the ON/OFF switch and attempts to rendezvous with a British unit east of Lashkar Gah proved futile. As it was getting dark, Maj Nolan pulled everybody over into a defensive position until he could get the location of the Governor's Palace, from where the battle was being run. The column then proceeded into Lashkar Gah where the mentors could see significant amounts of tracer-fire on the other side of the river. After several cell phone calls to a British number (whose owner was not sure what to do) Maj Nolan finally contacted 2nd (Strike) kandak who were ensconced in an ANCOP[7] police station situated right on the Helmand River. The OMLT teams in their RG-31s cruised through the unfamiliar city unescorted and were forced on several occasions to back up when confronted with dead ends – no easy task in the dark while pulling trailers.

There was a distinct feeling that Lashkar Gah was under siege. The civilian population was under cover, coalition and Afghan personnel were moving everywhere in a confused fashion and there was a high volume of fire on the west side of the river. It was believed that the Governor's Palace was nearly surrounded by insurgents. At the very least, its position on the Helmand River made it vulnerable to enemy fire from the west bank.

The ANCOP facility was, to put it mildly, a 'shithole' with no means for the several hundred ANA, their Canadian mentors and the ANCOP police to dispose of their human waste. Soldiers were discouraged from sortie-ing out at night to handle this task because of the amount of fire up and down the river. It was a rough night for all concerned. The situation was made even more surreal when the mentors noticed that they were across the street from a zoo and an amusement park, which even boasted a ferris wheel. They dubbed it Helmand Wonderland.

The next morning, on 18 October, the kandak command team, Maj Nolan and his crew, headed for the Lashkar Gah Provincial Reconstruction Team to liaise with whomever was running the battle. A British brigadier, the U.K. OMLT commander, promised to provide the new arrivals with whatever they needed. Situational Awareness was the priority: what was happening in the town itself? What was happening on the other side of the river? What grids were the enemy forces firing from? Where were the friendly forces, the 'Green SA'? Almost none of this information was available, and 2nd (Strike) kandak was still unsure as to exactly what the task was. The decision was made to find the Operations Coordination Centre-Provincial (OCC-P), where a British Colonel from the OMLT supposedly had a better grip on what was happening.

Finally, the 2nd (Strike) kandak team found General Mohajum, the commander of 3rd Brigade, 205 Corps, who was with his staff formulating a plan that would be launched the next day, 19 October, at 0500 hours. While that was underway, the Canadian mentors were brought into a briefing where the concept of operations was explained. For the most part, the insurgents were occupying a box that was positioned west of the river and south of Lashkar Gah. This box was aligned north-south and had three 'bands': the first was the river ('Blue') the second consisted of several canal systems, trees, wheat fields and settlements ('Green'); and the third was a arid desert-like area to the west ('Brown') which slowly ascended to higher ground. The box was between five kilometres wide in the north and 10 kilometres wide in the south, with an overall length of 17 kilometres, north to south. An estimated 600 to 700 insurgents were located in that box.

The general idea was to have three kandaks proceed south in line abreast and sweep through the built-up areas to engage enemy forces and drive them out of the 'Green' zone. The final objective was Nawa, 17 km to the south, where all of the forces would converge. A 3rd Brigade kandak was to handle the 'Blue' to 'Green' axis to the east, while 2nd (Strike) kandak and a depleted 3rd Brigade kandak, bolstered by an Afghan Border Police unit mentored by an American Police Mentoring Team, would handle the 'Green' axis. A heavily armed Afghan counter-narcotics kandak with American mentors (call-sign 'WARTHOG') would screen the west flank.

In addition to mentoring the command staff of 2nd (Strike) kandak, Maj Nolan's challenges revolved around ensuring he had communications with the Canadian chain of command and could re-supply his own people effectively with the jammed-up roads crowded with a variety of coalition forces, most of which could not communicate with each other. The kandak echelon remained behind in Lashkar Gah at the ANCOP station. Maj Nolan left a signals detachment and a radio mast, plus MCpl Pink, Cpl Kippenhuck and the crews from three of the SECFOR RG-31s, to act as a Quick Reaction Force on a just-in-case basis. U.K. signals personnel openly ridiculed these arrangements and thought that the OMLT signals detachment should be moved forward. Maj Nolan disregarded the criticism and would be proven correct during the course of the next day.

Operation BIA ITNAMAAN/Operation ATAL-28 Kicks Off

2nd (Strike) kandak assembled in their Forming Up Places (FUPs) with 1st Company on the right flank and 3rd Company on the left. The Afghan and coalition forces then crossed the start line, avoiding the roads as much as possible. After proceeding for one kilometre, the counter-narcotic kandak and its American mentors on the left flank started taking casualties, leaving 2nd (Strike) kandak exposed. The kandak headquarters, accompanied by the remains of Weapons Company in its Hummers, moved to replace the screen as the advance continued. Needless to say, it was unusual for a headquarters element to be providing flank security. Maj Nolan attempted to coordinate the TF WARTHOG mentors' activities with the British OMLT commander, but had no success because of the communications problems. He was, however, able to communicate with the kandak echelon and bring two OMLT SECFOR RG-31s from Lashkar Gah to assist with the screen.

The Afghan Border Police then started taking casualties, so a casualty collection point (CCP) was established. Two U.S. Air Force A-10s arrived on the scene, but communications between the British Joint Terminal Air Controller (JTAC) and the aircraft also broke down. The Canadian OMLT, however, had good communications and could relay through to the fighter-bombers. The same thing happened when a pair of U.S. Army AH-64 Apache gun-ships came in to support. It was clear to the Canadian OMLT personnel that the British OMLT and elements had lost control of their part of the operation right off the start line.

Then 1st Company was ambushed from a cornfield three kilometres into the sweep. In this case, the Taliban stayed and fought from their positions, firing PKM machine-guns and RPGs at the Afghans and Canadians. One RPG narrowly missed the OMLT-eers while the ANA engaged the position. 3rd Company stopped its advance to stay in line with 1st Company while this shoot-out was in progress in order to prevent a 'green on green' incident. A Canadian officer then got on the radio trying to vector in the AH-64s but was having problems determining what the Forward Line of Own Troops (FLOT) was. Once that was established, the attack helicopters made several 'gun runs' on the cornfield positions, killing more than 20 Taliban. There were so many dead that the enemy did not have the resources to remove them (as was their SOP) to deny the coalition an accurate battle-damage assessment.

When the OMLT assessed what was happening, they realized that staying off the roads had disrupted the enemy's defensive plan which was based on IED-initiated ambushes at vehicular choke-points. The Afghans had unseated the overall enemy defensive posture in the district. Taliban forces started withdrawing when they figured out what was going on and this part of the battle devolved into a series of small-scale, running gunfights all day long. Even the kandak headquarters that was screening the right flank was 'bumped' as the enemy tried to get out of the way of the onslaught, firing a number of RPGs at the Rangers, Hummers and RG-31s, but to no effect.

The Afghans and Canadians were four kilometres in when they had another strong contact at 1200 hours. By this time, the AH-64s had withdrawn, something that usually emboldened the enemy to manoeuvre as they did not have to worry about 'the mosquitoes' overhead. 1st Company started taking fire but a canal system separating the two companies prevented 3rd Company from manoeuvring to assist. ISTAR reportage passed down from higher headquarters informed the coalition forces that the enemy was reinforcing with a mobile team consisting of two trucks equipped with 82mm recoilless rifle teams, and that there was a large enemy Strongpoint to the west of this firefight. The composite kandak headquarters/weapons company/SECFOR screen then moved east and re-oriented itself to fire onto the Strongpoint while 1st Company poured on the fire. Then an uncoordinated move into the area by the Afghan Border Police and their American mentors forced the ANA to stop firing in order to prevent a 'green on green' incident. 1st Company then moved up and fought through the enemy position down to the 875 northing, while 3rd Company moved south to the 86 northing, again to keep the line dressed.

The kandak reached Ynak around 1600 hours, where it assumed a defensive posture in a series of compound complexes. The headquarters was in a cluster of compounds in the centre, surrounded by three company groupings arranged in compounds around the headquarters. 2nd (Strike) kandak sent out aggressive night-ambush patrols into the dead ground around the positions to discourage enemy infiltration. There was a lot of ANA fire at night but the mentors suspected it was mostly 'spec' fire[8] since the ANA did not have night-vision equipment.

As Maj Nolan returned to Lashkar Gah for orders, re-supply activities were conducted by the ANA echelon and the SECFOR. Forty RPG rounds, intended for the 3rd Brigade kandak which had hardly fired any, 'found' their way to replenish 2nd (Strike) kandak's depleted stocks. On arrival at the headquarters in Lashkar Gah, Maj Nolan was invited to sit in where he learned that the plan now involved a major push into the Nawa District Centre. Two British infantry companies from the British Battlegroup were now going to be part of the operation, thrusting into Nawa to relieve the beleaguered Patrol Base BERMUDA in town but, again, there was little apparent coordination between them, the various OMLTs and the kandaks coming down from the north. On the plus side, better ISTAR reportage was coming in to the British Tactical Operations Centre and was disseminated. The enemy force engaged by 2nd (Strike) kandak and its mentors was estimated at 150 insurgents.

The Canadians were shocked not only to discover that, after fighting all day for five kilometres, a nearly twenty-kilometre thrust was planned, but also that the U.K. OMLT was not, in fact, mentoring the 3rd Brigade planning staff or its Executive Officer. It was not clear who exactly was running the operation at all at this point, but 3rd kandak from the 3rd Brigade would move along the Helmand River. The three kandaks from the Home Special Security Brigade would run down the centre (see map: the battle-space broadens out at this point), while 2nd (Strike) kandak was to handle the right flank to the west. At the same time, Camp Bastion's staff was screaming for SITREPS from the OCC-P and wanted the Canadian OMLT to send them to the OCC-P, but the OMLT had no communications with the OCC-P. They also learned there was no higher-level battle-tracking but, in informal discussions, determined that an estimated 63 enemy were dead and 100 wounded.

In a surreal turn of events, Maj Nolan and the kandak leadership then met with Governor Gulab Mangal who, out of the blue, publicly awarded them all marble vases and two-kilometre tracts of land in Helmand Province out of gratitude for their efforts. Governor Mangal was happy and impressed that the coalition forces had pushed the Taliban away from the city. The plan for the next day was then played out in an elaborate ROC drill (Rehearsal of Concept drill) conducted by the Afghan commanders – with the media filming it! The Afghan Border Police was to handle flank security, while the HSSB and its U.S. mentors (call-sign DRAGON) would move down the centre.

A Canadian was detached to act as a liaison officer to them.

The primary 2nd (Strike) kandak modes of transport were Ford Ranger trucks (right) and un-armoured Hummers (above) equipped with a variety of crew-served weapons, including Dhska 12.7 machine-guns and PKM medium machine-guns.

2nd (Strike) kandak would be sandwiched between the two, while 3rd kandak, 3rd Brigade would move along the river.

The importance of this operation cannot be underestimated. No ANA-led operation of this scale had previously been attempted during the conflict. There were six battalion-sized units operating alongside each other, with perhaps the equivalent of two battalions of coalition forces mentoring and manoeuvring. Virtually none of the control measures used by NATO forces (phase-lines, report-lines, code-worded objective areas) were in use. To make matters even more interesting, the operation would be conducted out of range of artillery support from positions east of Lashkar Gah. There were even limited ISR resources because of distances and weather. In other words, this was a high-risk operation on all levels, from tactical up to political; and it was Afghan-led.

Maj Nolan had, by this time, brought the bulk of the 'QRF', consisting of SECFOR RG-31s led by MCpl Pink and Cpl Kippenhuck in their RG-31, forward to a leaguer. 2nd (Strike) kandak moved to the line of departure for an

Ford Ranger trucks with ANA soldiers preparing to depart.

0600 H-Hour, but did not cross until 0830. By 1113 hours, both 1st and 3rd Companies were taking enemy fire: 1st Company from the east and 3rd Company from the west. Cpl Latta, MCpl Pink and Cpl Kippenhuck, plus a medic, followed 1st Company. The initial contacts determined that the enemy were spread out in small defensive locations and were just blazing away with a single 82mm recoilless rifle and whatever automatic weapons they had. The Afghan Border Police working with 1st Company took cover under a bridge, except for a two-man police 82mm recoilless rifle team who stood exposed on the footbridge and who engaged the enemy 82mm successfully with several rounds.

The American Police Mentoring Team (PMT) mentors, in three Hummers trailing behind 2nd kandak and to the east, suddenly opened fire, at a two-kilometre range, at 1st Company and the Afghan Border Police (ABP). Maj Steve Nolan and 2nd kandak executive officer ran in front of the mentors waving their arms to get them to stop firing their Mk-19 grenade-launchers at the Afghans and Canadians while the Company Sergeant Major (CSM) pounded on the hoods of the American vehicles to get their attention. A 'blue on green' was narrowly averted.

The Taliban, meanwhile, went firm all along the 82 northing in an effort to delay the coalition forces. When they did withdraw under pressure, they did so behind a shower of RPG airburst rounds. 1st Company fought through a number of objectives and started to clear within its boundaries. Wounded and killed Afghan soldiers were evacuated to the casualty collection point at the rear, in Ranger pick-ups. When Maj Nolan, the kandak CO and his operations officer then moved forward with a police commander to gain an appreciation of the situation, a burst of enemy 7.62mm fire was directed at them. Two Afghan soldiers were wounded, one to the right and the other to the left of Maj Nolan, leaving the OMLT team commander and the kandak commander unscathed.

The compound sweeps were turning up nothing of value and, in time, there was no contact with enemy forces. They appeared to have melted away. It appeared as though between 150 and 200 insurgents opposed 2nd (Strike) kandak's advance on Day 2.

By 1500 hours, the weather was blisteringly hot and the kandak was running out of water. This forced the Afghan soldiers to use canal- and well-water to rehydrate. The Canadian mentors also had dry Camelbaks. The force reached the 785 northing when the higher leadership ordered all of the kandaks to move to the centre axis. The personnel from nearly six kandak-equivalents and their vehicles were now forced to converge on the Nawa district centre. Then the problems started.

The British maintained Patrol Base BERMUDA in the Nawa District Centre. It had been under siege, its occupants had endured regular attacks and they had been living on hard rations for some time. They had had little contact with the outside world and the high levels of local political and security-force corruption limited the amount of information the BERMUDA defenders had on what was going on. The Patrol Base itself was in a state of collapse, with no power and no defensive run-ups. The mentors and their charges did not have their overnight kit with them, only what was in their load-bearing vests and pockets. The kit was back in Ynak with the echelon.

There was no higher-level plan for refuelling, food or quartering once the Afghan and coalition forces got into Nawa. The kandak echelon was way back in Ynak and since there was no constant coalition presence along the route between there and Nawa, it was essentially cut off from its forward elements as the enemy started to lay IEDs in behind the coalition forces. A plan whereby the police would backfill the echelon had not been put into effect and it was evident from ISTAR reportage that the insurgents were moving back into the area from the west. To make matters worse, there was a 'green on green' between the HSSB and the 3rd Brigade kandak. When the Canadian mentors were asked to intervene, they learned that the American mentors with the HSSB had standing orders from Kabul to mentor from their seven Cougar vehicles but not to get out of them. The Canadian mentors were able to calm down the situation between the agitated Afghans.

Exfiltration: Getting Home is Half the Fun

The temperature in Nawa dropped to below zero at night. After fighting and sweating all day, and not having access to bedding other than some pieces of cardboard, the mentors and the Afghans were in danger of hypothermia. As it was warmer in the handful of British vehicles than in the building (which was virtually roofless and open to the elements) the soldiers took turns inside them. The British defenders of BERMUDA provided what they could. A giant piece of hessian acted as a blanket of sorts for the 20 mentors trying to sleep.

The primary problems confronting the mentors and their counterparts in the morning was: how to get resupplied; how to get the echelon safely back to Lashkar Gah; and how to get the whole force in Nawa safely back to Lashkar Gah. There was no food to speak of. A plan to establish a security 'tunnel' from Nawa to Ynak foundered when the Afghans would not go back up the road the way they came because of the threat. Three uncoordinated resupply columns, one for the HSSB, one for the 3rd Brigade kandak, and another for 2nd (Strike) kandak, were eventually sent out from Lashkar Gah but all three got bogged in the desert; all three extricated and returned to Lashkar Gah. When Maj Nolan asked the British commanders if he could get helicopters, he was told there were no helicopters available for the Canadians. The only other option was to get on the back of the unarmoured Afghan trucks and ride out. Then British CH-47 Chinook helicopters arrived to remove U.K. OMLT personnel. The British liaison officer visibly shrank when the helicopters landed in the HLS to take out the British mentors. Higher Afghan command then ordered 2nd (Strike) kandak to withdraw with the HSSB. The Canadians decided to go with them.

The exfiltration was a bad go. There was still no consensus as to whether the force should wait for food and then exfiltrate, or exfiltrate and then be resupplied. By 1500 hours, the decision was made to get out via the desert to the east on the other side of the river. 2nd kandak's International trucks and Rangers followed the HSSB column down to the 7069 northing and crossed a track into the Khotoki district wasteland.

The weather was hot and dry. Tired and hungry troops bogged vehicle after vehicle and it started getting dark. Then the HSSB mentors' Cougar MRAPs started to bog, one after another, and there were discussions about leaving the vehicles behind and blowing them up in place. 7-ton Internationals were outpaced by the Ranger pick-up trucks which produced an elongated, but truncated, column. Three hours later, the force reached a pass through a mountainous area. Communications failed completely, presenting a serious hazard. A large force moving through the desert effectively out of communications could come under air attack. Every soldier who had a helmet-mounted infrared strobe switched it on and prayed the batteries would last until morning. The temperature then dropped and clusters of soldiers huddled together for warmth in the pass. As an MQ-9 Reaper UAV orbited above as top cover, the troops collected brambles into large piles to act as insulation for emergency blankets. It was, as one of the mentors put it, "The longest night of my life out there in the desert".

As soon as the sun was up, the force drove north to cross the Arghandab River at the 84 northing where scouts found an ancient ford. The OMLT-eers moved to secure it and coordinated the crossing on the fly. In no time, 2nd (Strike) kandak was back at the Afghan National Civil Order Police (ANCOP) station in Lashkar Gah. By this time, Colonel Shipley had grabbed several Bisons and AHSVSs to bring food, water and amenities from Mas'um Ghar to Lashkar Gah. The British supply system, it turned out, had no Halal rations,[9] so some were scrounged from American and Canadian sources. The Ynak group was forced to buy gas from the local bazaar to keep their generators going and they were able to return to Lashkar Gah without incident.

2nd (Strike) kandak and its mentors then moved to FOB Price past the grim remains of six newly IED'd trucks. The camp's capacity was overwhelmed with 600 additional visitors, but the staff was able to provide good meals before the force proceeded back to FOB Mas'um Ghar. The mentors then prepared to head back to Kandahar Air Field on leave but were subsequently IED'd on the trip down the highway. There were, fortunately, no casualties other than the Remote Weapons System.

Conclusion

In the 'hot wash up' that followed, the 'lessons identified' were many. The main tactical issue was the lack of planning relating to securing lines of communication behind the sweep south. There was no larger plan to hold the area after it had been cleared. This may have been related to the contingency nature of the operation and the pressing need to push enemy forces away from Lashkar Gah as expeditiously as possible. The operation was successful from that perspective. The operation highlighted deficiencies in communications and logistics. This is not surprising in that the ANA kandaks had been virtually pushed out the door for the Kabul Military Training Centre (KMTC) armed with their combat skills, but communications and logistics had been a secondary training priority. The list of other deficiencies was a long one, prominent among which were the lack of counter-IED capability and the lack of battle-tracking by the staff.

That said, the operation was the largest attempted by Afghan forces in the past seven years and it did succeed in its objectives. Just as important was that the operation was seen to be successful by outside observers. The

Maj Steve Nolan with his interpreter "Froggy" at FOB Mas'um Ghar prior to an OMLT-mentored operation.

enemy was pushed out of Lashkar Gah and out of the adjacent district. The negative psychological effects that an enemy siege of the provincial capital was generating among the population, and also in the international media, were challenging – an effect not to be underestimated in the type of war being fought in Afghanistan. Operation BIA ITNAMAAN was a strategic accomplishment despite the myriad tactical, procedural and technical problems encountered. The ANA demonstrated that it could conduct combat operations at a Second World War tactical level and that it could even handle brigade-sized operations, at least to a certain extent. They had been incapable of this three years earlier. It must also be said that the problematic British mentoring was related to the fact that the U.K. OMLT had only been on the ground for two weeks, was not acclimatized and had not built up that rapport with their counterparts that is necessary for trusted operations.

The deployment of 2nd (Strike) kandak from Panjwayi district, however, stripped forces away from a critical district that was undergoing counterinsurgency and development operations that depended on a high troop density. Those operations had to be curtailed which, in turn, produced 'knock on' effects over time for the Canadian area of operations. It was, in a number of ways, reminiscent of operations in the summer of 2006: who should decide what the priority is when the enemy mounts 'spectacular' operations in Helmand? Is Helmand the priority province, or is Kandahar? Does the need to respond spectacularly to an enemy 'spectacular' trump long-term counterinsurgency and development operations? Is that the effect the enemy (or others) wants to generate?

British dispositions in Helmand contributed to the need to strip kandaks from Kandahar province. The Canadian mentors believed that British forces were wedded to their tactical infrastructure and that the U.K. OMLT-ANA combination was used for more mobile tasks. This was, perhaps, backwards. It did present an 'Afghan face' in such operations, but at the expense of contact with the population on a day-to-day basis. Indeed, some mentors believed that the re-designation of 2nd kandak was engineered (or at least exploited) in order to cater to British needs, and not to Canadian or Afghan requirements. As Maj Steve Nolan explained, "The OMLT is all about friction. The two gears are ISAF and the ANA and we're the oil."

Notes

1   This piece is based on discussions held between the author and the participants of these operations at FOB Mas'um Ghar in January-February 2009. I would like to thank Maj Steve Nolan, Capt Sean French, MCpl Steve Pink and Cpl Conrad Kippenhuck.

2   See "Operational Manoeuvre Group: Operation SOHIL LARAM II" chapter 7.

3   Note that portions of the tactical infrastructure were not located near centres where the population was concentrated along the 'TI' protected routes. Consequently, many 'security bubbles' were of limited effect on the population as a whole, particularly in Panjwayi district.

4   Technically, this is called CERP money or Commander's Emergency Response Project funding. Canada's equivalent is the Commander's Contingency Fund.

5   Note that the presence of the LST is one of the things that differentiates ETTs from OMLTs. The OMLT has no LST equivalent and cannot fund HA or CIMIC-type projects.

6   See "Panjwayi Alamo: The Defence of Strongpoint Mushan".

7   ANCOP stands for Afghan National Civil Order Police, a nationally controlled police force that handles the Focused District Development process.

8   Speculative fire or 'spec fire' is used to engage areas likely to have enemy present but without positive identification of enemy forces.

9   These are rations that meet Islamic standards for preparation.

Cpl Eric Frandsen and a British colleague keep an eye out for enemy movements. (courtesy Sean French)

Chapter Twelve
Action at Spin Masjed:
The Canadian OMLT and the
Afghan National Army
in Helmand Province, January 2009

The success of Operation BIA ITNAMAAN back in October 2008 did not mean that the insurgent threat to the Lashkar Gah area was eradicated. Indeed, what was euphemistically referred to as Operation BIA ITNAMAAN Phase IV still had to run its course in the wake of the October operations. Phase IV was designed to bring governance to areas that had been subjected to clearance operations. This generally meant the establishment of an Afghan National Police presence complete with checkpoints and policing facilities, in the hope that Provincial Reconstruction Team elements could assess a given area for inclusion in development projects. The focus for Phase IV was generally on the districts west of Lashkar Gah.

There was also the looming country-wide Voter Registration security operation. Strategically, the country needed a legitimate electoral process to maintain legitimacy, knowing full well that this time the enemy would pull out all the stops to interfere with it in order to deny legitimacy to the government. Detailed country-wide voter-registration plans were ready for activation, but the necessity for a massive security presence, coupled with disruptive coalition operations to put the insurgents back on their heels, was obvious. The planning for that had been underway for months in anticipation of the 2009 elections, especially in the volatile south.

As before, enemy activity in Helmand province, coupled with the nature of the British-led coalition deployment, resulted in the decision to deploy 2nd (Strike) kandak once again. Indicators pointed to a build-up of enemy in the Spin Masjed area south of Highway 1, but this time between FOB Prince and Lashkar Gah. If this build-up reached a critical mass and Highway 1 was cut, there was the possibility that the forces engaged in Operation BIA ITNA-MAAN Phase IV would have to suspend their operations and race back to deal with that situation. The enemy would move back into those areas to the west and start at Lashkar Gah all over again, as they had in October. The idea that operations in Kandahar should take second place to those in Helmand loomed once again in the internal ISAF debate. The decision was made to weight the Helmand operations at the expense of those in Kandahar. The result was that voter-registration security operations in Kandahar province would have to be suspended as 2nd (Strike) kandak was to have played a role in those protection plans. The second Helmand deployment, consequently, was seriously opposed by Task Force Kandahar.

In the end, the 'Helmand First' proponents got their way and part of 2nd (Strike) kandak was made available for operations in Helmand. The British wanted the kandak for two weeks, but the kandak leadership said they would go for five days. The debate over how long 2nd (Strike) kandak would be in Helmand continued even while the operation was in progress.

Spin Masjed

A helicopter reconnaissance of the Spin Masjed area conducted on the day before the operation laid out the ground for the Afghan commanders and the Canadian mentors. As with most terrain in southern Afghanistan 'green belts', it was complex and irregular. Spin Masjed sits on the Nahr-e Bughra Canal, a substantial watercourse that traverses the entire Helmand River Valley from the Kajaki Dam to Nimroz province. Densely packed agricultural and residential areas are sandwiched between the canal and the Helmand River and, in the Spin Masjed area, the depth of the green belt varies from two to four kilometres. An unpaved highway parallels the canal to the south, leading from Geresk to Lashkar Gah.

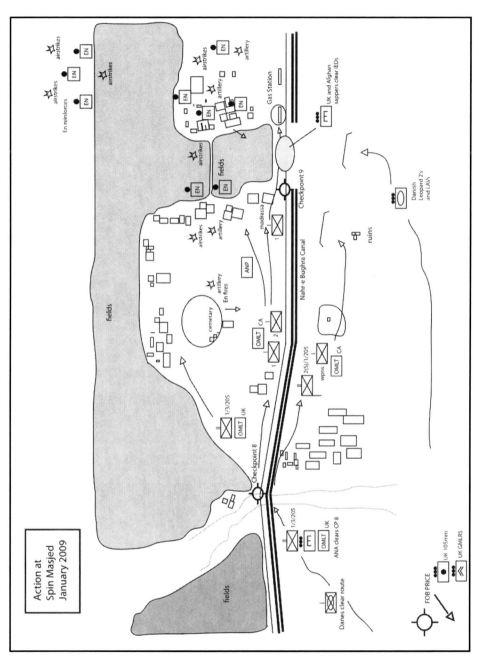

Action at Spin Masjed, January 2009.

The Spin Masjed Operating area from the air, facing east. FOB Price is to the east, with the Gas Station to the west (bottom of photo). The canal is clearly delineated, as are the crossing-points. (courtesy Sean French)

The canal itself is a formidable obstacle, as it is made from concrete and is usually full of water. Spin Masjed was one of two crossing-points in the area (the canal flows underground for about 500m here) while, three kilometres to the east, a wadi crosses above the canal. The ground to the north is arid and, compared to the green belt, sparsely populated. To the south, Spin Masjed is split in two by fields, with numerous compound complexes and growing areas east and west of the fields.

Consequently, the 3rd Brigade commander, General Mohaiyodin Ghori, wanted to mount an operation to clear and hold two crossing-points on the canal in order to re-build the checkpoints, and then to re-establish a police presence in the Spin Masjid area. The warning order, when translated into English, baldly stated "Destroy the Taliban, erase Taliban checkpoints and clear the area". The problem for General Ghori was that the kandaks in 3rd Brigade were numerically depleted and the British forces were occupying tactical infrastructure spread out all over the province. 205 Corps agreed to a request from 3rd Brigade to send forces from Kandahar province.

2nd (Strike) kandak was instructed to deploy to Forward Operating Base PRICE west of Geresk from where the operation would be mounted. The kandak and its mentors would receive their final orders there. The plan lacked clarity in some key areas, however. The exact locations where the checkpoints would be constructed were not determined prior to the operation, but just the general area that the forces would manoeuvre into. The Brigade XO would determine where the new checkpoints would be, based on how the situation unfolded. The enemy situation was vague, though initial analysis from 3rd Brigade was that "It's peaceful there".

Maj Steve Nolan was on leave by this time, so Capt Sean French was acting Officer Commanding for "72". Capt French learned that 1st Brigade was initially going to permit one infantry company and the kandak weapons company to participate in the Helmand province operation. This was later increased to two infantry companies, 1st and 2nd, plus weapons company led by Second Lieutenant (2Lt) Sayed Agha. The Weapons Company left most of its SPG-9 recoilless rifles and mortars at home and these platoons operated as regular infantry. The Hummers with the DshKa machine-guns, however, were brought along. Recce Platoon brought its Ranger 'techicals'.

Maj Hasrat, Capt Sean French, and Froggy at south east corner of Spin Masjed (courtesy Sean French)

This force, mounted in over 40 vehicles, would be led by the 2nd (Strike) kandak XO and mentored by "72". SMaj Dave Fisher would accompany Capt French; the 1st Company mentor team included Capt Ross Binnel; and the 2nd Company team was led by Capt Dave Andrews. The Weapons Company was mentored by Capt Chuck Pitkin and his men. Once again, SECFOR would backfill with their RG-31s and crews.

Command and control arrangements would differ from those used in Operation BIA ITNAMAAN. The Danish Battlegroup, the 1st Battalion Jutland Dragoons Regiment, was technically in charge of the area of operations but, in this case, the U.K. OMLT mentoring 3rd Brigade of the ANA deployed a forward headquarters and co-located it with the Danes in FOB PRICE to help the Afghan brigade headquarters run this battle. The Canadian OMLT was supposedly under the tactical control of the British Battlegroup and not the U.K. OMLT; but for practical purposes the Canadians had little or no contact with the British Battlegroup and worked with the U.K. OMLT. Unlike the operations in October, the Canadians were self-sustaining this time, with armoured AHSVS trucks and better communications links back to Kandahar with a command variant Bison. The British did, however, provide counter-IED, medical and indirect-fire resources to the Canadian OMLT, as required.

Deployment

On arrival at FOB PRICE on 10 January 2009, the Canadian mentors and the kandak command staff were given a British briefing that reminded those present of 'a Second World War movie using old mannerisms and terminology like FLOT (Forward Line of Own Troops]'. Phase-lines were drawn on the map and it looked everything like a conventional operation against conventional forces. The incoming forces learned that a militia, and not the ANP, had been manning the original checkpoints. When the tribal grouping or clan that had been hired to do the job had not been paid for some time. Most of them just walked away, leaving a small number behind. The Taliban overwhelmed both checkpoints, executed the remaining militia and levelled the bunkers.

The 3rd Brigade plan had matured to some extent by the time the Canadians arrived. A Danish force would clear from FOB PRICE to the former Checkpoint 8 on the edge of the target area and then hand off to the ANA kandaks who would push through the Danes. About 100 ANP officers were to be attached to 2nd (Strike) kandak as well. A kandak from 3rd Brigade would handle operations around Checkpoint 8 while 2nd (Strike) kandak pushed south and south-west towards the former Checkpoint 9 at Spin Masjed. Given the terrain, however, both sides of the canal needed to be swept, which separated the forces. The decision was made to have the headquarters vehicles and the Weapons Company north of the canal to support the dismounted sweep of the companies south of the canal. The companies would rendezvous with Weapons Company and headquarters at Spin Masjed. Notably, the ANA plan included the distribution of humanitarian aid to the local population by the kandaks and the police. There was also a PSYOPS plan linked to the humanitarian aid distribution. At the last minute, a section of un-mentored Afghan National Police was attached to each kandak company.

At 0630 hours on 11 January, the Danish mechanized infantry force mounted in M-113 APCs and its accompanying combat engineers proceeded out of the gates of FOB PRICE and initiated their sweep down to where Checkpoint 8 used to be. No contact was made as the force cleared the five-kilometre route. 2nd (Strike) kandak took up a leaguer position north-west of the former Checkpoint 8 as the 1st kandak, 3rd Brigade, moved up past the Danes to clear the site. An ANA engineer detachment, using rented construction equipment, followed. Unfortunately, the excavator they were using to re-construct the checkpoint struck an IED, disabling it. The other excavator was unserviceable back in FOB PRICE. Bobcat tractors did what they could to clear the rubble and erect Hescobastion barricades.

While 1st kandak moved off, 2nd (Strike) kandak swung into action. The southern component stepped off from the leaguer, passed through the Checkpoint 8 area and started to sweep to the west along the canal; 2nd Company was in the lead with 1st Company trailing. Weapons Company and the Headquarters proceeded along the north side.

2nd (Strike) kandak and Canadian OMLT depart FOB Price for Spin Masjed (courtesy Sean French)

Manoeuvre to Contact

The southern sweep zone consisted of complex and congested terrain. Working east to west and south of the canal, the terrain was dominated by several clusters of compound complexes all along the canal, with a cemetery in the centre. Then there was a substantial dry wadi followed by more clusters of compounds. Some low hills lay to the south. Given the time of year, there was not a lot of groundcover; the fields were empty which made it much easier to identify and engage enemy movement. Similarly, the cooler weather, down to zero degrees at night, improved thermal-imager optics and improved the capability for night engagements. The downside was the constant off-and-on rain that manifested itself throughout the operation.

2nd Company encountered the edges of the cemetery and the compounds around it as they swept through. The company commander decided to check the area out and wait for the ANA force on the north side to catch up. As the reconnoitre went forward, it triggered an insurgent ambush from compounds south of the cemetery. Other enemy forces panicked and started firing on 2nd Company from a madrassa to the west, thus revealing the enemy dispositions that were designed to pour enfilading fire onto the Afghan company if it charged the compounds to the south. 2nd Company went firm and started firing back. 1st Company moved up the road to assist with indirect fire support, aviation and close air-support. The lead U.K. forward observation team was co-located with 1st Company and had access to: British 105mm guns back at the FOB; Danish 60m mortars located back at Checkpoint 8; and British GMLRS. British AH-64 Longbow Apaches were inbound as well. The vast amount of available fire-support for this operation was a result of the British OMLT's 'lessons learned' process after the October 2008 operations south of Lashkar Gah.

While 1st and 2nd Company were engaging the enemy south of the canal and 105mm artillery fire was crashing down from FOB PRICE, Weapons Company and the kandak headquarters moved west into a ruined village, while three Danish Leopard 2 tanks and two Danish LAVs manoeuvred north of the wadi, prepared to provide direct fire-support; the tanks fired a number of 120mm rounds against enemy positions. Two of the Weapons Company hummers and two RG-31s from the SECFOR equipped with .50 cal and 7.62mm Remote Weapons Systems deployed to assist 1st Company, if required. The firing ebbed and flowed for the remainder of the day.

Tragically, the recce platoon leader, Lt Zalmi Khan, became a casualty. It was prayer time and Lt Khan searched for the mosque's ablution facility to cleanse his body as part of his five daily prayer rituals. The insurgents, however, laid a booby trap at the ablution site. It detonated and blew off both of Khan's legs and one of his hands. An ANA vehicle evacuated him to the leaguer where he was treated by Canadian medics, and then a British helicopter arrived to evacuate him to hospital. The loss of this respected leader had a demoralizing effect on Weapons Company which the mentors had to deal with. An ISTAR report of an explosion from the enemy lines revealed that an insurgent had a negligent discharge with an IED, killing three of his colleagues. It was seen as poetic justice.

These incidents forced an immediate re-examination of the battle area for IEDs. It turned out that all of the approach routes to the former Checkpoint 9 were IED'd. The Danish tank troop was wary of any further forward movement, so decided to withdraw back to FOB PRICE.[1] The Danish liaison officer with 2nd (Strike) kandak HQ also decided that he did not want to stay in the field so he walked back on his own to the Danish force back at Checkpoint 8, to the amazement of the Canadian mentors. British counter-IED teams were brought in and started clearing from Checkpoint 8 west along the canal. 1st Company identified four IEDs alone on the road leading up to the Spin Masjed crossing-point.

As night fell on day one, the plan changed. The destruction of the Afghan excavator back at Checkpoint 8 really slowed reconstruction down. Bobcats and bulldozers were brought in, along with more Afghan National Army engineer assets who were accompanied by British mentors. LCol Shareen Shah, the 3rd Brigade operations officer (and former 2nd kandak commander) decided to hold in location and wait for the IED clearance operations to be completed so the forces forward could be re-supplied (again, another lesson learned after the October 2008 operations). 1st Company occupied the madrassa complex while the un-mentored ANP unit moved in next door to an adjacent complex to the south.

12 January 2009

The Danish Leopards came back to their firing positions north of the crossing-point, while two more Canadian RG-31s joined the Weapons Company Hummers and the mentor's RG-31s in position to the west.

Danish Leopard 2s supported the coalition effort around Spin Masjed.
(Danish Ministry of Defence)

Early in the morning, the insurgents initiated a conventional assault on the 1st Company and ANP-occupied compounds. The series of enemy-occupied compounds to the west suddenly erupted with a high volume of small-arms fire, while four enemy groups of six or seven fighters attempted a right flanking on the ANP-occupied compound. It appeared to the Canadians that these small groups were operating in a dispersed fashion and 'hugging' coalition defensive positions so that it would be difficult to bring artillery down on them. These attacks were repelled by the Afghan defenders and eventually petered out. The Canadian mentors watched with amusement as an Afghan policeman stood on the roof of a compound house, danced, taunted and made faces at the insurgents. The Taliban opened fire trying to hit him, which gave away some of their firing positions.

Having had enough of this static firefight, the 1st Company commander decided to move in their Ranger pick-up trucks across the wadi, without support, in order to gain a foothold in the western compounds. Amazingly, the trucks made it across without detonating what turned out to be numerous IEDs that the enemy had laid to screen their defensive position. 2nd Company then moved to a blocking position to the south of the graveyard. They tried to encourage the enemy to engage them so artillery and aviation could be brought to bear, but the Taliban did not bite. Indeed, the enemy kept probing 2nd Company, but fire discipline was good and the Afghans did not reveal their positions.

Across the canal, Weapons Company was in a leaguer and the mentors were un-bogging an RG-31. The vehicle was pinged with small-arms fire and the Afghans and Canadians saw the enemy firing tracers in short bursts, looping towards the leaguer. "Goggles", an ANA Dshka gunner in a Hummer, fired entire boxes of ammunition, seemingly at random. When asked what he was shooting at, he replied, "The muzzle flashes! What else?"

Around 1730, insurgents succeeded in getting into some of the compounds in the south. The ANP poured out of their compound and pulled back north into the madrassa. A B-1B was on station and authorized to engage; it dropped two 500-pound and one 1000-pound JDAMS. ISTAR reportage passed on to the mentors indicated that all enemy communication from that area ceased after the air strike, and did not resume. Insurgent attempts to re-establish communications with that element continued throughout the day and night, but to no avail.

British sappers worked throughout the night to restore freedom of movement between Checkpoint 8 and the madrassa and from the madrassa across the wadi to the Afghan elements on the west side. This permitted resupply operations, particularly of badly needed ammo. In time, the Weapons Company was able to get a vehicle loaded with ammo and food across the narrow, cleared lane in the wadi. The sappers determined that every single possible approach route in the area was IED'd with pressure plate IEDs and that the 1st Company elements were lucky to be alive. This thin lifeline, however, needed to be broadened so that operations could continue – and that would take time. All in all, the British sappers BIP'd[2] (Blow in Place) sixteen IEDs just to cross the wadi.

1st Company shook out on the west side into better positions. The insurgents then set up in a school and started firing RPGs and small arms at the 1st Company elements. The British forward observers brought the 105mm guns and 60mm mortars rounds onto the enemy firing positions. U.K. Harriers were FAC'd (Forward Air Controller) in and dropped 500- and 1000-pound bombs. One bomb missed (probably a fin error) and landed 800m from Weapons Company/HQ leaguer north of the canal, "scaring the crap out of everybody".

13 January 2009

ISTAR reportage during the night indicated that a new Taliban group was moving in and trying to link up with the one that was already engaging the coalition forces. It turned out that the new group was trying to bolster the resolve of these fighters, who had had enough and wanted to retire. In effect, they were ordered to stay in place, or else. The enemy moved back into the school just in time to receive two JDAMS; one missed, but the second hit dead-on. ISTAR reportage indicated the enemy lost the equivalent of a platoon in that strike, disrupting their plan to take on the 1st Company elements.

The plan for Day 3 was to push two ANA platoons along the north side of the canal, west past the wadi and then have the remaining two platoons from 1st Company cross the wadi and link up with their western-most elements. The British sappers had, by this time, moved into the site of former Checkpoint 9 and discovered four IEDs on approach routes. Another sapper team back at Checkpoint 8 uncovered another three IEDs around where the excavator was hit. Both teams set about clearing their respective sites.

During a lull in the shooting, an Afghan engineer team, using comparatively primitive hand-held equipment, cleared another lane across the wadi. A platoon from 1st Company, moving west, secured a gas station and set up there. A British forward observation team and two Canadian RG-31s loaded with mentors crossed in behind them to link up with that platoon; they drove across the wadi at night in cleared lanes marked by the engineers with green glow-sticks. To confuse matters further, a platoon from the 3rd Brigade kandak also crossed the wadi and situated itself in a compound complex south-east of the gas station. There were no communications between that platoon and 2nd (Strike) kandak. Then one of the Afghan policemen, moving between the gas station and a compound, triggered an IED, which decapitated him. The Afghans, Canadian and British soldiers went to ground and did not move about that night.

14 January 2009

Heavy fog greeted the forces in and around Spin Masjed on the morning of 14 January. The visibility was limited to 150m for the Afghan forces, who did not possess thermal-imaging equipment. This was where the Canadian RG-31s played a significant role with the RWS's optical systems sweeping the area despite the roiling fog. The fog also provided cover for a counter-IED team to move forward and augment the clearance effort. The first contact came in at 1400 hours; an aerial platform spotted enemy forces to the south and they were subsequently engaged. This event served as a trigger for enemy forces located in a school south-west of the main Spin Masjed compound complexes nearest to the gas station to open fire with machine-guns. Then two more enemy positions decided to open up so three-way, long-range converging fire rained onto the ANA platoons and coalition forces near the gas station. All were promptly JDAM'd (Joint Direct Attack Munition) for their troubles with the fire controlled by the JTACs on the gas station roof.

Once one enemy position was hit, it would go quiet; then the next position was hit, and it went quiet; then the enemy reinforced the first position which had started up again and was JDAM'd again, and so on. The Afghans loaded up with RPGs, just waiting for targets to present themselves; but in time, the enemy commanders thought better of wasting more of their men by pushing them into what amounted to a JDAM meat-grinder.

A volley of six RPGs was fired against the Afghans, who eagerly responded in kind. By this time, the engineers had blown thirteen IEDs in the wadi, permitting SMaj Fisher and three RG-31s to move forward to the west where they promptly got into a TIC when a small enemy force opened up on them with small-arms fire. The enemy believed that the C-IED detonations were real strikes against coalition vehicles and they started to rejoice, until they were JDAM'd again.

Back at Checkpoint 8, the Afghans saw enemy observers to the west, so they prepared to push Weapons Company forward. By this time, however, the Danish tanks had withdrawn and, given the lack of a firebase and as it was getting dark, this course of action was not undertaken. Once night fell, a small group of insurgents were seen moving around and were engaged with .50 cals from the RG-31s and a few artillery rounds.

The Defence of the Gas Station

Initially, three Canadian mentors found themselves in the white-painted gas station (Capt Binell, Pte Johnson and Cpl Clayton Macklean) along with three British forward observers. They were later joined by a mix of mentors and, from SECFOR, by MCpl Cox, Cpl Rail (a medic) and Pte Cutler. After the policeman was killed, the Afghan engineers cleared around the gas station and found seven more pressure-plate IEDs. The mentors manoeuvred their RG-31s so that the 7.62 mm and .50 cal Remote Weapons Systems could be brought to bear over a wall while protecting the body of the vehicles, and the U.K. gunner's land rover, equipped with two 7.62mm GPMGs, was re-positioned to improve its arcs. Using a field-expedient ladder constructed from steel and bamboo that was laying around, the teams established machine-gun positions on the roof of the gas station, facing south. Expecting to be there for a time, a toilet, a stove and a rudimentary aid station were

310

all set up in the rooms. The glass in the windows was smashed so that it would not injure the defenders. The 1st Company platoon occupied the mosque to the east of the gas station and its firing positions were aligned south-south-west. The enemy positions in and around the school lay 600m away to the south-west.

Enemy fire was directed at the gas station continuously for two days and three nights. The Taliban were not moving around too much and initially just directed harassing fire against the coalition positions. On the first evening, ISTAR reportage indicated that the enemy was moving a number of mortars into the area to bombard the gas station and the mosque. The indirect fire was going to be used to support a planned flanking operation intended to clear out the defenders. The Canadians, using night-vision equipment, saw the enemy moving around and the British observers brought several rounds of 105mm fire onto the mortar positions. ISTAR reportage confirmed that the mortars were taken out. This threw off the planned enemy assault and it was cancelled.

Harassing small-arms fire was then directed at the gas station in retaliation. The Canadians fired back with their C-7A1 assault rifles, the British lobbed grenades fired from their SA-80 rifles' 40mm attachment, and a number of M-72s were employed. Corporal MacKlean was even able to use his shotgun against an insurgent trying to infiltrate the position. In one action, Pte Johnson was in the Radar Warning System (RWS) gunner's seat of an RG-31 when he spotted two enemy through the thermal imager and was able to drop both with some well-placed .50 cal. rounds at 550 m range. Later on, 'Tommo', one of the British observers was manning an RWS position. Macklean, using his night vision equipment, saw an insurgent popping up and down behind a wall. He directed 'Tommo' to engage with the .50 cal who was able to take out the enemy observer. Around 0300 hours, Cpl Rail, in the other RG-31, spotted more insurgent activity at a range of 1.5 kilometres that looked like a mortar team moving into position. He was able to lay down 7.62 mm machine-gun bursts and there was no more enemy movement that night.

During the next day, there was sporadic small-arms fire from the enemy, but just enough to say there were still there and still in the fight. The gas station defenders then heard a series of explosions from behind them, near the canal. It turned out that the ANA element in the mosque was using its 40mm grenade-launcher attachments to gather fish from the canal so they could eat a fresh meal. The first explosion was the round being fired and the second was the round itself after a delay.

15-16 January 2009

Elements in the Afghan intelligence system concluded that the enemy was pulling back, leaving a screen and IEDs behind. The fighters essentially cached their weapons and, dressed as civilians, walked away individually. The kandak XO contacted Capt French and informed him that they would be withdrawing in 30 minutes. Then counter-orders came down that the withdrawal would be delayed 24 hours. The plan was to use the RG-31s to cover the Afghan dismounted personnel, then withdraw the OMLT. However, some debate went on throughout the day between 2nd kandak and the operations officer of 3rd Brigade. The problem was that work on Checkpoints 9 and 10 was incomplete. The Afghan police were in no position to occupy those positions and could not hold the area on their own while the positions were constructed. Unfortunately, this also held true for Checkpoint 8.

The gas station defenders were ordered to prepare to withdraw and, on the last night, an RG-31 came in to withdraw the mentors. The enemy was not clear as to what the coalition forces were doing, but mortar teams were spotted by the JTACs, so JDAMs were employed to take them out. An enemy commander ordered reinforcements forward, but they refused. A U.S. Air Force B-1B, British 105mm guns and the British GMLRS were used to take out any identifiable enemy forces during the withdrawal. By first light, the force was back in FOB PRICE and the action at Spin Masjed was over.

Before withdrawing, the British and Canadian defenders left some graffiti behind. One of the soldiers drew a Royal Canadian Regiment cap-badge on the wall, while the British observers scrawled "Taliban: You've Been Fisted by OPAL-63".

End Game

The intended effect of establishing governance through the construction of the two police sub-stations/checkpoints was ultimately not achieved by the operations in and around Spin Masjed. Though the Afghan, British, Canadian and Danish soldiers fought to create the space to do so, the operation was undermined when the key piece of equipment needed for the construction of those facilities hit an IED on the first day, followed by the discovery of a massive number of deployed IEDs in the area. The coalition forces – specifically 2nd (Strike) kandak – eventually had to withdraw to conduct other tasks. That said, the insurgents in the Spin Masjed area, and whoever arrived to reinforce them, were dealt a series of serious blows which generated significant casualties and crippled their operations in the area for some time. They were unable to pose a significant threat to Highway 1 in any event, nor was the diversion of forces from Lashkar Gah required. This permitted governance activities to continue in the more vital districts around the provincial capital. Indeed, when British and Danish forces mounted Operation PANTHER's CLAW through Spin Masjed later in the summer of 2009, those enemy forces were incapable of mounting any significant resistance in the area.

NOTES

1   The Danes previously lost two of their Leopard 2 tanks to massive IEDs in Helmand province.

2   BIP: Blow in Place – detonate with C-4 in location.

Tank support moves south from Highway 1 to form a barrier to catch any exfiltrating enemy forces driven north by the river crossing.

CHAPTER THIRTEEN
OPERATION JALAY:
AN AIR-MECHANIZED ASSAULT
ON WESTERN ZHAREY, MARCH 2009

Operation JALAY, led by Brigadier-General Jon Vance and conducted between 18 and 20 March 2009, was a brigade-sized operation involving Canadian, American and Afghan forces. Notably, Operation JALAY was the first full-scale operation for 2nd Battalion, 2nd Infantry (2-2 Infantry) of the U.S. Army working with other allied forces while the operation was under Canadian command. 2-2 Infantry, informally known as The Manley Battalion, joined Joint Task Force Afghanistan in what initially turned out to be a laborious but ultimately profitable relationship. Operation JALAY employed 2-2 Infantry in an air assault while 3rd Battalion, The Royal Canadian Regiment conducted the mechanized portion of the operation alongside a kandak of the Afghan National Army from 1/205 Brigade, mentored by a Canadian Operational Mentor and Liaison Team (OMLT). Aviation support was provided by American, Canadian and Australian units. In terms of size and complexity, the operation was a significant Canadian-led multinational effort.

A Door Gunner provides security from a CH-146 Griffon helicopter equipped with a Dillon M134D small-calibre defence-suppression weapon during an escort mission. (DND-Combat Camera)

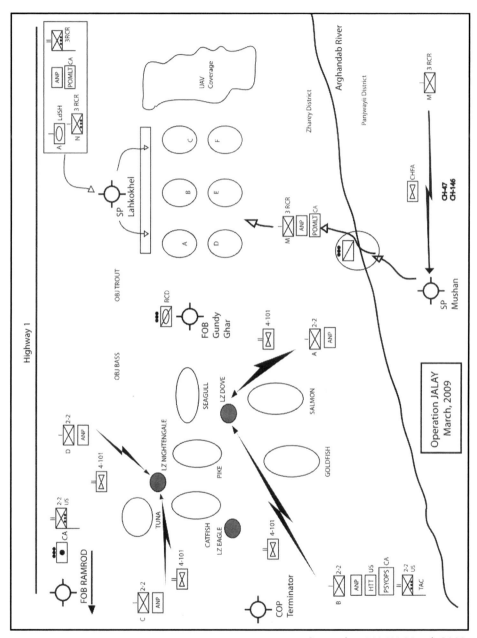

Operation JALAY, March 2009.

The situation as it stood in Kandahar province in March 2009 was not good. The incoming JTF-A headquarters, during its preparation phase, had decided on how it wanted to approach the situation in the province. The decision by the Canadian government to showcase development efforts during the previous JTF-A rotation, however, focused a lot of resources and attention on the Dala Dam project in lower Shah Wali Kot district. This meant that the parallel problems in neighbouring Arghandab district, the transit zone from Kandahar City to the dam, also demanded resources.

Several operations boxes in Zharey district established during the previous headquarters tenure had been merged into a single 'stability box' codenamed JUNO. The idea behind the stability box was to take this four-square-kilometre area centred on Pashmul, clear it, establish a government and security presence and then facilitate development on a key transportation node that linked Zharey and Panjwayi districts. These operations were in various stages of evolution at the time of Operation JALAY.

Stability Box JUNO essentially competed with Dala Dam and Arghandab for attention. At the same time, the priority of Regional Command (South) was keeping Highway 1 open from Kandahar City to Helmand province. Essentially, three battalion-sized organizations were available to do all of this: one Canadian Battlegroup (at 60-70 percent strength) and two Afghan kandaks (also at about 70 percent strength). One of those kandaks was repeatedly deployed to Helmand province to prop up the British and Afghan forces there. The Regional Battlegroup (South) was busy in the northern reaches of the province and over in Helmand. To complicate matters, 3 RCR was due to conduct a relief-in-place, as were the 1 RCR mentors from the OMLT. In effect, the incoming JTF-A had to juggle several balls in the air, hoping they did not all come crashing down. Fortunately, there was some relief. An American infantry battalion finally came on-line at the opportune time.

2-2 Infantry: The 'Manley' Battalion

From late 2007 into early 2008, the Canadian government conducted a review of the war in Afghanistan. The Manley Report noted that Canada's position in the province and, indeed, the ISAF mission itself was untenable without reinforcements in the form of a 1000-man battlegroup. In the spring of 2008, the U.S. Secretary of Defense examined the problem and, in consultation with Canada, recommended that an American infantry battalion be deployed to Kandahar province under the command of JTF-A.

3rd Brigade of the 1st Infantry Division, originally tasked to deploy to Iraq, was re-tasked in the spring of 2008 to deploy to Afghanistan to replace the 173rd Airborne Brigade in Regional Command (East). 2-2 Infantry from 3rd Brigade was at one point supposed to become the Theatre Task Force (TTF) for the entire country. Over the course of three months, 2-2 Infantry received potential taskings for several separate locations. Finally, in June 2007, they received orders to head to Kandahar. LCol Dan Hurlebut and his staff arrived at Kandahar Air Field to find there was no equipment; it was up in Jalalabad province, pre-positioned for another unit. Furthermore, it consisted of Mine Resistance Armored Protected vehicles that 2-2 Infantry's light infantrymen were not trained to operate and for which they had no maintenance staff. There were no specialized IED detection and destruction vehicles. There were no accommodations either, and no established logistics chain back to 2-2 Infantry's parent brigade over in Regional Command (East).

2-2 Infantry's build-up went on anyway. JTF-A[1] scrambled to support 2-2 Infantry as much as possible, including finding space on the air field, the construction of a Tactical Operations Centre, the provision of food, fuel and, in particular, intelligence data, district briefings and tribal-political situational awareness.

LCol Hurlebut's personnel started to flow in. Ultimately, 2-2 Infantry consisted of six companies: three light infantry companies, a heavy weapons company, a forward support company and headquarters company. Initially, there was only a single company of Hummer vehicles and no Mine-resistant Ambush Protected (MRAP) vehicles.[2] Some of the counter-IED equipment arrived, but there were no combat engineers to operate it. In time, former U.S. special forces personnel were brought in to provide an *ad hoc* C-IED analysis function for the battalion.

The anomaly of having a single U.S. battalion operating alone under another country's command meant that the initial operational certification was slow in coming from the battalion's parent brigade and, to his credit, LCol Hurlebut refused to artificially accelerate the process until he and his staff were confident they had everything they needed. 2-2 Infantry was declared ready in early fall.

By early October 2008, 2-2 Infantry was fully equipped with MRAP vehicles and counter-IED equipment and was fully deployed to FOB RAMROD in Maywand district. The decision to situate 2-2 Infantry there was taken earlier in 2008 after Operation SOHIL LARAM II and subsequent operations demonstrated that the Taliban did not, in fact, control that district. A small Afghan National Army and OMLT presence, plus Canadian CIMIC and PSY-OPS support, had been maintained in Hutel throughout the spring, but coalition forces were stretched thin and unable to establish a permanent presence between Highway 1 and the Arghandab River. This was the main enemy transit route from Helmand into western Zharey district. One of the first things JTF-A wanted from 2-2 Infantry was for them to establish a Combat Outpost (COP) near the Maywand-Zharey border, ultimately becoming the company-sized COP TERMINATOR. The effects of COP TERMINATOR on the Afghan and Canadian forces in Strongpoint Mushan to the south-east in Panjwayi district were significant. The existence of both positions seriously interfered with enemy re-supply and casualty-evacuation and it drew off enemy forces from the eastern parts of both districts. Indeed, the enemy forces in both Helmand and western Kandahar spasmed when 2-2 Infantry deployed into Maywand and they were not sure what to do about it.[3]

A patrol from 2-2 Infantry, supported by an American/Canadian Human Terrain Team and Canadian PSYOPS, prepares to interact with locals near a mosque.

2-2 Infantry received one of the first U.S. Army Human Terrain Teams (HTTs) in southern Afghanistan. The HTT had no Canadian equivalent. This four-man team had several functions. The HTT was to explain the nuances of local Afghan customs to the battalion's leadership in a general sense; it was to conduct detailed analyses of the socio-political-tribal make-up of the battalion's area of operations; and it was to collect information in the field during operations that fed both. 2-2 Infantry's HTT initially consisted of four people, a mixture of civilian academics, ex-military personnel with cross-cultural experience, and former security personnel who had lived and worked in Kandahar province. This particular HTT suffered a horrific casualty in December 2008 when Dr. Paula Lloyd was set on fire by a local national who was subsequently executed by her bodyguard, in revenge. Dr. Lloyd succumbed to her injuries weeks later.

3rd Battalion The Royal Canadian Regiment: Dispositions and Operations

LCol Colonel Roger Barrett's forces were distributed among the following districts: FOB Wilson in Zharey district; FOB Mas'um Ghar and FOB Sperwan Ghar in Panjwayi district; Arghandab district; and lower Shah Wali Kot district. There were three mechanized infantry companies, a tank squadron from the Lord Strathcona's Horse (Royal Canadians) and a Coyote recce squadron from the Royal Canadian Dragoons. For the most part, Recce Squadron and private security forces worked Shah Wali Kot and Arghandab, desperately awaiting a build-up of Afghan National Army forces, while 3 RCR and the tanks were situated in "Z-P". The Afghan National Army and its Canadian mentors from 1 RCR were superimposed on all five districts, amounting to between three and four Afghan kandaks; but those forces were in rotation, were not readily available and were not, in any event, under Canadian command.

The pattern of operations conducted by 3 RCR involved a combination of 'river runs' to support Strongpoint Mushan: forays west of Sperwan Ghar to disrupt groupings of Taliban forces; sweeps through the Salavat/Nahkony area; and operations along Route SUMMIT and Highway 1 to keep them open.

For the most part, 3 RCR stayed out of western Zharey district to focus on protecting the Stability Boxes in eastern Zharey and Panjwayi.

Canadian forces also assisted 2-2 Infantry in getting settled in Maywand. LCol Hurlebut was unable to get construction engineering resources from his parent brigade in RC (East), so Canadian engineers and contractors worked alongside 2-2 Infantry in setting up FOB RAMROD. 2-2 Infantry also lacked Civil Affairs and PSYOPS support, so Canadian CIMIC and PSYOPS detachments moved in to FOB HUTEL and FOB RAMROD. In time, a detachment of M-777 guns, under the command of Lt Mike Lavery from 2nd Royal Canadian Horse Artillery, was stationed at RAMROD and not too far behind them a UAV detachment controlling Scan Eagle MUAVs arrived. It took time to sort out the flow of operational and intelligence information as systems were incompatible, but personality-based work-arounds were found to be effective.

Planning Operation JALAY

Operation JALAY started as a conversation between Lieutenant Colonels Hurlebut and Barrett. Both commanders wanted a joint operation somewhere in the space between their commands, something that would have effects on both areas of operations. With the upcoming relief in place for 3 RCR, the timing was drawing near. Then Task Force Kandahar got involved. A vague concept that TFK wanted certain selected areas cleared in western Zharey district and in Arghandab district before the RIP, was floated separately, but there were few details. The area was considered devoid of government and of Afghanistan activity and there was no provision in the plan to maintain a government presence in western Zharey. There were an estimated nine IED-production facilities in the area; the existence of two was confirmed and seven were suspected. There was a network of safe-houses, bed-down areas and G-4 nodes that fed insurgent operations in eastern Zahrey district and western Panjwayi district. The general idea was to disrupt the enemy, gain the initiative in preparation for the RIP and, as one planner put it, "create tactical space" to influence the outcome of the spring campaign.

When 3 RCR and 2-2 Infantry examined the area, they roughly broke the zone down into Objective BASS and Objective TROUT-TROUT for 2-2 Infantry, and BASS for 3 RCR. That allowed an initial assessment of the compound and the community's terrain to start. The idea was that two battalions could simultaneously deploy into western Zharey, particularly into the enemy stronghold of Nahlgam, and present the enemy with mass. The insurgents would, in theory, be forced into action or they would have to go to ground, lose their weapons caches and do nothing. The scale of this operation was a factor as it was far different from a company-sized incursion like Howz-e Madad. And, unlike Operation TIMUS PREEM in 2008 where the enemy could escape to the west, 2-2 Infantry's dispositions in Maywand would seriously interfere with enemy movements to and from Zharey district. Indeed, the existence of Strongpoint MUSHAN would have a dampening effect on any enemy attempt to reinforce from western Panjwayi district.

The 3 RCR staff under the leadership of Operations Officer Maj Jason Guiney worked through the details. 3 RCR would come in from the east or south, the Afghan National Army and OMLT from the north, and 2-2 Infantry from the west. The question was how to phase the operation.

2-2 Infantry commanded by LCol Hurllebut conducts a Rehearsal of Concept drill for Operation JALAY at Forward Operating Base RAMROD .

The first possibility was to create a screen to the west, air-assault in and sweep in a north-south line heading west, with UAVs and air-support covering the flanks.[4] A second course of action was to create a cordon around both objective areas, insert the sweep companies by air-assault and sweep north to south.

The main issue here was that JTF-A had only a limited air-assault capability at this point and would have to go to RC (South) to get the necessary machines for the operation. The Canadian Helicopter Force Afghanistan had several CH-47 Chinooks and CH-146 Griffons, but it was new on the ground and the crews and staff had no experience in conducting a large air-assault under Afghan conditions, especially one involving American ground forces.[5] Either the British Joint Helicopter Force or Task Force WINGS, the American aviation task force, would have to get involved.

There were other important complications of which the 3 RCR staff was initially unaware but which had an impact later on. The first of these was the deteriorating situation in Arghandab district. A series of IED attacks against the Royal Canadian Dragoons and supporting forces over the course of two months produced six Canadian dead and over ten wounded.[6] This resulted in substantial scrutiny of operations by panicked politicians and bureaucrats in Ottawa. It was possible that elements in Ottawa would demand that Operation JALAY and other operations be postponed or suspended altogether. It also appeared to planners that the enemy was trying to isolate Dala Dam with IEDs and, since Dala Dam had been made into a 'showcase' by Canadian bureaucrats and politicians, it started to assume an artificially disproportionate importance vis-à-vis Zharey and Panjwayi districts.

The second involved humanitarian actions, which cut across military operations. The World Health Organization declared that there were going to be three 'Days of Tranquillity' so that polio immunization clinics could take place in rural areas throughout the province. How exactly this was to be deconflicted with military operations like Operation JALAY was unclear. It was even less than clear how this message would be conveyed to the Taliban, but the JTF-A Development Advisor was exercised about the issue. The WHO demanded that Regional Command (South) "respect humanitarian space", particularly in Arghandab district. The implication was that military operations would be suspended during this period. It was possible that the "Days of Tranquillity" might interfere with Operation JALAY in other ways, but the issue was not resolved during the initial parts of the planning process.

The "Days of Tranquillity" issue interfered more and more as planning continued. Operation JALAY was scheduled to last four days, overlapping with the WHO's "Days of Tranquillity" by two days. The JTF-A Development Advisor demanded that JTF-A respect this and cut the operation back. There was a belief in the JTF-A HQ that elements among the other government departments at JTF-A did an 'end-run' by approaching the development staff at Regional Command (South) in a bid to get JTF-A to comply with the demands of the WHO. At one point, the JTF-A deputy commander explained that Operation JALAY was designed, in part, to put the enemy back on his heels during the RIP and, in his view, if any Canadians were killed, responsibility would rest on those who attempted to truncate the operation.[7]

By 15 March, Operation JALAY had gained more definition. Objective TUNA now became one of six objective areas in the 2-2 Infantry portion of the operation. The whole area was now called Objective SHARK and included TUNA and WALLEYE, then CATFISH and PIKE, and finally SNAPPER and SALMON. The 3 RCR area broke down into Objectives TROUT and BASS.

Yet another complicating factor arose from the ongoing and semi-coordinated special operations missions. One of these went into Objective SNAPPER on 15 March to take out an IED facility and, as we have seen on previous operations, there was some concern that the enemy would be alerted for a repeat performance. Another went into GOLDFISH at the same time. The result was a shift in initial objectives for 2-2 Infantry. 2-2 Infantry would air-assault in: "C" Company into TUNA; "A" Company into SALMON; "D" Company would block to the north-east; while "B" Company, battalion HQ, mortars, medical and HTT would air-assault into SEA GULL, a new objective centred in Objective SHARK. The companies would then manoeuvre onto follow-on objectives CATFISH, PIKE and WALLEYE. SNAPPER which would initially be left alone.

3 RCR, meanwhile, was going to stage two companies to forward locations, one to the north of the objective areas and another to the south. They would then conduct a dismounted night-approach from both directions

while the tank squadron moved in to isolate Objective TROUT. (Afghan forces and Canadian mentors occupied strongpoints in Lakokhel, Pulchakan, Howz-e Madad and Gundy Ghar in Zharey district). A variety of options were explored as to how to coordinate the action, including sweeps north-to-south, east-to-west, and so on. For comparative purposes, the American battalion was going to flood its objective areas simultaneously, while the Canadian Battlegroup was going to cordon and sweep their more limited number of objectives. The east-west boundary between 2-2 Infantry and 3 RCR lay approximately 500m west of Strongpoint Gundy Ghar.

Up in Arghadab, the staff designated two operations boxes, POMEGRAN-ATE and APPLE, in lower Shah Wali Kot. Four U.S. Police Mentor Teams and their police counterparts were to sweep POMEGRANATE, supported by an Afghan National Army infantry company and its associated mentors.[8] Recce Squadron, meanwhile, was to ensure that the main service route from Kandahar north to Oruzgan remained open. The inclusion of the Arghandab portion of JALAY was designed to satisfy a number of higher-level requirements and demands and, as such, constituted an economy-of-force operation.

Maj Bryan Chivens, U.S. Army, and his operations staff worked the air-assault piece of Operation JALAY. His boss, LCol Colonel James Benson, commanded the 4-101st Aviation Regiment, 159th Aviation Brigade, better known as Task Force WINGS. This unit possessed a collection of CH-47 Chinooks, AH-64 Apaches, UH-60 Blackhawks and OH-58D Warriors, all based at KAF. The command relationship was complicated, but TF WINGS was tasked to bring 2-2 Infantry into the fight.

Similarly, LCol Roger Gagnon at Canadian Helicopter Force Afghanistan mulled over how best to move portions of 3 RCR about, in preparation for JALAY. The Canadian Chinook crews were still gaining experience with Afghan operations, as were their CH-146 Griffon counterparts. These Griffons had bite in the form of M-134D Dillon .50 cal. Gatling guns and their door gunners, all militia infantrymen re-trained in that task, were anxious to use them. The issue, as always, was weather. Dust levels were critical; if they were too high, there would not be enough visibility and that could delay pick-ups and insertions. Heat was another issue; the hotter it got, the less lift the helicopters had.

Tank support moves south from Highway 1 to form a barrier to catch any exfiltrating enemy forces driven north by the river crossing.
(DND-Combat Camera)

Staging

On 17 March, 3 RCR deployed to its staging areas. Strongpoint Lakhokhel was selected as the northern staging area and its Afghan police were suddenly reinforced at 0900 by a LAV-III mounted infantry platoon. An hour later, "M" Company was flown by Canadian Chinook into Strongpoint Mushan. The rest of "N" Company arrived at Lakhokhel in the early afternoon. The tank squadron with its Leopard 2 A6Ms, and Leopard 1s with their mine-clearance equipment, arrived at FOB Wilson in the late afternoon. "M" Company conducted a series of deception operations in Mushan; but were they staying in Mushan? The enemy was not sure what to make of this. They were used to Canadians operating from LAV-IIIs. To them, it may have appeared that "M" Company might be staying for a while to expand the Mushan security bubble. With the tanks in FOB Wilson and a company in Lakhokhel, were they trying to re-do Operation TIMUS PREEM against eastern Zharey?

2-2 Infantry, Afghan police, and Canadian PSYOPS boards CH-47 Chinooks at FOB RAM-ROD for the initial air assault into Western Zharey district.

LCol Dan Hurlebut, by this time, was repositioning 2-2 Infantry for its air-assault. He and his staff had to be able to take forces from FOB RAMROD, FOB HUTEL and COP TERMINATOR and, while maintaining security on his three bases, insert them all into western Zharey in a coordinated fashion. TF WINGS had three Chinooks, three Blackhawks, a pair of Apaches and a pair of Warriors available. An Australian Chinook was also available, as were more AH-64s later on. This force had to shuttle between all the bases and get the sub-units onto the ground in a phased fashion. This was not 'Apocalypse Now' with a single, mass air-mobile cavalry charge. When the U.S., Australian and Canadian air movements all combined, Operation JALAY was one of the larger air-mobile operations conducted in southern Afghanistan since 2003.

2-2 Infantry prepared to deploy three infantry companies and a support company acting as infantry, with an aerial quick-reaction-force platoon on call back in RAMROD. Each infantry company was augmented with Afghan National Police, NDS, female soldiers to search female civilians, Canadian dog teams, a Canadian PSYOPS team and the Human Terrain Team. Mortars, the JTAC, snipers and C-IED/EOD were grouped with the battalion TAC HQ. Canadian M-777 guns and mortars at FOB RAMROD, plus a variety of close air-support resources, would support 2-2 Infantry as required.

2-2 Infantry exploiting from the Landing Zone towards its objective areas.

Execution

Around 0100 hours on 18 March, Recce Platoon, under cover of darkness and using night-vision equipment, headed north out of Strongpoint Mushan across the open Arghandab River wadi to secure a position south-west of Objective TROUT. This 'foot on the ground' was to facilitate and protect "M" Company's movement. "M" Company's three platoons soon followed and passed through Recce Platoon around 0350 hours. At the same time, "N" Company's two platoons slipped out of their parked LAV-IIIs in Lakhokhel and moved south through the fields and ditches, by-passing the compound complexes on the routes. They were also ready to move into Objective TROUT around 0400. The "A" Squadron tanks turned over their engines in FOB Wilson and prepared to move out.

LCol Benson, back at Kandahar Air Field, and Maj Chivens at Task Force WINGS, closely watched the weather situation. The wind was picking up and the dust with it. It was not looking good over in Helmand province. Would the poor weather move east to Kandahar, or peter out? There was a coolish breeze, but no dust – yet. The helicopters were stood-to. Chinooks, Apaches and Warriors, all manoeuvred at first light and lined up, churning and burning, on the ramp. Then there was a hold. A ground crewman made a cutting gesture and the force returned to its pads and shut down. One could smell the damp rain approaching.

Just as suddenly, the operation was back on at 0530, after only a splattering of droplets. The TF WINGS commander decided to accept the risk and launched. The lead elements flew over eastern Panjwayi district, up to Highway 1, and then south into COP TERMINATOR where they picked up "A" Company. The force lifted off and conducted an extremely low-level flight to Landing Zone (LZ) DOVE, south of Objectives SNAPPER and SALMON. This took only minutes and the company poured out of the back of the Chinooks after the dust subsided. The helicopter force subsequently lifted off and headed for FOB RAMROD where it embarked "B" Company and the battalion TAC HQ and inserted them into LZ EAGLE, next to Objective CATFISH. A repeat performance brought "C" Company into LZ NIGHTINGALE near Objective TUNA. This whole process took less than an hour. 2-2 Infantry, the Afghan police and the Canadian enablers were now on the ground in western Zharey.

Meanwhile, over in Objective TROUT, "A" Squadron arrived to set up a screen north and south of the objective areas, while Scan Eagle UAVs crisscrossed the air-space overhead. "M" Company started clearing the compounds in Objective TROUT C at 0625 hours and Objective TROUT B at 0630 hours. "N" Company (which only had two platoons) worked through Objective TROUT E at around 0930 hours. These were typical search operations; they were slow, tedious and dangerous, and conducted building by building, room by room, outbuilding by outbuilding and field by field. In many cases, the Canadians cordoned off the compounds while the Afghan police, mentored by the Canadian Police Operational Mentoring and Liaison Team (P-OMLT), conducted the searches.

U.S. Army OH-58Ds and Canadian CH-146 Griffons buzzed around as 2-2 Infantry's companies conducted their searches in their four objective areas. The sudden arrival of 3 RCR at first light, putting the squeeze on Objective TROUT, should have generated significant enemy traffic to elude the cordon; in theory, there should have been some westward movement. With the inadvertent late arrival of 2-2 Infantry to the west, any enemy forces transiting west to escape should have been detected and engaged. The enemy was not communicating. There was no apparent movement in the morning in the 2-2 Infantry area of operations. There was a four-kilometre separation between 2-2 Infantry and 3 RCR, however, and they might be in that area. There was also the possibility that the enemy had gone to ground without weapons and were pretending to be civilians.

Then a Scan Eagle picked up twelve fighting-age males south-east of Objective CATFISH. They were headed west mounted in a van, on mopeds and on bicycles. Were they farm hands heading to work, or were they Taliban fighters escaping the 3 RCR onslaught? It was impossible to tell. Then twenty more fighting-age males with a truck were seen also heading west. A pair of OH-58Ds were dispatched to observe, but the same problem remained: who were the people on the ground? They appeared to be skirting the American search areas. The lack of ground-mobility and the geographical dispersion of the four objective areas meant that 2-2 Infantry could not give chase; nor could the suspected enemy be engaged by the helicopters because the people were unarmed. That said, the American companies' searches started to turn up medical supplies, ammunition and a 82mm mortar tube. Three detainees were held by the Afghan police after these searches. Another van blundered into a checkpoint near Objective SNAPPER and its seven passengers were searched; but there was nothing that could be used to hold them.

The Scan Eagle crews continued to report the movements of white vans and small groups of men, usually of around seven per group. The only ISTAR reportage came from around COP TERMINATOR that the enemy forces in Band-e Timor were preparing to ambush a patrol and the COP commander was diverting the patrol to avoid the ambush. Then there was ISTAR reportage that two enemy commanders were negotiating with each other about who would attack coalition forces first and who would support. They never resolved that debate.

Finally, "B" Company intercepted six vehicles south of Objective CATFISH which were carrying between 30 and 40 fighting-age males, and then 25 more arrived. The Afghan police questioned and searched everybody, taking all afternoon. Two of the men were determined to be involved with IED construction and/or deployment; a special counter-IED extraction request was submitted so they could be taken to Kandahar Air Field and interviewed by American C-IED specialists. These men were pointed out to the NDS by a local mullah who declared that they were "bad, bad men" involved in IEDs which, in his view, was un-Islamic.

As ISTAR reportage picked up in the afternoon showed that the whole enemy structure in western Zharey was severely disrupted. The commanders were unable to develop any coordinated action to bring to bear against the coalition forces. Demands for IED placement went unanswered. It was as if the enemy leaders were trying to do a roll-call to see who was still available for action.

Then civilians started leaving Objective SALMON, heading in the direction of Objective GOLDFISH. This could mean a couple of things. First, enemy presence in the SALMON compounds could mean the civilians did not want to be around in case the coalition hit the area with close air-support. In contrast, the enemy could have generated the flow of people to create a human shield to hide behind while escaping "A" Company's search efforts. It was unclear. "A" Company passed on a THREATWARN that the enemy was trying to find out exactly where 2-2 Infantry's companies were located, either to attack them or so they could avoid them. LCol Hurlebut instructed his interpreters to get on to the enemy communications and insult them in an attempt to goad them into action.

3 RCR, meanwhile, was progressing through Objective TROUT. The TROUT A compound searches started at 1030, just as the TROUT B and TROUT G compounds were completed. So far, the only thing that was turned up was a medical supply stash. When TROUT A was done, around 1530, searchers found Taliban letterhead and some non-explosive IED components, but little else.

Around 1940 hours, a pair of USMC F-18s spotted what looked like IED emplacement activity near Objective PIKE. Observers followed the pair of men to a compound where they met five more men. The weather deteriorated and, coupled with an ROE issue, the engagement was called off. There was no contact that night and the usual re-supply operations commenced for both 2-2 Infantry and 3 RCR. Mortars from both the battalion and the Battlegroup fired illumination rounds throughout the night to deter enemy movement.

Day 2: 19 March

"N" Company started clearing Objective TROUT D at first light. Within an hour, the Canadians found an emplaced IED which was blown in place and, a half an hour later, the Afghan police had detained a man connected to that event. Other forces entered Objective TROUT F around 0800 and commenced searches of the compound complexes there.

The big haul came at 1000 hours. "N" Company and its accompanying engineer platoon discovered an IED factory in a compound of interest within Objective TROUT D. Traces of ammonium nitrate, a wide variety of high explosive rounds of various calibers, and even a 105mm tank round, were uncovered. What surprised the searchers was the number of empty Canadian 155mm illumination carrier rounds that were being filled with home-made explosives and turned into IEDs. An adjacent facility was also booby-trapped with daisy-chained 155mm rounds. The C-IED and EOD people went to work, carefully disarming and cataloguing the latest developments in IED technology. The facility was blown in place in the early afternoon.

2-2 Infantry moved forces in to clear Objective PIKE in the morning of the second day. With CH-146 Griffons and OH-58Ds in rotating over-watch, U.S. infantry, Afghan police, Canadian PSYOPS and dog teams, plus the Human Terrain Team, moved in. The scheme of manoeuvre had the infantry company and the helicopters put in a cordon around PIKE F. The Afghan police, accompanied by a U.S. Police Mentoring Team and the Canadian dog teams, conducted the compound searches. Then the PSYOPS and Human Terrain Teams followed to talk to the local people in the cleared areas.

The Human Terrain Team deployed with the manoeuvre forces consisted of an academic, an ex-Marine turned academic, an interpreter, and an experienced academic (formerly a Canadian Forces officer) in support. Once the police completed their search activities, the HTT members selected businesses and private homes, approached the owners and interviewed them over tea. For the most part, the HTT was interested in the living conditions, lifestyle, political and tribal dispositions, and the local economics of the community. From that, the HTT moved into asking about opinions and attitudes towards the government and the insurgency. The HTT also solicited and recorded opinions from local people on how to solve problems in Afghanistan, from the local level to the national level.

In general terms, the HTT determined that the locals generally did not plan for anything beyond a year because there were too many factors they could not control. Many people did not even know exactly how old they were. There was no education since the Taliban had burned the school two years earlier. The previous teacher taught only Pashto and mathematics. Fundamentally, the message from the community to the HTT members was that the people wanted peace and "one government we can understand". In their view, the Taliban did nothing good for the community – they just took. They did not trust their own shuras because they were infiltrated. It was clear that the people were caught in between forces they felt they could not influence, so they took the path of least resistance. Islam contributed to this mind-set through the local mullah who counselled them not to resist the Taliban because they were unpredictable and were present more often than were the government forces. Indeed, locals alerted the HTT to the fact that the Taliban were using teams of two teenagers or children to monitor shuras and act as spotters for insurgent groups in western Zharey.

The local people also gave the HTT information on how the insurgents presented themselves physically. Generally, the insurgents wore civilian clothes and turbans, and always wore black beards. Personal weapons were always concealed. For the most part, they were nocturnal and were not seen during the day. They always threatened everybody and generated a climate of fear, even when they were not around. The 'young ones' would report on the behaviour of the population when the insurgents were not present and there would be retaliatory activity later for any transgressions. Interestingly, the lack of dental care caused the insurgents health problems and they frequently asked where the nearest dentist was located.

The Afghan police, with a bomb dog, uncovered a Taliban cache in PIKE at this time. It consisted of AK-47s and magazines, iCom radios, radio and cell-phone components, doorbell ringers and a substance suspected of being ammonium nitrate. The search team described it all as an "insurgent kit". Another insurgent was apprehended near this small cache and information led to another cache that consisted of even more IED components. In that cache, a former Tier I special forces operator, now serving as a civilian advisor to the counter-IED team, identified five factory-made IED systems made in Iran.

Meanwhile, over in TROUT F, a number of bunkers and empty storage tunnels were uncovered, followed by the discovery of another IED, all of which were in turn blown in place, denied to the enemy. Once again, the gruelling cordon and searches progressed through TROUT A and TROUT F until around 1400. The large IED find was BIP'd around 1430 hours. At the same time, the detainees taken by the police working with 2-2 Infantry over in Objective BASS were evacuated. The final search of TROUT H was completed.

The decision was made higher up to end Operation JALAY early because of the pressure being exerted by those who accepted the 'Days of Tranquillity' argument regarding respecting 'humanitarian space'. JTF-A issued instructions to start the extraction of the coalition forces. ISTAR reportage also suggested that, in any event, the enemy was low on weapons, low on electronics, and low on personnel who were all demanding immediate IED re-supply. Interestingly, the insurgents used the large BIP denial explosions as information operations both to bolster their own personnel and to influence the population; the explosions told people these were successful IED strikes against coalition forces.

Day 3: 20 March

2-2 Infantry started its extraction on the morning of 20 March. TF WINGS' Chinooks, protected by Apaches and Warriors, arrived to pull out each company team in succession. There was no contact and no incidents on 2-2 Infantry's side of the boundary.

It was a completely different story for 3 RCR Battlegroup. "M" Company successfully exfiltrated back to Strongpoint Mushan starting at 0300 hours. "N" Company started to moved back towards Objective TROUT H when, at first light, an IED strike was triggered by dismounted troops. This wounded six and killed Cpl Tyler Crooks, MCpl Scott Vernelli and one of the interpreters. The overall situation deteriorated further and there was an IED strike against

Afghan National Army forces in a location east of Kandahar City. Then a Coyote from RCD Recce Squadron patrolling the area in lower Shah Wali Kot and Arghandab districts was hit with a large IED. This strike threw the vehicle nearly ten feet into the air, killing Trooper (Tpr) Jack Bouthillier and Tpr Corey Hayes, and wounding four more Canadians. Then a Leopard 1 from the tank squadron, equipped with a mine-roller, struck two IEDs down in Zharey district with minimal damage to the implement and none to the crew.

The IED strike against "N" Company wounded the company commander, but quick action by subordinates ensured there was no loss in continuity of command. A small enemy force then tried to engage a Leopard with small arms and an RPG but they were dealt with using 120mm tank-fire and coaxial machine-gun fire. CH-146 Griffons were brought in to MEDEVAC the wounded and the dead from the strike site, while other Griffons, armed with M-134D Dillon Gatling-guns, orbited in over-watch positions. The decision was made to use the rest of the Canadian Helicopter Force to extract "N" Company from the area.

Up in Arghandab, the insurgent cells had reportedly emplaced eight more IEDs in an attempt to kill and maim the recovery forces headed to the Coyote strike-site. None of these devices detonated during the recovery effort and the wounded and dead were extracted without further incident. Later that day, in an unusual move, the insurgents rocketed Kandahar Air Field during daylight. One rocket struck the accommodations of some contract workers, killing and wounding several of them.

3 RCR, after crossing the Arghandab River, moves north to isolate objective areas and search for IED cells. (DND-Combat Camera)

Aftermath

As it turned out, four enemy leadership targets were operating in the Howz-e Madad area and in Objectives BASS and SNAPPER right before Operation JALAY. At some point shortly before the operation was executed, these leaders exfiltrated and headed south, skirting the Mushan area; they possibly made their way into the Registan Desert and then elsewhere, either to Helmand or Pakistan. It became evident that they received early warnings of the operation. They left in a hurry but kept their units, sub-units and cells in place in Zharey district. The JTF-A assessment was that Operation JALAY produced a short-term, but critical, disruption on the enemy in Zharey district and had a positive effect on the relief in place allowing the incoming Battlegroup to deploy relatively unmolested.

Operation JALAY also provides an opportunity to compare and contrast air-mobile and mechanized operations conducted on the same terrain against a light insurgent force that had the ability to masquerade as civilians. The air-mobile forces, once on the ground, were relegated to 'islands' that they could search and control, but the enemy could exploit the spaces between them despite the observation put on these spaces by aerial assets. The mechanized forces, on the other hand, had the ability to dominate similar spaces, and the larger cordon surrounding them, with the optics and fire-power of the tanks and the LAV-IIIs. Those forces, however, were hampered by their inability to manoeuvre on the roads and tracks in a high IED-threat environment. This produced a certain level of vulnerability and the danger that a successful IED strike could produce a cascade effect during the recovery process which, in turn, would generate more targets. The lack of enemy AAA capabilities meant that a comparable situation did not exist for the air-mobile forces. Neither force structure, of course, was able to address the basic rule of counterinsurgency: the counterinsurgent force has to remain in the target area permanently in order to protect and minister to the civilian population. Mobile operations like JALAY are disruptive in nature, must be integrated into a larger operational plan and understood as such, not only by commanders, but by commentators and the media.

Notes

1   Note also that the U.S. Air Force organization at KAF, the 451st Air Expeditionary Group under the command of Colonel "Oz" Ozowski, U.S. Air Force, helped out in addition to JTF-A. This was facilitated through the Kandahar Air Field Cigar Club, a Canadian-led organization that, among its traditional Caribbean leaf-fuelled activities, generated opportunities to provide informal solutions to problems that cropped up in KAF between JTF-A, the U.S. Air Force and other non-ISAF allied elements.

2   Similar to the Canadian RG-31 vehicle.

3   The number of successful SOF operations against enemy leadership targets transiting Maywand dramatically increased once 2-2 Infantry was on the ground.

4   Normally Coyote surveillance vehicles would have been used but the damage caused to Recce Squadron up in Arghandab and Shah Wali Kot seriously reduced this capability for Op JALAY.

5   Certain American commanders viewed the Canadian helicopter force as inexperienced at this point in the campaign; they were cautious and believed there was too much risk. The Canadian aviation commanders were justifiably proud of their newly won capability and were happy to finally get into the fight after years of sitting on the sidelines but were restricted as to whom they could carry and under what conditions. The loss of Canadian experience with air-assault operations, particularly involving CH-47s, was in part the product of narrow-minded politics in the early to mid-1990s and not the fault of the forces in the field. However, training in Canada and operations in Bosnia and Kosovo, an American aviation commander told me, in no way compared to the nearly eight years of hard operational experience in Afghanistan that their American counterparts had. In months, however the Canadian helicopter force was conducting air assault operations in the Canadian AOR.

6   Trooper Brian Good was killed on 7 January; Sapper Sean Greenfield was killed on 31 January; Warrant Officer Dennis Brown, Corporal Dany Fortin and Corporal Ken Quinn were killed on 4 March; and Trooper Mark Diab was killed on 8 March.

7   The possibility that enemy-infiltrated NGOs or IOs in Kandahar had access to the time-lines for Operation JALAY and other operations through the humanitarian coordination process and compromised operational security cannot be ruled out. Certainly there was a very real suspicion expressed by JTF-A personnel.

8   At this point there was a land dispute over where the ANA company was going to be quartered and its FOB was not yet under construction.

CONCLUSION

Though selective, these eight battles provide us with a broad understanding of how battles in Afghanistan, specifically Canadian-led battles, were conducted in the south during the 2007 to 2009 period. The overall driving condition during this time was the inability of the coalition forces and the Afghans to muster enough troops and police to implement a traditional counterinsurgency approach in all or most of the populated areas throughout Regional Command (South). This situation forced the Canadian military leadership and its allies into a generally reactive posture with intelligence-cued operations on the one hand and opportunistic disruption operations on the other. These types of operations were undertaken for shielding the developing Afghan security forces – police and army – as much as for shielding the governance and reconstruction activities in a more general sense.

As we can see, the evolution of the Afghan National Army's logistical, tactical and operational capability has been a challenging task, but one that was starting to pay off by 2008. Compare, for example, the ANA in Operation SEASONS in 2007 to the Lashkar Gah-area deployments in 2008-09. Canada's role in the mentoring of 1/205 Brigade and its kandaks is, overall, a significant success story despite the gargantuan obstacles placed in the way of progress, at all levels and by all players, including the enemy. Maintaining that progress will remain a challenge.

The multinational character of all of the operations should be apparent to all readers. The significant aspects of this include the willingness of the Americans and the British to place infantry and engineer units under Canadian command, albeit with certain legitimate restrictions. The Gurkhas and the soldiers of 2-2 U.S. Infantry had no serious issues with these working relationships and they were used to great effect. Similarly, the ability of these units to seamlessly absorb Canadian 'enablers' like PSYOPS, CIMIC, artillery and UAVs is impressive. Canada's deficiencies in the air-support realm are not glaringly apparent in these eight narratives because of the seamlessness that developed between the U.S. Air Force and Joint Task Force Afghanistan. Specifically, the provision of armed UAV support, close air-support and ISTAR resources was conducted behind the scenes and should not be assumed in any future Canadian overseas activity. Steps taken by Canada to correct air-mobile lift and UAV support had not yet had as dramatic an impact on operations during the 2007-09 period as they would in late 2009 to 2011. The lesson here is that Canada should not relinquish hard-won capabilities just because the war is perceived to be over; look back at the First World War and the Canadian Army's abandonment of technical capacities and equipment in France *en masse* in 1919, or the discarding of the CH-47 Chinooks in the early 1990s.

The use of armour deserves special mention. Once again, all of the amateur 'analysis' and commentary about the uselessness of tanks on the modern battlefield, and specifically this particular battlefield in Afghanistan, proved to be false. Afghanistan, once again, is not Vietnam. Recall also that even the Taliban used tanks when they controlled half of the country and would do so again if they could today. Tanks can be used, and to great effect, as long as their limitations are understood and integrated into the plan, and the cavalrymen are reigned in from time to time.

The narratives also give any reader insight into coalition politics and how they affected events in southern Afghanistan. The competition for scarce resources in pursuit of national objectives is the staple of such a conflict and it is an arena in which Canada needs to learn to play better. In this case, the debate over the allocation of resources to Helmand province or to Kandahar province is the one that affected Canada the most. Canada's unwillingness to spend money to acquire the full range of ISTAR 'enablers', and thus remaining dependent on other allies' 'enablers', reduces national power at times when there are divergent opinions on the future course of events. Military forces become pieces in a chess game that is played concurrently with the competition with the enemy for success. The importance of having a vertically integrated national system in place in the country, from the operating areas, through the coalition headquarters to the diplomatic corridors of the capital, is part of that game and Canada needs to understand this better.

Related to this is the increased de-confliction required between reconstruction and development activities, on the one hand, and military activities on the other. Though this was not readily apparent in 2007 and early 2008, it emerged more dramatically by 2009. In this case, national development personnel essentially acted as advocates for international and non-governmental organizations and were starting to interfere with military operations. The belief by some that reconstruction, development and humanitarian aid are somehow neutral on the battlefield still must be overcome. It will only get worse in the future.

Most importantly, these narratives demonstrate that Canada's military leadership in Afghanistan was able to conceptualize beyond the tactical level and to really appreciate the operational level. In all cases, Canadian commanders looked to what effects they wanted to generate (and not only on the enemy) and how those effects related to larger concerns – both inside and outside Kandahar province – on the psychological level as much as on the physical. The fact that most of these operations were successful needs to be brought out more and not submerged under specious political debates like those conducted over the issue of detainees. The opportunities afforded to the Canadian Army, as an institution, by the operations in Afghanistan will go a long way to revitalizing the professionalism and prestige of the Army at home and, more importantly, abroad. This spin-off benefit from this conflict is important, though it is not normally appreciated. The toughness, resourcefulness and tenacity of the Canadian soldier, already a staple of Canada's prestige in this and other coalitions, can now be augmented with the image of the Canadian operational commander who can employ Canadian and non-Canadian troops and resources at a higher level and can do so with confidence and with competence.

In the end, these eight battles are emblematic of what amount to a three-year disruption campaign intended to prevent the insurgents from seizing Kandahar City. These and other operations forced the enemy to frequently change tactics, change operational planning, expend scarce material resources, commit experienced leadership to vulnerable positions where they could be killed, and a host of other things they would rather not have done. In effect, a Canadian Battlegroup-sized force consisting of some 1000 soldiers in rotation, later augmented with another allied Battlegroup under Canadian command and, progressively, Afghan National Army and other security forces, prevented a catastrophic collapse of governance in southern Afghanistan during a period of political indecisiveness and strategic confusion.

Index